The Caddo Indians

NUMBER FIFTY-SIX:
The Centennial Series of the
Association of Former Students
TEXAS A&M UNIVERSITY

The Caddo Indians

Tribes at the
Convergence
of Empires,
1542–1854

F. Todd Smith

Texas A&M
University Press
College Station

The paper used in this book meets the minimum requirements of the American
National Standard for Permanenceof Paper for Printed Library Materials,
Z39.48-1984.
Binding materials have been chosen for durability.

Library of Congress Cataloging-in-Publication Data

Smith, F. Todd (Foster Todd), 1957–
    The Caddo Indians: tribes at the convergence of empires,
1542–1854/ F. Todd Smith.
        p. cm. — (Centennial series of the Association of Former Students, Texas
A&M University; no. 56)
    Includes bibliographical references (p.) and index.
    ISBN 0-89096-642-7
    1. Caddo Indians—History. 2. Caddo Indians—Government relations.
I. Title. II. Series.
E99.C12S65 1995
973'.04975—dc20   94-41590
                                                                              CIP

Contents

Maps

The Caddo Indians

Introduction

ON MAY 21, 1542, AFTER FUTILELY ENGAGING in a three-year search for Indian kingdoms in the southeastern region of North America, Hernando de Soto died. His successor, Luis de Moscoso, interred his body in the Mississippi River in an effort to conceal his death from the nearby Indians, for de Soto had "given them to understand that the Christians were immortal," and the remaining five hundred Spaniards feared an attack should the natives learn otherwise.[1]

Abandoning the search for riches, Moscoso led his men westward in an attempt to return overland to New Spain. In mid-July, 1542, the party passed through a province the natives called Amaye and on to another called Naguatex.[2] For three months the Spaniards wandered around the country of the Naguatex, a people described as living in scattered settlements, and their allies. The Spaniards burned a few of these villages to the ground in a desperate attempt to impel the natives to supply them with corn. In addition, Moscoso forced the Indians to provide guides, and though some of these natives attempted to lead the Spaniards astray, they only ended up hanging from the many trees in the woods. Finally, Moscoso decided to leave the Naguatex, retreat back to the Mississippi, and construct boats, in which the Spaniards finally floated downriver into the Gulf of Mexico. It was not until September, 1543, that the remnants of de Soto's failed expedition finally reached New Spain.[3]

Moscoso's episode among the Naguatex, which took place in present-day Louisiana and Texas, represents the first contact between Europeans and a tribe now known as the Caddos.[4] Naguatex is a transliteration of the Caddoan words *nawi* and *techas*, which mean "friends down there," while *amaye* is the word the Caddos use to designate an "older uncle on the male side of the family." Other tribes mentioned by members of the Moscoso party, including the "Nissohone" and the "Nondacao," are so similar to those included among the Caddo tribes that little doubt exists as to whether Moscoso visited the Caddo villages.[5]

The Spanish appearance in 1542 began four-and-one-half centuries of contact between the Caddos and the European invaders. For 150 years the Caddos occupied a critical position on the convergence of various

Euro-American empires—France and Spain, Spain and the United States, the United States and Mexico, and, finally, Texas and the United States. Curiously—despite a welcome increase in the publication of studies on the various native tribes of North America (including many excellent anthropological and ethnographic studies of the Caddos)—historians have continued to overlook the tribe.[6]

One reason for this neglect is the bias of American historians toward English colonization over the contemporaneous history of those areas once controlled by France and Spain. By the time the Caddos became subjects of the United States in 1803, they had already been weakened by a century of contact with the French and the Spanish. Following the War of 1812, the Caddos continued to decline and were forced by Anglo Americans from their lands in the trans-Mississippi forests and onto the prairies of Texas, where they settled on a reservation in 1854.

The Anglo bias is reflected in the only general history of the Caddos, written by William B. Glover in 1935.[7] Glover concentrated almost exclusively on the period after 1803, providing only minimal information on Caddo relations with France and Spain. In addition, the focus of Glover's work is solely on the group of Caddos that lived within the borders of the United States, the Kadohadachos.

In view of the paucity of historical literature on the Caddos, this work is intended as the first comprehensive history of the tribe to include all three confederacies, from the time of first contact with Euro-Americans to the settlement of the Caddos on the Brazos Reserve in 1854. I have tried to keep the story focused on the Caddos and their perspective, rather than tell it from the point of view of either the Euro-Americans of the time or modern historians, who consider the decline and removal of Native Americans as having been inevitable. The Caddos, occupying a strategically important position on the border between Louisiana and Texas, were able to deal with the intruders as equals—from a position of relative strength, not as inferiors facing superior conquerors. As long as two Euro-American powers each sought the allegiance of the tribe, the Caddos made sure that contact benefited their own people; thus, the tribe was able to assimilate what it needed from the Euro-Americans and discard the rest, keeping the strong foundations of its native culture essentially intact. Unwittingly, however, the tribe became dependent upon Euro-American goods, and when the tribe ceased to be of any importance to the whites, the pattern of both Europeans and natives benefiting from the contact broke down. Like their Indian brethren throughout North America, the Caddos suffered great hardships and eventually lost their land. It is for this reason that the history of the Caddos, a tribe on the historically neglected southwestern frontier, is as important as that of other tribes, many of whose stories have already been told.

Chapter 1
The Caddos

In the earliest times, darkness ruled over the land. In this darkness only one man lived as a Hasinai. Around him, a village emerged. As its occupants grew in number, they noticed that the man seemed to be everywhere. Then he disappeared, returning with all types of food in the form of seeds. The unknown man called the people together and patiently explained that the seeds were food for Hasinai use. He then gave the seeds to each of the people present. The man also told the people that the darkness would not rule all the time, as it had in the past. . . .

. On one memorable occasion, the tammas were sent out to tell the Hasinai that the caddi wanted them to assemble. . . . The people formed themselves into groups and selected a leader known as canaha, or community headman, for each group. The caddi called these leaders together and gave each one a drum. He explained to the canahas that they must sing and beat their drums as the people moved from the world in darkness to the new world. . . . Upon the signal from the caddi, the people began moving to the west, emerging in groups in a new world of light. . . . When the first people emerged into the new world, the men, aside from the leaders, carried pipes and pieces of flint. The women carried the seed corn and pumpkin seeds that had been given them in the old world.

—Hasinai origin tradition[1]

THE CADDOS AND THEIR ANCESTORS lived in their homeland for thirty-five hundred years before being disturbed by European intrusion. Linguistic evidence shows a similarity between the Caddoan and Iroquoian languages, leading anthropologists to hypothesize that a Proto-Iroquoian-Caddoan community existed long ago at a place somewhere between the historical locations of the two groups.[2] This hypothesis runs that around 3800 B.C., the two groups began to separate, and by 2000 B.C., an increase in moisture and game on the Great Plains drew the Proto-Caddoan groups westward up the tributaries of the Mississippi River. Within five hundred years or so, they had spread as far west as the Rocky Mountains and as far north as the Missouri River. The ancestors of the Caddo proper only went as far as the edge of the plains, however, remaining in the forested area along the Red River Valley and spilling over into Arkansas River drainage, an area that has come to be called the Trans-Mississippi South.[3]

This area of mixed-oak-pine-hickory woodlands—directly related

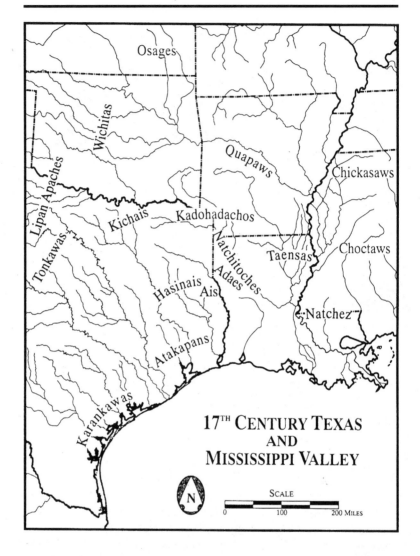

Osages

Wichitas

Quapaws

Chickasaws

Lipan Apaches

Kichais — Kadohadachos

Natchitoches

Taensas

Choctaws

Tonkawas

Hasinais Adaes
Ais

Natchez

Atakapans

Karankawas

**17ᵗʰ CENTURY TEXAS
AND
MISSISSIPPI VALLEY**

N

SCALE

0   100   200 MILES

to the temperate deciduous forest biome found east of the Mississippi—
provided the hunting and gathering ancestors of the Caddos with an
abundant supply of food. Nut-bearing trees, such as the walnut, chest-
nut, oak, and hickory, abounded in the lush forest. Plum and cherry
trees, along with mulberry and blackberry bushes, were common as well,
and the Indians picked grapes from wild vines and dug up edible roots.
This vegetable and fruit diet was supplemented by wild game, especially
deer and turkey, though wild hogs, rabbits, partridges, quail, and bear
also lived in the rich forest. The local streams provided fish, and wild
geese and ducks appeared from the north in the fall. The ancestors of the

Caddos successfully used these limited resources by organizing themselves into small, relatively mobile bands.[4]

The hunting and gathering lifestyle of the Proto-Caddos was revolutionized by the introduction of horticulture into the Mississippi Valley from Mesoamerica sometime around 500 B.C. Within a thousand years or so, a culture known as Mississippian came to dominate much of the eastern half of North America. The Caddos were located at the westernmost extension of this Mississippian cultural complex and were influenced by both Mesoamerican and Southwestern cultures. The Mississippian culture, which climaxed around A.D. 1200, was based primarily upon the successful production of corn, as well as beans, squash, pumpkins, watermelons, and sunflowers.[5]

The Caddos' agricultural success allowed them to develop a highly complex though sedentary culture. To concentrate on intensive agriculture, the Caddos gathered in fixed, permanent villages located along the fertile river valleys of the area. Their productivity allowed them to develop hierarchical political and social structures and elaborate exchange networks, and they established large ceremonial centers consisting of temple mounds. The construction of these mounds was directed by an elite class supported by the rest of the tribe.[6]

The success of Caddo agriculture afforded the tribe an opportunity to specialize in other areas as well. The Caddos produced pottery ranking with the finest and most ornately decorated of any produced by an aboriginal culture in the United States. Tribal crafters produced fine baskets made of reeds, and bows constructed from the wood of the Osage orange. Along with the salt found in the region, all the above items were used for trade in the extensive network that developed between the Southwest and the Mississippi Valley.[7]

Prosperity helped the Caddo population reach two hundred thousand by the end of the fifteenth century. The area occupied by the tribe encompassed the western edge of the Trans-Mississippi forest, stretching all the way from the Trinity to the Arkansas River. Settlement patterns varied, ranging from densely populated riverine town communities in the Arkansas, Ouachita, and Red River valleys, to more sparsely populated rural communities located away from the major streams, mainly in the Neches, Angelina, and Sabine River valleys.[8]

Unfortunately for the Caddos, their population would not grow beyond the point it had reached around 1500. Even before the thriving Caddos came face to face with Moscoso in 1542, the Spanish presence in North America had already proven detrimental to the tribe's well-being. Preceding Moscoso and his followers into Texas were two boatloads of men from the failed Pánfilo de Narváez expedition, who washed ashore on an island near the western tip of Galveston Island in 1528. Four men, led by

Cabeza de Vaca, ultimately survived and spent seven years in Texas before finally reaching Mexico in 1536. Although the Caddos never encountered the four men, they—as well as the other Indians of Texas—were exposed for the first time to deadly European diseases.[9]

Unfortunately for the Caddos and the other natives of America, their isolation from Europe had completely cut them off from the diseases to which Europeans had developed immunities over the centuries. As a result, these diseases found new victims in a Native American population that lacked the resources to fight them, and exposure to these diseases—smallpox, measles, and cholera, among others—created epidemics. Decreased population fertility resulted, accompanied by sporadic infections that killed those fortunate enough to be born between epidemics; incredible population losses occurred, reaching often as high as 95 percent of a tribe. More than any other factor, disease caused the Indians to weaken and decline, opening the door for invasion and displacement by the Europeans.[10]

Although there is no historical evidence of epidemic diseases reaching the Caddos before the sustained presence of the Europeans in the late seventeenth century, the archeological record does suggest that a major demographic decline occurred among the Caddos prior to the 1680s. Large parts of the area occupied by the tribe were abandoned, particularly among the urban communities in the Arkansas, Red, and Ouachita valleys. Mound construction ceased, and the hierarchical burial system gave way to community mortuaries, suggesting a simplification of the complex sociopolitical system of the tribe. Depopulation was not as severe among rural Caddo communities as it was along the major river valleys, and as a result, the Neches and Angelina River basins in East Texas would have a higher population density in the early historic period.[11]

By the time the Europeans did reappear in the late seventeenth century, the Caddo population had fallen to perhaps ten thousand, a catastrophic decline of 95 percent.[12] The Caddos had roughly reestablished themselves into three loose confederacies: the Kadohadachos, Natchitoches, and Hasinais. The Kadohadacho confederacy was located around the bend of the Red River near the Arkansas, Texas, and Oklahoma common border. Thirty-five hundred Kadohadachos lived in four tribes: the Kadohadacho proper, Nanatsohos, Upper Nasonis, and Upper Natchitoches.[13] Further downstream were the Yatasis, who would eventually merge with the Lower Natchitoches and the Doustionis to form the least populous of the three confederacies known as the Natchitoches, who settled around the modern town of the same name. There were perhaps two thousand members of the tribes in the Natchitoches confederacy.[14]

To the west, along the upper reaches of the Neches and Angelina Rivers in East Texas, was the largest confederacy, the Hasinais. Nine principal tribes—consisting of forty-five hundred people—were included among the Hasinais, and they were banded together in four geographic groupings. The westernmost group lived on or near the Neches River and included the Neche, Nabedache, and Nacono tribes. The second group included the central tribe and acknowledged leader of the confederacy, the Hainais, who, together with the Nabitis, lived on the Angelina River. Almost due east of the Hainais was the third group, the Nacogdoches, living around the modern town of the same name. North of the Nacogdoches, and the farthest removed of the Hasinais, were a group of three tribes, the Lower Nasonis, Nadacos, and the Nacaos.[15]

All the Caddo tribes maintained strong ties with one another and often used trails, which one Frenchman believed were "as well beaten [as the road] from Paris to Orleans," to make their visits. Although they enjoyed close relations and shared the same culture, each of the Caddo confederacies was a separate and independent political entity, and each was treated as such by both Europeans and other Indians. Hostilities occasionally broke out between the confederacies, as demonstrated by the need for the peace negotiations carried out in 1690 by Frenchman Henri de Tonti between the Kadohadachos and the Yatasis. Rarely, however, did the confederacies oppose one another, especially after the appearance of the Europeans. In fact, one of the dominant trends of the contact period was the ability of the confederacies to bond more tightly together and act in concert until they finally became one tribe, the Caddos.[16]

While the Caddos may have declined compared to their past glory of the fifteenth century, they still retained an impressive and viable culture, one which made them dominant in the area. Remnants of their hierarchical society still remained when they were first observed by Europeans, and the elite class continued to provide the tribe with a strong, efficient government that helped keep the Caddos self-sufficient, organized, industrious, and successful, despite the catastrophic drop in population.[17]

At the head of each confederacy was a religious leader, the xinesi, who provided blessings for the planting of crops and construction of houses and presided over various feasts and ceremonies. The office was hereditary and carried with it, for obvious reasons, tremendous veneration and respect. All the xinesi's wants and needs were provided for by the tribe, and the commands he issued were, in the words of a Spanish missionary, "more strictly obeyed by these Indians than the ten commandments are observed by the Christians."[18]

As with all aspects of their society, the religion of the Caddos was well-defined. The supreme deity was called Ahahayo, which means "Father above." The Caddos believed that Ahahayo had created everything and that he rewarded good and punished evil. Communication between Ahahayo and the tribe was carried out through the xinesi, who was in charge of keeping a perpetual fire in a temple near his own house in which two divine children called *coninisi* ("the little ones") were said to reside. Except on special occasions, only the *xinesi* was allowed to enter their house, and it was through the *coninisi* that he learned the wishes of Ahahayo.[19]

A more numerous but lesser class of priests or shamans—called *connas*—existed below the *xinesi*. They were medicine men who attempted to heal the sick or wounded by using a variety of methods, including spells and incantations (the Caddos believed that sickness was caused by the witchcraft of enemy tribes). The *connas* had also developed great knowledge of the medicinal herbs that abounded in the forest, and this knowledge allowed them to have great success in curing the ill.[20]

The *connas* performed many other religious duties as well, the most important of which was presiding over burials. The Caddos believed that a dead person's soul went up to the sky and entered the House of Death presided over by Ahahayo. Here, all were required to wait until all the Caddo souls had been gathered together, at which time the whole tribe would "enter another world to live anew." All the Caddo people were entitled to enter the House of Death, "where everyone is happy and there is no hunger, sickness, or suffering"; only enemies of the tribe were sent to the house of *texino*, the devil, to be punished.[21]

Although the *xinesi* was recognized as being the head of each confederacy, actual political power was exercised at the individual tribal level. The highest political office of each tribe was that of the *caddi*, also a hereditary position. He presided over a well-defined chain of command that carried out his orders with "peace and harmony and absolute lack of quarrels." Each *caddi* had four to eight principal aides called *canahas*, who in turn had a number of *chayas* to assist them. Policy meetings were held in a large public assembly house located near the house of the *caddi*. *Tammas*, or town criers, performed the function of policing the tribe, keeping people in order and at work by whipping all idlers with sticks. These clearly defined lines of authority allowed the tribal government of the Caddos to function smoothly.[22]

The offices of government were held by a hereditary, aristocratic elite that was accorded certain forms of deference and respect. There were even specially raised seats in each house that could be occupied only by this elite class, who were also served first at public functions and had menial services performed for them. The only way common tribal members could gain prestige was by distinguishing themselves in battle and being awarded the status of *amayxoya*.[23]

Although there was a recognizable elite among the Caddos, the commoners were not slaves to this class and a community spirit prevailed within the tribe. The entire tribe worked together under the supervision of the *caddi* and the *tammas* to raise individual houses. Planting was also done communally by the entire tribe, including the *caddi*. Crops were sown first at the house of the *xinesi*, then at the *caddi*'s, and on down the line in order of rank from "the highest to the humblest."[24]

The key to the Caddos' strength came from their ability to successfully procure sufficient amounts of food. Over the centuries the tribe had learned to manipulate their environment using, for example, the basic hoe (usually made of bone or fire-hardened walnut) to great advantage. As agriculture had become the most important food source, the tribe had adopted a lifestyle centered around the successful raising of crops. The Caddos were very proficient at agriculture, for over the years, they had developed a very sophisticated knowledge of plant rearing. The Caddos had great respect for the earth, demonstrating through prayer and ceremonial rituals their appreciation to Ahahayo for allowing them to use it.[25]

Corn was the most important crop raised by the Caddos, and there were two plantings each year, one in April and one in June. The first crop was a corn with a small stalk, which was harvested at the end of May. The second crop was the tall corn, and it was gathered at the end of July. Though, as stated above, the entire community—men and women, elite and commoners—engaged in the planting of the crops, women performed the remaining agricultural tasks alone. The tribe took great care of the harvest, storing the shelled corn in baskets made of very strong reeds into which the women mixed a few cups of well-sifted ashes as a preventative against worms. Then the baskets were carefully covered to keep out mice. The fullest ears were used for seed, since, fearing an unsuccessful crop next year, the tribe always saved enough seed for two years' sowing. This was considered as a "sacred deposit" to be used only in times of "grave necessity."[26]

Pumpkins were planted in the spring and harvested in the late summer or early fall. As with the corn, the best pumpkins were chosen for their seeds and saved for the future. The other important crop was beans, of which there were five or six kinds. Watermelons, squash, and sunflowers were also raised, and tobacco was grown for smoking. The Caddos were able to keep their fields productive through rotation and by using plant and animal matter as fertilizer.[27]

Agriculture even determined the way the Caddos arranged their living quarters. They lived in scattered dwellings in the midst of their fields, grouped around a central village where their chief officials lived. This was done so that each family "had a place large enough for his crop and one where there is water at hand for household use and bathing." In addition, the heavily wooded country with few clearings lent itself to more spread-out communities described by one European as being "twenty leagues long, not that [they are] constantly inhabited, but in hamlets of ten or twelve cabins."[28]

The Caddo "cabins" were well-constructed dwellings made of grass and reeds "in the shape of a beehive, or a rick of hay." Their size varied with the rank of their occupants, but they averaged about forty or fifty feet in height and about sixty feet in width. Along the walls were skillfully made beds raised above the ground. The floor was kept clean and well-swept and covered with finely made mats and rugs. A fire continually burned in the middle of each dwelling.[29]

Several families—three or four at most—occupied each house. The Caddos were, for the most part, monogamous. Marriages of virgins were arranged and carried out with the consent of the woman's parents and the *caddi*. The marriages were very loose, and couples rarely stayed together for life. New mates were chosen without parental consent, and divorce did not carry any particular stigma. Marriage was considered permanent only among the elite, and the wives of the *caddices* were called by the common name *aquidau*.[30]

Mothers gave birth alone in a small hut located near a stream. Immediately following birth, the mother bathed herself and the newborn child in the water before presenting it to the village. A week later the child was visited by a *conna*, who bathed "it all over in a large vessel" and asked the parents what name it was to receive. This baptismal ceremony was followed by a feast. If the parents divorced, the children went with their mother. Since divorce occurred often in Caddo society, the maternal uncles and aunts were, next to the mother, the most important adult figures to the child, and they were charged with teaching the children the Caddo way of life.[31]

While agriculture played the central role in the Caddo lifestyle, hunting was also important to the tribe. During the summer months the men, armed with bows and arrows (tipped with stone points), hunted near the villages for wild turkey. Throughout the year the Caddo men also hunted other game, such as wild hogs, quail, and rabbits, located in the surrounding area. Following the harvest in September, the men left the villages for much longer, intensive hunts. In the autumn, the men stalked deer throughout the forests, and as the weather got colder with winter's approach, they ranged even farther from the villages. Bear was the most important animal tracked on these hunts, since they were plentiful north of the Kadohadacho villages and provided the Caddos with great quantities of fat, used both as a seasoning for food and as a drink. Bear skins were also valuable and were employed as clothing and blankets.[32]

Due to their great distance from the tribe, buffaloes were less important than bears. The nearest buffalo hunting grounds lay almost eighty miles to the west of the Hasinai villages near the Brazos and Navasota Rivers. In the winter, when food supplies were getting low, parties were organized for a buffalo hunt. Since the Caddos had only dogs as pack animals before the arrival of the Europeans, the amount of meat carted back to the villages was limited. Other parts of the buffalo were used for clothing, blankets, and various utensils.[33]

The women continued to work hard in the fall and winter months as well. They roamed near the villages digging up edible roots, collecting nuts, and picking wild fruits. They took the nuts and roots and ground them with corn into a flour called *pinole* by the Spanish, which was used to make bread throughout the rest of the year. Women also used the winter months to dress the deer, bear, and buffalo skins the Caddos used for clothing. The tribespeople were very concerned with their appearance and spent much time on their clothes. The women knew how to dress and dye the skins so well that, when they were finished, the skins resembled "fine cloth." The women then bordered the edges with very small beads, which they obtained from plants, and cut "all the edges in fringe, so the garment is very pretty," according to one Spanish priest.[34]

In the warm months the men generally went either naked or slightly covered with a breechcloth. In the winter they used finely dressed and dyed buffalo skins as a blanket, which was worn over the shoulder. The women, on the other hand, were more modest. From a very early age, they were covered from the waist down by a finely made skirt of deer skin. This was usually accompanied by a deerskin blouse. Both sexes wore moccasins made of soft leather, usually deer skin.[35]

Both sexes also adorned their bodies with ornaments, such as earrings, bracelets, and necklaces, usually made from shells. Tattooing was commonly practiced, particularly by the women, whereas the men employed the more temporary alteration of face and body painting. The men were also partial to wearing bird feathers in their hair, which they kept rather short except for a thin braid growing from the middle of the head (described by one observer as looking "like [what] a Chinaman" might wear). The women, on the other hand, always wore their hair long, carefully combing it into a braid and tying it together with a string of rabbit's hair, which they dyed bright red. The Europeans first encountering the Caddos were impressed by their appearance and considered them to be very attractive, claiming that they were "well built and robust" with "good features and thin faces."[36]

Although war played a role in Caddo society, it was not as central to their culture as it was for some tribes with whom they had contact. Traditional Caddo warfare was not economically motivated but, rather, provided an opportunity for lesser tribal members to demonstrate valor and enhance their social status. Battle usually consisted of hit-and-run raids upon an enemy in which an attempt was often made to capture a foe. The unfortunate captive was returned to the Caddo village, where the entire tribe, including the women, participated in an extended torture session, which served as a bonding mechanism for the tribe.[37]

Even though the Caddos often preyed upon nearby tribes and occasionally even fought among themselves, their traditional enemies were the Osages, who lived in present-day Missouri on the river that bears their tribal name. Like other Siouan tribes, the Osages were very belligerent, and the mere mention of their name struck terror in the hearts of the Caddos. In the days before horses and guns were available to the natives, however, warfare between the two tribes caused little serious damage. The Caddos also considered the Choctaws and Chickasaws—Muskhogean tribes from east of the Mississippi River—to be enemies, but battles with them occurred much less often than with the Osages.[38]

The Caddos were able to dominate the weaker surrounding tribes through their cultural success rather than their martial prowess. Among these neighbors were two Caddoan-speaking tribes, the Ais and the Adaes, who were located between the Hasinais and the Natchitoches. They lived outside the Caddo confederacies and were generally looked down upon by other Indians and Europeans alike because their culture was considered to be much cruder than that of the relatively advanced Caddos.[39]

Southwest of the Hasinais, living on the lower reaches of the Trinity River, were two Atakapan-speaking tribes. The Bidai (and their subgroup, the Deadose) lived nearest the Hasinais and often tried to place themselves under the Hasinais' protective wing. The Bidais practiced agriculture, though on a much less intensive scale than the Caddos, and lived a much more marginal existence. Their Atakapan kin living on the Gulf Coast, the Akokisas, were hunters and gatherers but did not raise crops. The Tonkawas lived west of the Hasinais on the buffalo plains of Central Texas. Consisting of the Tonkawa proper, the Mayeyes, the Yojaunes, and a few other bands, the Tonkawas were nomadic hunters and gatherers who were a bit more prosperous than the Akokisas because of their access to the buffalo.[40]

The Wichitas were more successful buffalo hunters and a much more formidable tribe. They lived north of the Tonkawas between the Red and the Arkansas Rivers in the heart of the buffalo range. Like their linguistic relatives the Caddos, the Wichita tribes—the Wichita proper, Taovayas, Iscanis, and Tawakonis—practiced agriculture and lived in relatively fixed villages. Unlike the Caddos, however, they relied much more heavily on the buffalo than upon their agricultural produce. Similar to the Wichitas were the Kichais—another tribe of Caddoan stock—who lived between the Brazos and Red Rivers. Both the Kichais and the Wichitas kept close ties with the Caddo confederacies.[41]

Although there were linguistic as well as cultural differences among all these tribes, they shared two things in common: they had lived in the area for a long time, and they harbored a common hostility to recent invaders, namely the Lipan Apaches. Sometime during the fourteenth century A.D., the Apaches, along with their Athabaskan kin the Navajos, gradually migrated south from Canada to the Rio Grande Valley of New Mexico, where they preyed upon the agricultural Pueblo tribes. The easternmost group of Apaches, the Lipans, established themselves upon the western plains of Texas and occasionally encountered the Caddos on their annual winter hunts. Besides being newcomers, the Apaches quickly earned the enmity of all the Indians of Texas by stealing from the other, more established tribes.[42]

What initially made the Apaches more of a threat to the Caddos than their traditional foes were the items the Apaches acquired through trade and theft from another group of newcomers to the Rio Grande Valley, the Spanish. Establishing themselves among the Pueblos by the early seventeenth century, the Spaniards brought with them many prized items, most importantly metal goods and horses. The Apaches quickly obtained both from the Spanish and used them on raids throughout New Mexico and Texas. On their raids the Apaches captured Indian slaves and sold them for Spanish goods in an illegal underground market that had been established in New Mexico by Spanish smugglers. Horses allowed the Apaches to become even more mobile, and the Lipans continued to move farther eastward, where they posed an even greater threat to the Caddos.[43]

Luckily for the Caddos, they were able to obtain horses and other Spanish goods soon after the Apaches and easily co-opted these items into their culture. By 1629, Spanish explorers had come into contact with the Jumano Indians, a migratory tribe that followed the buffalo on the plains of western Central Texas. Once trading ties were established with the Jumanos, the Caddos were able to obtain Spanish items from them long before actually meeting the Europeans. The Jumanos traveled to East Texas every year to attend a trading fair held at the Hasinai villages, where the Caddos sold their pottery, baskets, bows, and salt to the plains tribes. Many of the goods the Jumanos brought to the fair were trivial items, including coins, spoons, and lace, obtained from the Spanish in New Mexico. The Caddos were particularly attracted to blue cloth and quickly incorporated it into their dress, as they did other items of Spanish clothing.[44]

Of course, the most important item the Jumanos brought to the Hasinai villages was the horse. Having witnessed Apache raids, the Caddos already recognized the horse's utility and necessity in "modern" warfare and were desperately eager to obtain the animals. The horse also made it easier for the Caddos to obtain buffalo, for not only did it take a shorter time to reach the buffalo range, the buffaloes were also easier to kill from horseback. More meat could be slaughtered and more skins could be gathered than in the past, since horses were also better pack animals than the Caddo dogs.[45]

After the first trickle of horses arrived in East Texas in the mid-seventeenth century, they became increasingly easier to obtain in the years that followed. Trade with the Jumanos continued, and the Caddos were able to raid the Apaches and plunder their herds as well. They could also increase their holdings through natural reproduction, since horses thrived in Caddo country. Horses were commonplace by the last decade of the seventeenth century, at least among the westernmost Hasinai confederacy, and Tonti noted in 1690 that, while there were four or five horses for each Hasinai dwelling, the Kadohadachos had fewer. Nevertheless, both groups had enough horses by this time that they could afford to sell them at low prices to the astounded Frenchmen.[46]

The Caddos heard that the Spanish had brought soldiers with them in addition to goods and had allied themselves with the Pueblo Indians against the Athabaskan invaders. The Caddos certainly reasoned that the Spanish would be very valuable allies to have, not only for the goods they could provide, but also for the amount of protection they might afford. With this in mind, the Caddos eagerly looked forward to the time they could meet the Spanish face to face.

The Caddos probably never associated the Spanish of New Mexico with those they had encountered during the Moscoso expedition, for the Spaniards of the late seventeenth century were quite different from those of the early sixteenth. No longer did the conquistador, aggressively searching for gold and native kingdoms, lead the way for the Spanish effort in the New World; in the seventeenth century, he was replaced by the missionary as the symbol and driving force behind Spanish expansion.

There were various reasons for the ascendancy of the missionaries. Influenced by the writings of such men as Bartholomé de Las Casas, who pointed out the brutality of the initial Spanish contacts with natives, the Spanish crown adopted a more humane policy for dealing with the natives by the seventeenth century. The peaceful conversion of the Indians to Christianity became the major goal of the Spanish crown, and it was left to the missionaries to accomplish this task. The priests were to go forth with only a few soldiers for protection, seeking out those natives who wished to convert to Christianity. The tribes would then, in Spanish terms, be "reduced" to mission life and made to "congregate" around a mission built among the Indians for their religious instruction. A presidio manned by Spanish soldiers would be established nearby to protect the priests and the local tribe from enemies. No force was to be used upon those wishing to convert, nor were guns or tools of war to be issued to them. Only items of civilization were to be distributed, for the missionaries were also charged with teaching the natives the lifestyle of the Spanish in the hope that they would become transformed into productive subjects of the crown.[47]

This idealistic method of dealing with the natives meshed well with the realities of the slow-moving Spanish advance northward from Mexico City in the early seventeenth century. The fact that the Spanish lacked the manpower needed to conquer the nomadic tribes of northern Mexico helped convince the crown to attempt a religious conquest rather than a military one. Spain had greatly overextended its resources early in the sixteenth century in exploring much of its North American claim, and by the seventeenth century, Spanish authorities recognized that only the missionaries were willing to extend the frontiers of New Spain northward. It was hoped that, by converting and "civilizing" the Indians of the north, the missionaries would also serve the crown by providing a bulwark against foreign encroachment.[48]

The Spanish priests in New Mexico did meet with some success in their conversion efforts among the Pueblo Indians. Beleaguered by the Athabaskan invaders, the Pueblos, who were settled natives engaged in intensive agriculture, welcomed the Spanish more for their military protection than for their spiritual offerings. The optimistic Spanish priests, however, failed to perceive this, and it became doctrine among them that settled, agricultural tribes like the Pueblos were more responsive and inclined to the faith than nomadic ones. For this reason, the priests were always in search of more "civilized" tribes like the Pueblos.[49]

Although the fire that had driven the original conquistadors such as Coronado and de Soto had dimmed a bit, there were still a few expeditions sent out from New Mexico in search of Quivira and Teguayo, Indian kingdoms thought to lay somewhere to the east upon the Great Plains. It was from one of these expeditions that the Spanish first heard of the Caddos, inspiring missionaries and adventurers alike to attempt to reach them and reap the harvest they expected to obtain.[50]

In 1650, an expedition led by Capts. Hernando Martín and Diego del Castillo was sent out from Santa Fe. After encountering the Jumanos near the Concho River in western Central Texas, the Spaniards passed through three other tribes before they came to the borders of a nation of people called the "Tejas," which "they did not enter . . . as they learned that it was very large and contained many people." They were also told that the "Tejas had native princes or chiefs to govern them. They plant and gather their crops of corn; their lands are fertile; and they utilize wild cows called *cíbolas*."[51] The kingdom of Quivira was said to be found upon the northern boundary of the Tejas, a word taken from the Caddo word *techas*, which means "friend." The Spanish would continue to mistak-enly use it interchangeably with the name "Hasinais" for the next century and a half.[52]

A quarter of a century passed before the Hasinais were heard from again by the Spaniards, even though the Caddo tribes continued to obtain Spanish goods through trade. It was from the south (on the Nuevo León–Coahuila frontier), rather than from New Mexico, that the Spanish advanced unknowingly toward the Hasinais. By 1670, they had reached the Rio Grande downstream from the mouth of the Pecos River. Franciscan Father Juan Larios led the missionary activity along the Rio Grande, and in 1675, Larios crossed the river accompanied by Fernando del Bosque to explore the country and examine the possibilities of missionary work among the tribes to the north.[53]

Through the Coahuila Indians they met on the expedition, Bosque and Larios heard of a nation to the northeast, "a populous . . . people, and so extensive that those who give detailed reports of them do not know where it ends. . . . The people of that nation, which they call Tejas . . . live under an organized government, congregated in their pueblos [and] governed by a *cacique* who is named by the Great Lord, as they call the one who rules them all, who they say resides in the interior. They have houses made of wood, cultivate the soil, plant maize and other crops, wear clothes, and punish misdemeanors, especially theft." The Coahuilas did not give more of a detailed account of the Tejas, for they said they were allowed to travel only to the border, since the Great Lord did not permit foreign nations to enter the interior of the country.[54]

Reports of a tribe as culturally advanced and as well-organized as the Hasinais excited the missionaries immensely. They reasoned that the tribe, because it was sedentary and agriculturally inclined, could be easily converted, just as the Pueblo tribes of New Mexico had been. The bishop of Guadalajara recommended the quick pacification of the Coahuilas through the establishment of four missions, thus making it easier for the Spanish to reach their ultimate goal, the rich and powerful Tejas. The Hasinais had now become one of the objectives for the Spanish of both New Mexico and Coahuila.[55]

As the Spanish were seeking out the Hasinais, the tribe was also attempting to establish direct contact. In 1683, the Hasinais sent two messengers to the Jumanos asking them to contact the Spanish and request that missionaries be sent to their country. The Jumano chief, Juan Sabeata, was a man who knew how to manipulate the Spanish. He traveled to El Paso and told the priests of the request from the "great kingdom of the Tejas," while at the same time asking for missionaries for his own tribe. He told them that the Tejas were a settled people who raised many crops and were ruled by a powerful king. To further whet their appetite, Sabeata stated that the Tejas lived near the border of "the great kingdom of Quivira," and Spanish interest was heightened even further when

Sabeata added that "houses made of trees" had entered the rivers of the Tejas for the purpose of trade (implying that French ships had visited the Hasinais).[56]

The Tejas request and the report of the French prompted the Spanish to action, and an expedition headed by Juan Domínguez de Mendoza and Father Nicolás López was sent from El Paso in 1684 for the purpose of discovering "the East and the kingdom of the Tejas." The party, however, made it only as far east as a river in Central Texas—possibly the San Saba or the Llano—where they built a temporary fort and chapel. During their stay of six weeks, Mendoza and López met with many tribes and claimed to have received messages from many others, including "people of the Rio de los Tejas," who promised to come and meet the Spaniards. Mendoza and López, however, were not able to wait for them, and they returned to El Paso after leaving messages stating that they would return the following year.[57]

Stimulated by the prospect of returning to find the Hasinais, López and Mendoza traveled to Mexico City to promote the enterprise. Father López wrote the viceroy of New Spain, telling him of the Indians' desire for permanent missionaries. He claimed to have "touched upon the threshold of the extensive and powerful kingdom of the Tejas" and asked for authorization to establish missions there. Captain Mendoza, concerned with more temporal matters, addressed a memorial to the viceroy offering to lead a force of two hundred men to find the kingdom of the Tejas and build forts to secure the country from the French.[58]

Both of these offers went unaccepted, however, for Spanish officials in Mexico had already received word that the French had indeed invaded the holdings of Spain by landing somewhere upon the Gulf Coast of Texas. Consequently, Spanish authorities momentarily lost interest in the Tejas and turned their attention to the French. Ironically, it was in searching for the remnants of the intruders' colony on the coast that the Spanish would finally reach the Hasinais, but not until after the tribe had already made contact with the colonists from France.

Chapter 2

The Caddos and the Arrival of the Europeans, 1686–94[1]

Among these nations, the [Hasinai] seem to us the most numerous and polished; it is governed by a king or cacique, and the subordination that we remarked among them made us infer that they had officers; the houses are built with order and very prettily, and they have the art of making a cloth of feathers and the hair of animals. We found there silver lamps, old muskets and Spanish sword-blades. Having asked them by signs where they got them, they took coal and depicted a Spaniard, houses, steeples, and showed the part of the heaven under which New Mexico would lie.

—Father Jean Cavelier, 1686[1]

The [Hasinais] refuse to believe that there is only one God. They declare that there are two: one who gave the Spaniards clothing, knives and hatchets, and one of their own who gave them corn, frijoles, acorns, and water for their crops.

—Father Damian Massanet, June 14, 1693[2]

THE INTRUSION OF FRANCE INTO TEXAS in the late seventeenth century added one more newcomer to the rapidly changing Caddo world. All three Caddo confederacies met and established friendly relations with the French through the remnants of the ill-fated colony on the Gulf Coast. Although the French were only in the area for a short time during this period, they laid the foundations for future associations between themselves and the Caddos.

As the weakness of Spain became more and more apparent, the powers of its European rivals, France and England, increased. This left the great expanses of unoccupied land claimed by Spain open to foreign encroachment. While the English contented themselves for the most part with the East Coast of North America as well as choice islands in the Caribbean, the French began to advance southward from Canada down the Mississippi River toward the Spanish holdings.

The French threat finally prompted the Spanish to meet the Caddos and to establish a foothold in the Hasinai country. Both the Spanish and the Hasinais were deeply disappointed in this effort, however, for the Spanish were not prepared to provide the tribe with the weapons—forbidden to do so by idealistic crown policy—or the protection they desired, and the Hasinais were not as eager to accept Christianity as the Spanish had hoped. The seventeenth century came to a close with the Hasinais bitterly opposed to the Spanish and all three Caddo confederacies looking toward France as a prospective trading and military partner.

Like the Spanish, the French were few in number and constituted no threat to the natives by coveting their lands or displacing them. Unlike the Spanish, matters of religion, conversion, and civilization hardly figured in their dealings with the natives in Louisiana, for what the French desired were the furs and hides the natives could deliver for sale in the profitable European market. Having little desire to change the Indians' religion, the French provided them with guns and ammunition to improve their hunting ability. The natives also desired other European goods, such as cooking and farming utensils, cotton clothing, axes, knives, beads, and vermilion. Like the Spanish, however, the French used the Indians to secure a territorial claim: by establishing trading ties with the tribes, which later would be strengthened by a military alliance, the French sought to extend their empire into the uninhabited expanses of North America already claimed by Spain. The French knew of the rich mines in northern Mexico and wished to obtain a foothold as close to them as possible from which to launch an invasion. Thus the Caddos, the most important tribe on New Spain's northeastern frontier, became the focus of attention for both the European powers.[3]

Nine years after Father Jacques Marquette and Louis Joliet had ventured down the Mississippi in 1673, René-Robert Cavelier, Sieur de La Salle, descended the river to the Gulf of Mexico. Returning to France, La Salle proposed to place a colony upstream from the mouth of the Mississippi River with the intention of "[harassing] seriously or even completely [winning] New Spain." He envisioned setting up posts throughout the rest of the Mississippi Valley to secure the trade of the natives, and when war broke out between France and Spain in October, 1683, La Salle's proposal was accepted by the aggressive, expansion-minded king of France, Louis XIV.[4]

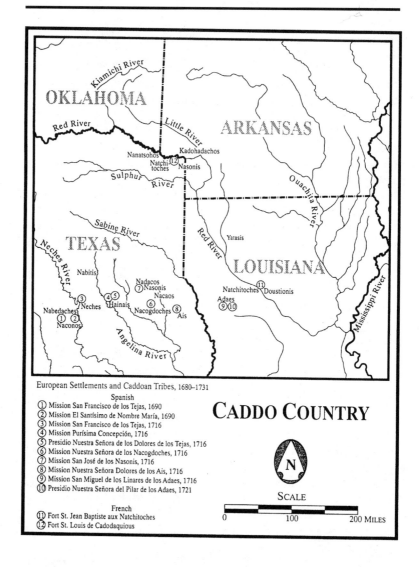

European Settlements and Caddoan Tribes, 1680–1731

Spanish
1. Mission San Francisco de los Tejas, 1690
2. Mission El Santísimo de Nombre María, 1690
3. Mission San Francisco de los Tejas, 1716
4. Mission Purísima Concepción, 1716
5. Presidio Nuestra Señora de los Dolores de los Tejas, 1716
6. Mission Nuestra Señora de los Nacogdoches, 1716
7. Mission San José de los Nasonis, 1716
8. Mission Nuestra Señora Dolores de los Ais, 1716
9. Mission San Miguel de los Linares de los Adaes, 1716
10. Presidio Nuestra Señora del Pilar de los Adaes, 1721

French
11. Fort St. Jean Baptiste aux Natchitoches
12. Fort St. Louis de Cadodaquious

CADDO COUNTRY

SCALE

0   100   200 MILES

In the summer of 1684, La Salle left France with one hundred soldiers and nearly three hundred colonists in search of the mouth of the Mississippi, which he calculated to be much farther west than its actual location. Thus, La Salle landed in Matagorda Bay, halfway down the Texas coast.[5] The group soon found itself stranded when the vessel that had been left with La Salle ran aground and was destroyed by the surf. Following the construction of a fort called Saint Louis (generally accepted now to have been on Garcitas Creek), La Salle decided to find the Mississippi by land and ascend it to the French fort he and his trusted, one-handed lieutenant, Henri de Tonti, had founded in 1683 on the Illinois River. At this post (also called Fort Saint Louis) La Salle hoped to secure the reinforcements necessary to carry out his plans of colonizing the area and reaching New Spain.[6]

In April, 1686, La Salle and twenty men, including his brother Jean Cavelier and the friar Anastase Douay, set out to find the great river. Traveling northward through open plains, the party lived off the numerous buffalo and enjoyed friendly relations with the Indians they met. After about three weeks they turned toward the east and entered, in Douay's words, "countries still finer than those we had passed, and found tribes that had nothing barbarous about them but the name." The most important of these were the Hasinais, whom the French called the "Cenis." According to Jean Cavelier, the Cenis were the "most numerous and polished" of the natives they met. Although the Spanish had heard of and had been trying to reach the Caddos for nearly four decades, it was the French who first encountered the tribe, without any previous knowledge of their existence.[7]

A Nabedache warrior, hunting with his family west of his village, was the first Caddo to meet with the French face to face. He warmly welcomed La Salle and his party, for upon observing their clothes and weapons, he must have assumed they were the longed-for Spanish. This "very honest Indian" returned to his village to announce the arrival of the Europeans to the Nabedache *caddi*. The chief formed a welcoming committee for the French and hastened back to their camp with two horses laden with food. La Salle was "received as if in triumph" by the *caddi*, and the French party was met by a "great concourse of people," who lavished them with gifts as they made their way to the village.[8]

Evidence of the Hasinais' extensive indirect trade with the Spanish was everywhere in the Nabedache village. The French saw silver lamps, old muskets, swords, spoons, candlesticks, and clothes. La Salle quickly made the Nabedaches understand that he and his party were different from the Spanish and offered the tribe his own French-made metal goods in return for food and horses. The natives prized the French metal axes and knives the most, but they also desired needles and pins for sewing, as well as rings and beads from La Salle. The French felt they had swung a bargain, since they obtained horses worth twenty gold pieces in France for just one ax; the Nabedaches, already rich in horses but desperate for metal goods, felt they had gotten the better deal. With both sides pleased by the transaction, the foundation for a mutually beneficial trading partnership was established between the Caddos and the French by La Salle and the Nabedaches.[9]

La Salle and his men stayed with the Nabedaches for four or five days before resuming their quest for the Mississippi River. They headed across the Neches River and passed by the Nasoni village, the easternmost tribe of the Hasinai confederacy. La Salle attempted to continue the journey, but four Frenchmen, attracted to the easy life of the Hasinais, deserted five leagues from the village and returned to the Nasonis. La Salle then came down with a fever, and the whole expedition returned to the Nasoni village until he recovered. The party, minus the four deserters, finally returned to Fort Saint Louis with the intention of returning to the Hasinais the following year.[10]

The Hasinais gladly welcomed the deserters into the tribe, and the Frenchmen in turn quickly adopted native ways. They took Hasinai wives, adopted native dress, and had their faces tattooed in the manner of Caddo men. Since they had kept their firearms when they deserted, the Frenchmen gained great reputations as warriors.[11] From their experience with the French deserters, the Hasinais certainly came to believe that the Europeans were tractable people: men with valuable goods who could be adopted easily into their tribe.

In January, 1687, La Salle and another group left Fort Saint Louis in yet another attempt to reach the Mississippi River. La Salle's immediate goal, however, was to reach the Hasinais to obtain fresh horses. Henri Joutel was among the party, as was an eleven-year-old boy, Pierre Talon, who was brought by La Salle "so he could learn their language." Before reaching the tribe, however, quarreling broke out within the group, and La Salle and a few others were assassinated.[12]

The remnants of the French party continued to the Hasinai villages, where they were gladly welcomed by the Nabedaches. The natives took them to greet the *caddi* and then to a public meeting house, where a feast was held to celebrate their arrival. The next day the Frenchmen were taken to the house of the *xinesi,* where they witnessed the great veneration and respect the tribe had for him. Wherever he went, the *xinesi* was "borne by eight men on a platform, [and] all the tribe ranged in two lines, both hands on the forehead, uttering a cry of joy or humility."[13]

The Hasinais eagerly resumed the trade that had begun the previous year with the French. The Frenchmen further impressed the tribe by accepting their invitation to join them in a war campaign against an enemy tribe called the Cannohatinno, probably the Cantonas, who ranged the prairies between the Trinity and Guadalupe Rivers. Assisted by the French and their firearms, the Hasinais completely routed the enemy, killing the unprecedented total of forty-eight men and women. Two women were brought back alive; one was allowed to return home with a present of a ball and powder to inform her tribe that the Hasinais intended to return with firearms, and the other was tortured and killed by the Hasinai women.[14]

Seven of the French, led by Joutel, decided to resume their quest for

Canada in June, 1687. A few other Frenchmen—those who had either deserted or had been involved in the assassination of La Salle—remained with the Hasinais. Eventually, however, they fought among themselves and two were killed. The boy, Pierre Talon, also stayed with the Hasinais "and was treated with the greatest kindness" by them.[15]

Joutel and his party hired Nasoni guides, who took them through "the finest country in the world" on their way to the Kadohadacho confederacy on the Red River. Although the Kadohadachos had heard of the French, they had yet to meet any face-to-face. The mounted Kadohadacho *caddi*, attended by a great number of followers, encountered the French outside his village and greeted them with "very much kindness and affection." After engaging in a friendly smoke, the French were carried triumphantly into the village in accordance with Kadohadacho tradition. Two hundred Kadohadachos gathered as the visitors had their heads and feet washed by women. The French were then placed on a platform "covered with a very neat, white mat," where they were harangued by the old men's long speeches. Joutel responded to this greeting by distributing presents to the tribe: axes, knives, needles, and beads were handed out with the promise that more would be given when the French were able to return. Upon their departure, the French were provided with guides who led them to the Cahinnios, a Caddoan-speaking tribe that lived to the east on the Ouachita River. From there they were taken to the Arkansas Post, a small French fort that had just recently been established by Tonti among the Quapaw Indians near the mouth of the Arkansas River.[16]

After meeting with Joutel's party, Tonti decided to investigate the fate of La Salle's colony that had been left on the coast. In January, 1690, Tonti headed down the Mississippi from the Arkansas Post with two Kadohadacho women the Quapaws had recently freed from the Osages. He continued south to the Taensas tribe, from whom a few guides escorted him westward to the Red River and the third Caddo confederacy, the Natchitoches. The Natchitoches had yet to meet a Frenchman, and they were immediately impressed by the one-handed traveler, for Tonti helped negotiate a truce between them and the Taensas. As a reward, the Natchitoches *caddi* instructed a few tribesmen to take Tonti upstream to the Yatasis, another tribe of the Natchitoches confederacy. They welcomed him warmly but were unwilling to direct him to the Kadohadachos, since the two tribes were at war. Tonti was given guides only after he assured the Yatasis that he would mediate a settlement with the Kadohadachos, and the party arrived at its destination on March 28, 1690.[17]

The Kadohadachos, remembering Joutel's visit, greeted Tonti with great fanfare and were pleasantly surprised when he returned the two captured women. In return for his diplomatic services, the *caddi* informed

Tonti that there were still Frenchmen living among the Nabedaches and provided him with guides to their village.[18]

Tonti's visit to the Nabedaches was the first and only time during this period that the French and the Caddos did not enjoy amicable relations. In the preceding year, the Nabedaches had met with a large group of Spaniards searching for La Salle's colony far to the south of their village. As will be detailed below, the tribe had become well-disposed toward the Spanish, since they had received presents and a pledge that their Spanish benefactors would return with more the following year. The promised Spanish expedition was actually en route from the south as Tonti approached from the opposite direction. Knowing that Tonti and the Spaniards were at odds, the Nabedaches were unsure how to receive him when he entered their village on April 23, 1690.[19]

From the beginning the meeting between Tonti and the Nabedache *caddi* was clouded in confusion. The *caddi* truthfully informed Tonti that there were indeed Frenchmen in his village, yet there was no sign of them. When the *caddi* further explained that two had killed each other and that the rest were out with a hunting party, Tonti mistakenly assumed that the Nabedaches had killed his countrymen. He refused to smoke with the tribal elders and gruffly demanded that the *caddi* furnish him with horses and guides to take him to Fort Saint Louis. The offended *caddi* made Tonti give him "seven hatchets and a string of large glass beads" for the horses but refused to supply him with escorts. The unhappy Tonti was forced to return to the Kadohadacho villages and from there made his way back to Illinois.[20]

Although Tonti failed to contact the French survivors, his trip was very important for the Caddos. The third Caddo confederacy, the Natchitoches, had established relations with the French, while the Kadohadachos had reaffirmed their friendship with them as well. Through his brusqueness with the Nabedaches, however, Tonti had temporarily alienated the Hasinai confederacy, which helped convince the tribe to provide the advancing Spanish with a very congenial welcome to their country.

As previously mentioned, the Nabedaches had already established friendly relations with the representatives from Spain a full year before Tonti's arrival. Provoked by the French colony on the Gulf Coast, the Spanish had undertaken a large-scale search to find and destroy the intruders; beginning in 1686, five maritime expeditions and as many overland searches were sent out from New Spain. The fifth overland expedition, headed by Alonso de León, governor of Coahuila, left from the presidio of Monclova on March 23, 1689, in search of La Salle. One month later he found Fort Saint Louis destroyed, the houses in ruins, and all but a few members of the French party killed by the surrounding Karankawa Indians.[21]

The Hasinais were well aware of the search for La Salle, and the Nabedache *caddi* in turn sought out the Spanish with a group of warriors and two of the French refugees, who were "naked except for an antelope's skin, and with their faces, breasts, and arms painted like the Indians." The Nabedaches visited a group of natives—possibly Tonkawas—on the lower Colorado River, and from there one of the French sent a message to the nearby Spanish encampment on the Guadalupe. On May 1, 1689, Governor de León arrived at the village and met the Nabedache *caddi*, who agreed to return to the Guadalupe with the Frenchmen and eight warriors to meet the rest of the Spanish party.[22]

The moment both groups had long awaited had finally arrived. The Nabedaches surely found the well-supplied Spanish much more impressive than the desperate French refugees who had visited them from the Gulf Coast. The Spaniards, in turn, were very enthusiastic about meeting the tribe of whom they had heard so many great things. De León felt that the *caddi* "was an Indian in whom was recognized capacity" and presented him with generous amounts of cotton cloth, knives, beads, blankets, and other goods. This pleased the *caddi* greatly, and he promised to visit the Spanish in the future at Coahuila.[23]

The chaplain of the expedition, Franciscan Father Damian Massanet, was especially excited at meeting the tribe the Spanish knew as the Tejas. He showed the *caddi* "all possible consideration," giving him both of his horses and his only blankets. Using one of the Frenchmen as an interpreter, Massanet told the *caddi* that his people should become Christians and have priests come into their lands to baptize them in order to save their souls. When Massanet volunteered to go the following spring, the *caddi* said he would "very willingly" take him to his country. The priest believed that the Nabedaches "seemed well pleased, and I was still more so, seeing the harvest to be reaped among the many souls in those lands who know not God." The next day the natives heard mass, and both parties headed back to their respective homes.[24]

Massanet obviously misread the Nabedaches' eagerness for the Spanish to come to their lands as being a desire for Christianity. It is questionable whether the *caddi* understood what Massanet meant by baptism and the saving of souls. He did, however, understand to some extent (from what he had been told by the Jumanos) that the missionaries were the central figures of every Spanish expedition. If the Nabedaches desired more Spanish goods and a military alliance, they understood that the acceptance of the priests was the way in which these items might be gained. It is extremely unlikely, however, that the Nabedaches realized the religious and cultural changes that the acceptance of the missionaries would represent.

Both de León and Massanet returned to Mexico eager to go back to the Nabedaches and the Hasinai confederacy. For months they lobbied for the viceroy's authorization to return despite the fact that each had a different view of the proposed expedition. De León desired a military expedition that would win the territory and the Indians over to the Spanish by halting the French threat. Father Massanet opposed the martial nature of de León's proposal, however, preferring a more religious tone for the expedition with only a few soldiers to escort the missionaries.[25]

Officials in New Spain leaned toward Massanet's proposal, since the crown had long expressed its desire to spread the Gospel through peaceful means; however, the French threat caused them to decide in favor of a joint military and religious expedition. De León was ordered to set out as soon as possible with 110 men, a sufficient number to contend with the French presence. Father Massanet was entrusted with the missionary aspect of the expedition and was authorized to select 5 missionaries to accompany him from the Franciscan training seminary, the Colegio de la Santa Cruz de Querétaro. They were to meet with the Hasinai chiefs and inquire if they still desired missionaries to instruct them and perform baptisms. Father Massanet was given the right to decide if the priests should remain among the tribe alone or if a troop of soldiers should be left for their protection. No force was to be used, since the Hasinais were to be converted by "God's faith and their own free will." In late March, 1690—just as Tonti arrived at the Kadohadacho village—the expedition set out from Coahuila with two hundred head of cattle and four hundred horses.[26]

A month and a half later—following Tonti's angry departure from the Nabedaches—a welcoming committee of fourteen warriors, headed by the Nabedache *caddi*, greeted the Spanish party near the Trinity River. The Nabedache headman, seeing the great extent of the Spanish expedition, was very impressed and eagerly demonstrated his desire for close relations with this valuable ally. He recognized Father Massanet and rushed to embrace him. He told de León—using Talon and another Frenchman as translators—that "all his people were awaiting [the Spaniards] with much pleasure" and was rewarded with a gift of clothes and other goods from the Spanish governor. For three days the Nabedaches led the Spanish through groves of live oak until they reached a valley "thickly settled with the houses of the Tejas Indians." A formal procession took the Spanish to the house of the *caddi*, where they were seated and fed "all very cleanly." Presents of clothing and other goods were distributed to the tribe, and de León asked the *caddi* to summon his people to celebrate the feast of Corpus Christi on the following day of May 25, 1690.[27]

The next morning the tribe observed the Spanish priests as they celebrated mass, and this ceremony was followed by one that formally marked the Hasinais' acceptance of an alliance with Spain. The *caddi* pledged that his tribe would remain obedient to the king of Spain, and he allowed the Spanish flag to be raised above the village. In return, de León promised the king's aid and friendship and gave the *caddi* a staff with a cross, signifying the formal recognition of Spain's rule. The *caddi* was notified that he should respect and obey the priests and encourage all his people to attend Christian teaching "in order that they might be instructed in the affairs of our holy Catholic faith so that they might become baptized and become Christian." According to de León, the *caddi* accepted the cross "with much pleasure" and promised to do all that was desired of him. He also agreed to send his brother, nephew, and cousin back to New Spain with the Spanish to witness the great riches there.[28]

The *caddi* sent for the *xinesi* so he could give the alliance his blessing. Under Father Massanet's direction, the Hasinai high priest was treated with great respect by the Spanish party. Massanet invited him to eat with the Spanish priests and allowed the *xinesi* to bless the food in the traditional Hasinai manner. After dinner Massanet gave him and his wife clothing, "and he was well pleased." With the consent of the Nabedache *caddi*, the missionaries found a spot near a brook outside the village for the mission and the priest's quarters. The Indians completed the construction of Mission San Francisco de los Tejas three days later, and on June 1, 1690, the first mass was celebrated there.[29]

Once the mission had been built, Governor de León inquired about the French and was informed by the *caddi* that Tonti had been in the area. After hearing this news, de León wanted to leave fifty soldiers among the tribe to head off any further French intrusions. Father Massanet angrily opposed this, claiming that it was against the official orders allowing him to determine the number of soldiers to remain with the missionaries. Massanet felt that only three soldiers should stay, "since it was at no time necessary for the safety of the priests to leave soldiers amongst the Tejas, for from the very first they welcomed us with so much affection and good will that they could hardly do enough for us." In fact, the soldiers were the tribe's only cause for complaint because one of them had tried to rape the wife of the *caddi*'s brother. Massanet forced Governor de León to acquiesce, and only three soldiers were left with the three priests who remained at the mission.[30]

Satisfied that firm ties had been established with the Spanish, the Nabedache *caddi* tearfully bid the three members of his family goodbye as they left for Coahuila with de León and Massanet in June, 1690.[31] However, he quickly turned his attention to the six Spaniards who remained with his tribe. They had been supplied with nine horses, twenty head of cattle, two yoke of oxen, metal farming implements, and flour.[32] Although the three priests had been instructed to learn the Caddo language and convert the Hasinais to Christianity, the *caddi* was much more interested in how he could profit from them materially. Since their goals were so much at odds with one another, the relationship between the priests and the Hasinais was doomed almost from the beginning.

Father Miguel de Fontcuberta was left nominally in charge of the three priests, but his colleague, Francisco Casañas de Jesús María, quickly took the reins in carrying out their mission. He visited all the tribes of the Hasinai confederacy to learn their language and tribal customs. To serve more of the Hasinais, he founded Mission Santísimo Nombre de María near the Neches village five miles to the east of Mission San Francisco.[33]

Although the missionaries were warmly welcomed by the tribal leaders initially, the Hasinais were not as receptive to Christianity as they had seemed to the Spanish.[34] They were satisfied with their religion, their leadership, and their way of life, which had served them very well up to this point. The tribe had wanted the Spanish for the material goods and the protection they could provide, not for spiritual guidance. The more the missionaries insisted upon conversion, the more they were resented.

None of the three priests possessed the depth of understanding and adaptability of Father Massanet. The Hasinais expected that the Spaniards, like the Frenchmen, would adopt the Hasinai way of life. Instead, the priests ran roughshod over tribal customs and ridiculed the Hasinai religion, and the worst offender in this regard was Father Casañas. Although he admired the Hasinais' work habits and their monogamous marriages, he was horrified by the "errors and superstitions these retched [sic] people (who are blind to the true faith) entertain." Casañas confronted and challenged the tribe, starting at the top with the *xinesi*, who was deceiving the people, according to Casañas, and frightening them into giving him tribute and respect. The priest demanded that the *xinesi* allow him to enter the sacred house of the *coninisi*, but refused to disrobe as called for by tradition. Casañas asked to see the two children and was handed a wooden box, which he then threatened to throw into the perpetual fire. When the *xinesi* understandably became furious, Casañas relented, though he threatened to build a mission on the spot of the sacred house in the future.[35]

The medicine men, or *connas*, were also the object of Casañas's scorn: he characterized them as being "liars and guilty of a thousand deceptions." He interrupted them as they performed a lengthy burial ceremony by placing his hand over the mouth of one of the *connas*, telling him to be quiet, for "all he was saying was of no use and that what I was going to say to God would alone be useful to the dead man." On another occasion, Father Fontcuberta attempted to move a corpse from the house of the *caddi* to the mission, but he retreated, since "it caused so much excitement among the Indians that we were afraid it would incite a riot."[36]

In addition, the priests were unable to control their own soldiers, who continued to molest the Hasinai women. Admitting that "the dissatisfaction of all the Indians is great when the Spaniards live among them without their wives," the missionaries advised that, in the future "it would be to our interest if no man came without his wife."[37]

The strained relations between the Hasinais and the priests were exacerbated by an epidemic that swept through the country in early 1691. On January 28, Father Fontcuberta came down with a fever and died eight days later. The disease then spread like wildfire through the Hasinai confederacy and on to the surrounding tribes, including the Kadohada-chos and the Natchitoches. The connas, whose remedies worked so well on native ailments, were unable to stop the foreign contagion. Before the epidemic had run its course in March, three or four hundred of the Hasinai had succumbed, together with three thousand members of the neighboring tribes.[38]

As their people died, the Hasinais panicked and became unsure of what to do. The tribe correctly assumed that the Spanish had brought the disease but blamed it on the baptism ritual, since the priests had been baptizing the sick, who often died soon thereafter. The connas implored their people to resist baptism, and the caddi went so far as to call a council to discuss killing the priests. Casañas entered the meeting and calmly told the caddi that the deaths had been God's will. As this explanation surely did not endear the tribe to Christianity, the priests' lives were saved only when the xinesi allowed Casañas to baptize him on his deathbed and soon recovered to "perfect health." Despite the xinesi's recovery, tensions remained high in the country of the Hasinais in the summer of 1691, when the news arrived that a large Spanish expedition was approaching from the south.[39]

Once again, this expedition had Father Massanet as its spiritual leader. The priest, upon returning to Mexico with Governor de León in 1690, had petitioned the viceroy to allow more missions to be sent to the Tejas. Massanet believed that they would succeed for the "Tejas people are in-clined to work, plant corn and beans, . . . and are well governed." He also proposed sending missions to the Kadohadachos since he had heard that they were "very politic, reasonable, and very united with the Tejas." The Caddos were so peaceful that Massanet suggested that only carpenters and other craftsmen be sent, as no soldiers would be needed.[40]

Both the Hasinais' warm welcome of the Spanish and de León's report of Tonti being in the area led the officials in Mexico City to accept Massanet's proposals. They instructed Massanet to return to the Tejas with an expedition headed by the new governor of Coahuila, Don Domingo Terán de los Ríos. Fifty soldiers would accompany the ten priests and three lay brothers, but the principal purpose of the expedition was a religious one. Seven missions were to be established among both the Hasinais and the Kadohadachos; the search for French intrusion was to be secondary. As always, the use of force was forbidden, since the Indians should instead "be controlled by persuasion, kindness, gentle and considerate treatment."[41]

The slow-moving expedition left Coahuila on May 16, 1691. Among Terán's guides was the nephew of the Nabedache *caddi* who had gone with his cousin to New Spain, where he had been baptized and given the name Bernardino. Like his countrymen back at the Hasinai villages, Bernardino had quickly become dissatisfied with the Spanish, since his cousin had been murdered while in Mexico. For the time being, however, Bernardino kept his complaints to himself and guided Terán and Massanet toward the Hasinai country.[42]

In mid-June the expedition reached the Guadalupe River and was met by a large group of Jumano Indians led by Juan Sabeata. The Jumanos had just left the Hasinais, and Sabeata gave Massanet two letters from the missionaries informing him of the epidemic and the death of Father Fontcuberta. A return message was sent to the priests at Mission San Francisco alerting them of the imminent arrival of the new expedition. The Nabedaches were very unhappy when they heard the news; they objected that the troops were once again coming without wives. The men warned Casañas that if the Spanish desired to be their friends, the troops must be kept from molesting their women.[43]

Despite his misgivings about the Spanish arrival, the Nabedache *caddi* accompanied Father Casañas to greet Father Massanet and the Spanish missionaries—who had gone ahead of Terán—outside his village on August 2. The Spanish set up camp and were formally received by the *caddi* on August 6, 1691. Governor Terán, ignoring the tribe's bad relations with the priests, presented the *caddi* with a baton both as a token of royal protection and to recognize his "obedience and his inclination toward the Christian religion." After the Spanish priests said mass, Governor Terán distributed presents to the tribe, and a general celebration followed.[44]

The Hasinais remained friendly as long as the soldiers remained in their village and Terán continued to lavish gifts. However, when Terán and the soldiers departed for the coast to meet a supply ship on August 24, the tribe, led by the disgruntled Bernardino, became insolent and hostile. They stole the horses and killed the cattle the Spanish had brought with them. Before heading west to hunt buffalo with Bernardino, the *caddi* warned the priests that he did not want them to be there when he returned. While on their hunt, the Nabedache warriors found further reasons to hate the Spanish: west of the Trinity River, the party was attacked by a troop of Spanish deserters who took the *caddi*'s hat, French rifle, and Spanish sword.[45]

The Spaniards' behavior at his village also displeased the Nabedache *caddi* when he returned from his hunt. Governor Terán, just back from the coast, confronted the tribe and had five natives accused of killing cattle bound and brought to him. His troops also relieved the *caddi* of three mules he was suspected of having stolen. Terán, however, took no further action against the Hasinais because he was preparing to leave for the Kadohadacho villages as called for in his instructions.[46]

Accompanied by the ever-zealous Father Massanet, Terán and a group of soldiers headed north for the Kadohadacho confederacy on November 6, 1691. Not until late November did they reach the home of the new *caddi* of the Kadohadachos, a "very good looking" boy of about fourteen, who welcomed them and gave them shelter.[47] Both Massanet and Terán were impressed by the respect he commanded from his "strong robust" warriors. The *caddi*'s older brother received a baton for him from Governor Terán signifying the Spanish recognition of his authority. Father Massanet then met with the elders of the tribe to ask if they wanted to become Christians and receive priests. Unsure whether their French friends would ever return and eager to remain on good terms with both European powers, the elders replied that they were willing. The Spanish party, weakened by the travel and the bad weather, were unable to establish a mission on this visit, but they promised to return the next year. Massanet put a cross above the door of the *caddi*'s house, and the party returned to the Hasinais and Mission San Francisco. Now both the Spanish and the French had staked a claim among the tribes of the Kadohadacho confederacy.[48]

In January, 1692, the Hasinai people gladly watched as Terán left for his return trip to Mexico. Most of the missionaries, discouraged by the unfriendly attitude of the Hasinais, joined him. Only Father Massanet, two priests, and a few lay brothers had the faith and strength to remain and continue the effort to convert the Hasinais. Their task was made more difficult when Terán took most of the horses and livestock intended for the remaining missionaries. Because of the increasing hostility of the Hasinais, Terán left nine soldiers to protect the three priests.[49]

The Hasinais' enmity for the Spanish did not decrease following Terán's departure, and relations quickly worsened. The situation was exacerbated by the failure of the tribe's corn crops. The first planting was flooded by torrential rains that also washed away the mission among the Neches. Their second crop was destroyed by drought, and as a result, both the Hasinais and the Spaniards were starving and preyed upon the remaining livestock. In addition to this famine, a second epidemic swept through the country from May to November of 1692. Although it was less destructive than the previous epidemic, it still did not endear the

Spanish to the Caddos. The tribe was also irritated by the soldiers' continued harassment of the women.[50]

Besides the tensions arising out of the physical hardships, the Hasinais refused to part with their "witchcraft, superstitions, and frauds of the devil" and stubbornly resisted the priests' conversion attempts. The tribe also refused to leave their scattered houses and congregate in towns as the Spanish wished, nor did they ever come to church or bother to listen to the prayers of the missionaries. Although the *connas* were willing to accept the existence of the Spanish God, they persisted in their belief in Ahahayo. They told Massanet that there were two Gods: one who gave the Spaniards clothing, knives and hatchets, and one of their own who gave them corn, beans, nuts, acorns, and water for their crops. Once the people began dying of sickness, the *connas* again convinced most of the tribe that the sacrament of baptism was responsible. They prevented the Christian burial of the few who had been baptized on their deathbeds and performed the traditional funeral ceremonies instead.[51]

In October, 1692, Massanet hired two visiting natives to take a message asking for assistance to Mexico. Not until May 3, 1693, did the new governor of Coahuila, Gregorio de Salinas Varona, set out with twenty soldiers and supplies to relieve Massanet. In June the expedition arrived at the mission just in time, for the priests had decided to abandon the country in July if nothing had been heard from Mexico by then.[52]

Living with the Hasinais for a year had caused Father Massanet to abandon his belief that the tribe had actually desired Christianity. He now understood that all they wanted from the Spaniards were metal goods, gifts, and protection. Massanet conveyed his reappraisal of the situation in a letter to the viceroy in which he also indicated that the only possibility for the Hasinais' successful conversion lay with the use of soldiers and a presidio to force the tribe to live together, "not like now where they are very scattered." In the event that the officials of New Spain opposed this proposal, Massanet requested permission to leave the country.[53]

A week after arriving with the supplies, Governor Salinas and his soldiers left the mission along with two more priests and Massanet's proposal for the forced conversion of the Hasinais in hand. Upon receiving this shocking document, the viceroy in Mexico City expressed surprise at Massanet's request. Unwilling to adopt such rash methods, Governor Salinas was ordered on August 31, 1693, to send a force to Texas to escort the priests out of the country. As Governor Salinas did not receive the order until October 1, 1693, he decided against mounting an expedition so late in the year.[54]

In the meantime relations between the priests and the Hasinais continued to disintegrate. Shortly after the departure of Salinas in June,

1693, Massanet "began to recognize a major restlessness among the Indians." The Hasinais, who had desired only weapons and a military alliance from the Spanish, were receiving neither. Only a few priests lived among them, and the only valuable items they had were horses and cattle. The natives immediately stole most of these and soon threatened the remaining missionaries. In August, 1693, the Nabedache *caddi* formed a plan calling for the Hasinais and the surrounding tribes, including the Kadohadachos, to rise up and massacre the Spanish at the beginning of winter. A Spanish-speaking Mexican Indian informed Father Massanet of this plot, and the remaining Spaniards went on full alert.[55]

Things remained tense until October 6, when the *caddi* told one of the few remaining soldiers that "all of his people were very annoyed with the Spanish and it would be better if the Spanish went and left his lands." When a group of Kadohadachos arrived later, a worried Father Massanet asked the *caddi* if what he had said was true. With "much ridicule" the *caddi* confirmed this and told Massanet that his people had often spoken of throwing out the Spanish. Massanet berated the *caddi* for his ingratitude, but realizing that his life was in danger, agreed to leave the country. On October 25, after burying the iron and copper church ornaments and setting fire to the mission, the Spaniards took flight. For four days Hasinai warriors followed them but did not attack. Massanet and his party wandered helplessly in the wilderness for four months until they finally staggered into the presidio at Monclova on February 17, 1694. One month later the viceroy resolved to postpone any further attempts to Christianize the Hasinais until a more opportune time.[56]

Thus, the flurry of activity that had occurred among the Caddos from 1686 to 1693 finally came to an end. The Spanish attempt to win the Hasinais over by the peaceful conversion to Christianity had failed completely, and the tribe's experience with the Spanish made them want to renew their ties with the French. The Kadohadacho and Natchitoches confederacies had also responded favorably to the French who had visited their villages. However, by the time the Europeans did return to the region in the eighteenth century, the Caddos' situation had been altered by events well beyond the tribe's control.

Chapter 3

The Caddos and the Establishment of the Europeans, 1694–1731

[The Kadohadacho caddi] informed the people that the time had come to change their tears into happiness, even though it was true that most of their comrades had been killed or made slaves by their adversaries, and that they were no longer numerous. The arrival of the Canouches [the name given to the French] would prevent their total destruction. . . .

—Bénard de La Harpe, 1719[1]

We have not succeeded in getting [the Hasinais] to put their houses close to the church, although they promised at first to do so. Therefore, there is no Christian doctrine imparted to them, first, because of the great repugnance they have for Christianity, and, second, because of the great distance there is between their houses and because of other motives and reasons they have. Their repugnance to baptism from past times is well known, for they have formed the belief that the water kills them.

—Father Francisco Hidalgo, November 4, 1716[2]

FOLLOWING THE MISSIONARIES' FORCED WITHDRAWAL from the Hasinai country in late 1693, the Caddo confederacies had only minimal contact with Europeans for two decades. By the time the French and Spanish did return to the Caddo country in the second decade of the eighteenth century, the relationship of the two empires had changed. In 1700, Philip V—the Bourbon grandson of Louis XIV—ascended the throne of Spain, and the two countries became allies in the War of the Spanish Succession. French dreams of conquering New Spain were put aside, and an unnatural international boundary line was eventually established between the Caddo confederacies: the Hasinai country was recognized as being Spanish (because of the establishment of the missions in the 1690s), while both the Kadohadachos and the Natchitoches fell within the lands claimed by France. The establishment of the boundaries of empire between the Caddo confederacies only reinforced the tribe's preeminent position in the region, one they would maintain well into the next century.

Despite the withdrawal of the French and Spanish from their country in the 1690s, the Caddos did continue to feel the detrimental effects of the European presence in North America. By the turn of the century, the British in South Carolina had, by way of the Tennessee River, established a trading partnership with the long-standing enemies of the Caddos, the Chickasaw Indians. The Chickasaws—amply supplied with guns and ammunition—increased their attacks on the Caddos in order to obtain slaves to sell to the British.[3]

The Kadohadacho and Natchitoches confederacies particularly bore the brunt of the Chickasaw onslaught. Bénard de La Harpe reported in 1719 that the "greater part of [both tribes] had been killed or made slaves by their Chickasaw adversaries."[4] The population of the Kadohadacho tribes had been reduced from a population of thirty-five hundred members to around one thousand,[5] while the Natchitoches numbers fell from about two thousand to only five hundred.[6] Displacement within the two tribes attests to the severity of the Chickasaw attacks. The raiders "destroyed almost all" the isolated Yatasi tribe and forced them to split in two for protection: half moved down the Red River to join the Natchitoches, while the other half moved upstream to live with the four Kadohadacho tribes. Both the Natchitoches and the Doustionis relocated several times during the era before they finally settled down with the Yatasis. The Nanatsoho tribe—the farthest upstream of the Kadohadachos—was forced by the Chickasaws to abandon their village and move closer to the rest of the confederacy.[7]

Although the Hasinai tribes were somewhat sheltered by the distance from the Chickasaw raiders, they suffered during this period as well. The epidemics that the Spanish had brought to the tribe in 1691 and 1692 continued to ravage the Hasinai into the next century. In 1716, a Spanish missionary complained of the "diseases which rage during the summer" in the Hasinai country, and a serious epidemic broke out among the Hasinais during the winter of 1717–18 that killed at least one hundred of the tribe. Sickness was the leading cause for the Hasinai decline in population, which fell from about forty-five hundred in 1693 to fifteen hundred in 1721. The great decline in the population of the Kadohadachos and the Natchitoches was also certainly exacerbated by disease, and cannot be wholly attributed to the Chickasaws.[8]

As a result of the tribes' suffering, the Caddos desired to reestablish the trading partnership with the French initiated during their meetings in the previous decade. They desperately needed to acquire French guns, powder, and bullets in order to defend themselves from the Chickasaw onslaught. Unfortunately for the Caddos, the French were in no position to supply the tribe with the number of weapons they needed for a full fifteen years after reestablishing contact with them in 1700.

France's interest in the Mississippi Valley was rejuvenated in 1698 by the British penetration into the interior of North America.[9] This prompted the French to hurry their effort to found a colony in Louisiana, and in October, 1698, an expedition left France under the direction of Pierre Le Moyne, Sieur d'Iberville. After establishing a base on the Gulf Coast, Iberville entrusted his brother, Jean-Baptiste Le Moyne, Sieur de Bienville, with the important mission of traveling up the Red River to reestablish ties with the Caddo confederacies and find out if the Spanish were still in the area. In March, 1700, Bienville and twenty-two French Canadians set out for the Caddos by way of the Red River, but travel was made difficult by the continual spring rains that turned the entire region into a swamp. The first Caddo tribe that Bienville reached was the Doustionis, who took him two miles upstream to meet the *caddi* of the Natchitoches, named Chef Blanc by the French. The *caddi* smoked a pipe with Bienville and renewed the friendly relations between the Natchitoches and the French that Tonti had inaugurated in 1690.[10]

From the Natchitoches village, Bienville attempted to go up the Red River to visit the Kadohadacho tribes. Chef Blanc's son guided them along the river to the Yatasi village, which consisted of forty houses stretched out along the Red River for about four miles. The trip took them nine days because of the high water and a natural logjam known as the Red River raft, a barrier that was to hinder navigation of the river for the next century and a half.[11] Members of the Kadohadacho, Nabedache, and Nadaco tribes were at the Yatasi village. They told Bienville of both the Spanish missions among the Hasinais and Terán's 1691 visit to the Kadohadachos but did not succeed in making it clear to him that the missions had been abandoned. Bienville then attempted to reach the Hasinais by way of the Kadohadachos, but the strong current and a bout with dysentery caused him to turn around and head back downstream to the Gulf Coast.[12]

As soon as they returned, Iberville ordered one member of the expedition to lead a party back to the Kadohadachos to check on the Spanish. This was the twenty-one-year-old Louis Juchereau de Saint-Denis, who would prove to be the European wielding the most influence with the Caddos over the next four decades. Saint-Denis returned with twenty-five Frenchmen to the Natchitoches and continued on with Chef Blanc to the Kadohadacho villages. The Kadohadachos informed him that the

Spanish had indeed abandoned the missions, and Saint-Denis returned to Biloxi.[13]

With the Spanish absent from the area, Saint-Denis and the French were free to develop a trade—albeit a limited one due to the War of the Spanish Succession—with all three Caddo confederacies. The Natchitoches and the Kadohadachos obtained a small supply of much-needed guns and ammunition (as well as clothes and beads) from Saint-Denis in return for salt and horses. In 1705, he reestablished contact with the Hasinais and lived with them for a few months. By providing them with trade goods and friendship, Saint-Denis erased any ill will between the French and the Hasinais that might have remained following the visit of Tonti fifteen years earlier.[14]

In particular, the Natchitoches tribe allied itself closely with Saint-Denis and the French. They had been ravaged by the Chickasaw raiders for nearly a decade when their crops were destroyed by flooding in 1702. In desperation, Chef Blanc traveled down to a temporary French post on the Mississippi River to request assistance from Saint-Denis. The French commander suggested to the *caddi* that the Natchitoches settle with another French ally, the Acolapissa tribe, that lived on the banks of Lake Pontchartrain. Chef Blanc agreed, and a few years after their move, Natchitoches warriors joined a force led by Saint-Denis in a campaign against the Chitimachas, a tribe that had earlier killed a few Frenchmen. The friendship between the French and the Natchitoches was further enhanced when Chef Blanc allowed a group of hungry Frenchmen to winter at his village in succeeding years.[15]

Although contact had been reestablished with the French, the Kadohadachos and the other tribes of the Natchitoches confederacy—the Yatasis and the Doustionis—still were not able to obtain enough French firearms to successfully defend against the Chickasaws. An increase in the volume of trade did not occur until after the French crown granted Antoine Crozat a monopoly on the commerce of Louisiana in 1712. Crozat named Antoine Laumet, Sieur de Cadillac, governor of Louisiana and directed him to open trade with the Spanish in America as a way to turn the colony into a money-making concern. It was through this French attempt to develop commerce with New Spain that the Caddo confederacies finally gained access to a dependable source of much-needed European goods.[16]

After first being rebuffed by the Spanish at Veracruz in 1713, Cadillac decided to attempt trade with New Spain through the reestablishment of the Spanish missions among the Hasinais. The French governor had conceived of this plan after receiving a letter from a Spanish Franciscan missionary, Father Francisco Hidalgo, who had become impatient with the indifference of the Spanish officials in Mexico City concerning the conversion of the Hasinais. In 1711, Hidalgo addressed a letter to the French governor in Louisiana asking for his help. Governor Cadillac received the letter two years later and quickly perceived it as the opportunity he had been waiting for. He supplied Saint-Denis with ten thousand livres' worth of merchandise in September, 1713, and directed him to open trade with Mexico using the search for Father Hidalgo as an excuse.[17]

Saint-Denis realized that he would need the assistance of his old friends the Natchitoches and dispatched a messenger to their village on Lake Pontchartrain to ask them to return to their original homes. The Natchitoches, assured of French arms and assistance, agreed to accompany Saint-Denis back up the Red River, along with twenty-four Frenchmen and five boatloads of merchandise. When the party finally reached the old homesite of the Natchitoches, they found the last remnants of the ravaged Doustioni tribe, who had been forced by the Chickasaw onslaught to move their villages every year. Saint-Denis assembled the two beleaguered tribes and urged them to resettle permanently in the old village of the Natchitoches and replant their fields. He promised them that "henceforth there would always be Frenchmen living among them" and they would have nothing to fear from other tribes as long as they all remained closely united. He engaged the tribes in building a warehouse and living quarters for the French, and thus laid the foundations, in late 1713, for the first permanent European settlement among the Caddos at Natchitoches.[18]

Two years later the French induced half the ravaged Yatasi tribe—heretofore isolated between the Natchitoches and Kadohadacho confederacies, and therefore susceptible to Chickasaw attacks—to move downstream and join their brethren near the French post. In return for the trade and protection of the French at Natchitoches, the three united tribes of the confederacy provided their allies with food, furs, and horses.[19]

Immediately following the erection of the post at Natchitoches in 1713, Saint-Denis and the French began to use it as a center from which to develop trade with all three of the Caddo confederacies. Using fifteen Natchitoches warriors as guides, Saint-Denis reopened relations with the Hasinai tribe, whom he had not visited in several years. Bernardino warmly greeted his old French friend with a celebration that lasted three days. In return, Saint-Denis distributed presents to the tribe, which also had a large number of horses and furs to sell. Saint-Denis then returned to the French post at Natchez to report to Cadillac and pick up a fresh supply of trade goods. He brought this merchandise back to Natchitoches, and a moderate trade was maintained with the Caddo confederacies over the next two years.[20]

The trade between the French and the Caddo confederacies increased dramatically after 1716, when Saint-Denis returned from his celebrated venture to Mexico (to be detailed below).[21] In the fall of 1716, Saint-Denis and six other Frenchmen formed a commercial partnership, acquired another sixty thousand livres' worth of trade goods at Mobile, and returned to Natchitoches, which had been reinforced by a sergeant and six French soldiers. As a result of Saint-Denis's merchandise, the Hasinais had more guns than a moderate-sized Spanish expedition did when it entered their villages in 1718. The Spanish complained that the Kadohadacho tribes also traded with the French at Natchitoches because they were "so interested in muskets, powder, bullets and clothing" that they now made war on other tribes in order to obtain slaves to sell at Natchitoches.[22]

Saint-Denis's work coincided with developments in France that intensified the French effort with the Caddo tribes. In 1717, Crozat relinquished his monopoly, and a new, powerful colonial trust called the Company of the Indies was placed in charge of Louisiana. The able, experienced Bienville was named governor, and in 1718, he moved the capital from Mobile to the newly established town of New Orleans in order to facilitate control. Bienville understood the importance of the friendship of the Caddo tribes, and all three confederacies were awarded an annual present. Trade with the Caddo tribes was also stepped up, and measures were taken to make the French presence at Natchitoches more secure. Bienville ordered Philippe Blondel to take command of the fort and provided him with forty additional soldiers. The Brossaut brothers, merchants from Lyon, were granted the trading concession at Natchitoches, and the volume of trade with the natives there increased.[23]

Bénard de La Harpe was granted the concession for the Kadohadacho villages upstream from Natchitoches, and it was through him that the Kadohadacho confederacy finally established a full trading partnership with the French. The *caddices* of the four tribes of the Kadohadacho confederacy—the Kadohadacho proper, Nanatsohos, Upper Natchitoches, and Nasonis—greeted La Harpe at the Nasoni village in April, 1719. La Harpe told the gathering that he had been sent by the French king to assist them in arranging a peace with their great enemies, the Chickasaws and the Osages. La Harpe promised that the French king "would declare himself against" those tribes if they refused to cease hostilities against the Kadohadachos.[24]

This opening statement greatly pleased the Kadohadachos, since they—like the Natchitoches tribes—had suffered greatly from the escalation of warfare in the area. The Kadohadacho *caddi* told La Harpe that "the time had come when it was necessary to change their tears into joy." He declared that many of "their companions had been killed or made slaves by their adversaries," but the "arrival of the French would prevent their entire destruction." He diplomatically claimed that the tribe had been waiting since the time of La Salle and Tonti for the French to return and establish an alliance with them. A great celebration formalized the ties between the French and the Kadohadacho confederacy, and the Indians accepted presents to ensure their allegiance to France.[25]

A few days later the Nasoni *caddi* sold La Harpe a piece of land near his village, upon which the French built a fort and trading center they called the "Nassonite Post."[26] In the summer of 1719, La Harpe, guided by the Kadohadachos and the Nabedaches, met with the Wichita tribes located to the northwest. For the next century the Kadohadachos (and, to a lesser degree, the Hasinais) would play an important political and economic intermediary role between the Euro-Americans and the Wichitas that would enhance the well-being and the prestige of the Caddos.[27]

With the erection of the Nassonite Post (officially known as St. Louis de Cadodaquious) and the increase in trade with the Kadohadacho confederacy, all the Caddo tribes finally secured easy access to French trade goods. For the most part this trade was beneficial to the Caddos, since they acquired the firearms necessary to defend themselves in return for easily obtained items like salt, horses, and furs. No longer would the Kadohadachos and the Natchitoches be at the mercy of other tribes with better access to European weapons.

Unfortunately, there were drawbacks to the French presence, especially for the Hasinais. The French paid well for native slaves, and the Caddo tribes quickly entered the dangerous business of attacking the surrounding tribes to obtain human merchandise. Warfare, which had previously lacked an economic motive, increasingly became a serious business for the Caddo warriors. The Hasinais, who had been spared the ravages of the Chickasaw slave raiders, boldly initiated raids of their own on their erstwhile friends, the Tonkawan Yojuanes, soon after Saint-Denis's visit in 1714. The Yojuanes attacked the Hasinais out of revenge and destroyed the fire temple maintained by the *xinesi*. The introduction of French weapons, then, greatly militarized the area and made it even more necessary for all the Caddo confederacies to have European guns and ammunition.[28]

The establishment of the French in the Caddo country had other repercussions for the Hasinais, for it encouraged the return of the Spanish priests to their villages. As stated above, Governor Cadillac hoped to establish a trading partnership with the Spanish in Mexico through the reestablishment of the missions in East Texas. Both Saint-Denis and Governor Cadillac worried that the Spanish might oppose the entrance of French traders but felt they would certainly respond to the opportunity to convert heathen souls. Therefore, when Saint-Denis returned to the Hasinai villages following his trip to Natchez in 1714, he used all his persuasive powers to convince Bernardino, the Nabedache *caddi*—who remained "very adverse to all matters of the [Catholic] faith"—to ask for the Spanish missionaries to return to his villages.[29]

Saint-Denis explained to the *caddi* that the French now recognized the Spanish claim to the Hasinai territory and that, despite the wishes of the tribe, the French could neither settle there nor provide the tribe with a military alliance. Saint-Denis showed Bernardino that having the Spanish as well as the French nearby would be to his advantage, since the Hasinais would share in the profitable trade that promised to develop. To convince the Spanish to return, however, the Hasinais had to once again play upon Spain's desire to convert the natives to Christianity. With this in mind, Bernardino, along with two Hasinai warriors, appeared with Saint-Denis and three Frenchmen at the presidio at San Juan Bautista to solicit the return of the Spanish priests in person. Saint-Denis also told the commander, Capt. Diego Ramón, that he wanted to open trade with Mexico and obtain horses and cattle for Louisiana. In response to the arrival of Bernardino and Saint-Denis at San Juan Bautista (and the latter's interview at Mexico City), the Spanish decided to reestablish missions among the Hasinais. This decision had a twofold purpose: one, to bar any further entrance of French trade into Mexico, and two, to convert the Hasinais to Christianity. In other words, the French plan to open trade through the Spanish missions had backfired, and it was left to the Hasinais to undermine the Spanish presence in their country and assure themselves access to illegal French goods.[30]

The Spanish sent three expeditions to the Hasinai country from 1716 to 1721 in an attempt to permanently plant the missions there. Each time the Hasinais warmly greeted the Spanish and gladly accepted whatever presents they distributed. However, they firmly but politely refused to leave their spread-out homes and fields to congregate in compact villages so the priests could preach to them. The Hasinais also refused to give up their ties with the French and continued to travel to Natchitoches to trade. Ultimately, the Hasinais were able to wear the Spanish missionaries down and force them to accept the fact that the tribe would neither convert nor abandon their French partners.

The first expedition to the Hasinai country was formed under the command of Capt. Domingo Ramón (Diego's son), who was instructed to lead twenty-five soldiers and two groups of Franciscan missionaries—one from the Colegio de la Santa Cruz de Querétaro, the other from the Colegio de Nuestra Señora de Guadalupe de Zacatecas—back to the country of the Hasinais and establish four missions. Ironically, the Spanish chose Saint-Denis to guide the expedition. The charming Frenchman had ingratiated himself with the Spanish and had married Domingo Ramón's niece (Diego Ramón's granddaughter) at San Juan Bautista. He also had a much greater knowledge of the country than anyone else, and he had come to Mexico with Bernardino's invitation to the priests.[31]

The Ramón expedition left from the presidio at San Juan Bautista on April 25, 1716, and entered the Hasinai country in late June. The Hasinais were certainly somewhat ambivalent about the Spanish arrival, but the tribe's doubts were relieved by the presence of Saint-Denis at the head of the expedition. He was sent ahead of the party to inform Bernardino of the expedition's approach and arrange for their reception and the renewal of ties. On September 27, 1716, Saint-Denis led thirty-four Hasinais and five *caddices* on horseback into the Spanish camp. Captain Ramón, accompanied by the priests, politely greeted the headmen and led them to a grove of trees, where the Spanish had arranged blankets and saddles for the meeting. The Hasinai leaders lighted a pipe adorned with white feathers that was smoked specifically to signify peace. This was followed by a "very serious discourse" by Bernardino, who welcomed the Spanish to his country.[32]

Large numbers of Hasinai tribesmen greeted the Spanish party on its way to the main villages over the next few days. Captain Ramón piled large amounts of blankets, cloth, hats, and tobacco in front of the gatherings, and these were distributed by the tribal leaders, who impressed Ramón with their orderliness and sense of fairness. On June 29, a large gathering of the tribe heard Ramón tell them that the purpose of his visit "was for the salvation of their souls." With Saint-Denis translating, Ramón urged "that they should recognize absolutely" the Spanish king as their only ruler and suggested they elect a single captain general to govern the entire Hasinai confederacy. The tribe accepted this advice and chose Cheocas, son of the Hainai *caddi*, and Cheocas received Ramón's cane and one of his best jackets in the name of the Spanish king.[33]

Finished with his diplomatic duties, Ramón, assisted by the priests and the Hasinai headmen, inspected sites for the various missions. The first mission was built near the Neche village and, like its predecessor, called San Francisco de los Tejas. Upon the occasion of its formal opening, the Spanish distributed large amounts of clothing to members of the Neche, Nabedache, and Nacono tribes, whom it was to serve. The Spanish again insisted that the three tribes choose an official captain general to govern them.[34]

Similar ceremonies were held for the establishment of the other missions. The second mission, called La Purísima Concepción, was built nine leagues to the east, just beyond the Angelina River, to service the Hainai tribe. For the Nacogdoches tribe, Mission Nuestra Señora de Guadalupe was founded nine leagues southeast of the Hainais. Mission San José de los Nasonis was established seven leagues northeast of the Hainais for the Nasonis and the Nadacos. A presidio, manned by twenty-five soldiers, was established a quarter of a league from Mission San Francisco.[35]

In the fall of 1716, Ramón traveled to Natchitoches to observe the French settlement there and decided that missions were needed farther east of the Hasinais to check the French at the Red River. Eight leagues west of Natchitoches, Mission San Miguel de los Adaes was established with the consent of the Adaes Indians. Halfway between the Adaes and the Hasinais, west of the Sabine River, Mission Nuestra Señora de los Dolores was founded for the Ais Indians. All in all, six missions had been created—split equally between the Querétaran friars and the Franciscans of Zacatecas—to instruct the natives in Christianity and the Spanish way of life in an attempt to draw them into the Spanish fold and secure the frontier from the French.[36]

Although relations between the Hasinais and the Spanish remained cordial this time, the tribe persisted in resisting Christianity. At the time of the founding of the missions in the summer of 1716, the natives claimed they could not assemble until they had harvested their crops, an excuse which proved to be useful for many years. By the fall—after the crops had been gathered—the Hasinais still refused to congregate close to the missions and remained "numerous and spread out." Remembering their past experiences with the Spanish and disease, the natives had a "great repugnance for Christianity" and still believed that the baptismal water would kill them. This hostility was reinforced by the epidemic that occurred during the winter of 1717–18, killing more than one hundred Hasinai tribal members. The priests concluded that conversion could only be accomplished by both the destruction of the Hasinai temples and the forced congregation of the tribe, neither of which could be attempted with the limited number of soldiers at the presidio.[37]

The attitude of the Hasinais was clearly demonstrated to the missionaries in the fall of 1716. Most of the livestock brought by the Spanish had died in the heat of the summer, and the priests had arrived too late to plant a crop. By the fall harvest, they faced starvation, but the Hasinais refused to give them any aid, "being content merely to visit" the Spanish. It was only through the influence of Saint-Denis that the priests were kept alive, for he convinced the Natchitoches tribe to sell him corn that he then gave to the Spanish. This made it obvious to Captain Ramón and Father Isidro Félix de Espinosa that the missions in East Texas were not blocking the French but, rather, existed only at their mercy. Both appealed to the viceroy for more troops with which to both influence the Hasinais to congregate and provide a more worthy opposition to the French establishment at Natchitoches.[38]

In response to the friars' appeals, another expedition to East Texas was organized under the command of Don Martin de Alarcón, and it arrived at San Francisco de los Tejas in October, 1718. Neche, Nabedache, and Nacono tribesmen gathered to hear Alarcón tell them that his inspiration for coming was the king's desire to save their souls. Once again, he urged them to congregate, and, as usual, they promised to do so in the future. For the time being, however, the tribesmen excused themselves on the grounds that they were about to leave on a buffalo hunt.[39]

For the next few weeks, Alarcón visited all the missions, performed the same ceremonies, and most importantly, distributed large amounts of presents to the Hasinais. To aid the missionaries in their conversion effort, Alarcón agreed to be the godfather of the few Hasinais who could be persuaded to be baptized. The baptismal ceremony was performed "with the greatest solemnity possible" in order to impress the large crowds that assembled to watch. When the baptism had been completed, the mission bells were rung and muskets fired. To make the pot even sweeter, Alarcón distributed extra clothing to the families of those who had been baptized.[40]

In late November, 1718, Alarcón returned to Mexico without leaving enough troops to either coerce the Hasinais to congregate or secure the country from French influence. By the summer of 1719, the French were firmly situated at Natchitoches, and La Harpe was establishing their position higher up the Red River among the Kadohadachos. Although the Spanish had established six missions in East Texas, their grip on both that area and the Hasinais remained pitifully weak. One Spanish missionary complained, "the French have a complete hold upon the Indians and have subjected them entirely to their will by means of gifts and flattery" since they literally "take their shirts off to give them to the Indians." Another feared that the French would attach the Hasinais firmly to their side since "they fondled them much, giving them firearms in exchange for horses."[41]

The commanding influence of the French in the area was made evident in June, 1719. Upon receiving word of a minor war—the War of the Quadruple Alliance—between France and Spain, Blondel, the commander of the French troops at Natchitoches, led six men into Mission San Miguel de los Adaes and captured it and the sole Spanish soldier stationed there. A lay brother escaped and hurried west to inform the other missions of the French invasion. Realizing that the sympathies of the Hasinais rested with the French, the priests abandoned East Texas once again and removed to the newly founded town of San Antonio.[42]

On July 1, 1719, Saint-Denis was named commander of the post at Natchitoches, and it was suggested by expansionist Frenchmen that he use the Hasinais to aid him on an expedition to capture San Antonio. Saint-Denis never carried out this ambitious plan, for he felt it would upset the stable relations between Louisiana and Texas. The French commander preferred peace with Spain as a means to secure more tightly the friendship and trade of the native tribes. La Harpe's concession at the Kadohadacho villages soon lapsed, and jurisdiction of the entire Red River Valley fell to the capable Saint-Denis.[43]

In the meantime the Spanish had once again decided to reoccupy the missions of East Texas, and the last and largest of the Spanish expeditions into the area was put together under the command of the Marquis of San Miguel de Aguayo. The size of the force, which consisted of five hundred men, four thousand horses, six hundred supply-laden mules, and a large number of cattle, attests to the seriousness of this Spanish attempt to establish themselves permanently among the Hasinais. Aguayo left Coahuila on August 16, 1720, with instructions to reestablish the missions and reinforce and increase the size of the garrisons stationed there.[44]

After resting in San Antonio, the party headed toward the Hasinai villages and was met near the Trinity River by Cheocas, now the *caddi* of the Hainais, along with eight important men and four women. From past experience the Caddos realized they would be showered with presents if they were friendly, and Cheocas played his role to the hilt. According to the Spanish, he "sobbed so bitterly he could hardly speak," being so overwhelmed with joy at their return. Aguayo replied in the same manner as his predecessors by explaining to the *caddi* that he had been sent by the king to protect the Hasinais from their enemies and had sent missionaries to instruct them in the Catholic faith. Cheocas accepted a long coat, jacket, and woolen breeches from Aguayo and was presented with a silver-headed baton to denote his position as captain general of the Hasinais.[45]

Cheocas accompanied the Spanish toward the Neches River and expressed "surprise" and consternation when he realized just how large the size of the entire expedition was. He remained quiet, however, and went ahead with Father Espinosa to inform the rest of the tribe to prepare a reception at the site of San Francisco de los Tejas. On July 28, sixty men and women of the Neche tribe received Aguayo at the mission and gave the Spaniards flowers, watermelons, beans, and corn. The Neche *caddi* smoked a peace pipe with Aguayo and told him that he was pleased with the arrival of the Spanish and hoped they would remain. The entire village was treated to a great feast and received clothes and beads from Aguayo after the *caddi* promised to remain faithful to the Spanish.[46]

One hundred members of the Nacono tribe met the Spanish party upon their arrival at the Neches River a few days later. Mindful of the French invasion, Aguayo told them that not only should they be on friendly terms with the Spanish, but they should also be allies in any "wars that should be waged." To further ensure the tribe's compliance, Aguayo was extremely lavish in his gift-giving and clothed "all the men and women in coarse woolen garments and small cloaks with ribbons and presented them with glass beads, knives, ear-rings, finger-rings, mirrors, combs, awls, scissors, chain-links, and blankets, all of which things they treasure highly."[47]

While the Spanish were camped on the Neches, Saint-Denis arrived to meet with Aguayo and declare his willingness to observe a truce. Aguayo agreed on the condition that the French evacuate all of Texas (including Los Adaes), retreat to Natchitoches, and not impede the Spanish reoccupation. Although Saint-Denis wished to keep the Spanish from recovering Los Adaes, he reluctantly complied with Aguayo's terms after seeing the size of the Spanish force. He remained in the area for three days, however, advising the *caddices* of the various Hasinai tribes as well as some visiting Kadohadachos.[48]

After the departure of Saint-Denis, Aguayo set about reestablishing the missions. Mission San Francisco de los Neches—formerly de los Tejas—was officially reopened on August 5, 1721. Father Espinosa spoke to the assembled tribe and told them that the primary motives for the Spanish arrival were to save their souls and protect them from their enemies. He contrasted the Spanish and the French by pointing out that the priests had never made any demands on the tribe and had only given them an abundance of presents. However, the French had forced them to earn presents by trading horses, skins, and Native American slaves. To drive the point home, Aguayo clothed the entire gathering of 158 natives and "refused to accept so much as a single buckskin" from them as payment. The Spanish governor also formally appointed the Neche *caddi* to be captain general and gave him a silver baton and a Spanish suit.[49]

The following day the party traveled eastward across the Angelina River and reestablished the presidio near the Hainai villages by stationing a troop of twenty-five soldiers there. On August 8, mass was celebrated at the nearby mission of La Purísima Concepción in front of four hundred Hainais and eighty visiting Kadohadachos. The pattern established at the previous mission was followed here as Aguayo assured the gathering that the Spanish presence would be permanent. They were told that they would have to congregate in pueblos, and they agreed to do so as soon as the crops were harvested. All the Indians were clothed and given presents. Large crowds of natives were drawn to the reestablishment of the other two Hasinai missions. On August 13, 1721, the formal reopening of Mission San José de los Nasonis drew a throng of 300, all of whom received presents, as did the 390 who attended the rededication of Mission Nuestra Señora de Guadalupe de Nacogdoches two days later.[50]

Aguayo then left the Hasinai villages to reestablish the missions among the Ais and the Adaes tribes. To ensure the success of the missions in the face of the French threat, a presidio was established near the Adaes village, only eight leagues west of Natchitoches. The presidio was manned by one hundred soldiers and provided with six cannons for protection. Because of its strategic position on the frontier, Los Adaes became the capital of Texas, a status it maintained until 1772.[51]

Although the huge Aguayo expedition firmly established the Spanish presence once and for all in East Texas, the Hasinais remained aloof from the conversion efforts of the priests. Brig. Gen. Don Pedro de Rivera visited the Hasinai country in 1727 while conducting an inspection tour of northern Mexico and found that the Indians had not gathered at any of the four missions. Rivera called Mission San Francisco de los Neches a "shack" where one Querétaran missionary lived "for the ministrations of the Indians when they wanted to be Christians." The Hasinais were friendly to the Spanish, so the soldiers had nothing to do "out of regard for the fact they do not have any Indians in the mission buildings and those they minister to live at a distance in their rancherías."[52]

Rivera was overwhelmed by the close ties the Hasinais maintained with the French. Fifty mounted Nabedache warriors "armed with French guns, with flasks of powder and bags of bullets, [looking] like the most expert troops" met Rivera upon his arrival in East Texas. The Spanish commander observed that all the tribes of the Hasinai confederacy had obtained French guns, "which they have learned to use with skill." Rivera realized that the Hasinai tribes had completely accepted the French influence and, therefore, he recognized the futility—as well as the monetary waste—of maintaining the two presidios in East Texas. He recommended that the presidio among the Hasinais be abandoned and felt that sixty troops would be sufficient at Los Adaes, since obviously one hundred would not be enough in the event of war. Rivera was certain that the French could easily "make themselves masters of the interior of the country" by circumventing Los Adaes and crossing the Red River at the Kadohadacho villages. From there the French would make their way to the Hasinai tribes and surround the Spanish troops at Los Adaes. Rivera had no doubt that the Caddo tribes would not object to a move of this sort.[53]

The Caddos' attachment to the French was again demonstrated in 1731, when the post at Natchitoches was besieged by the Natchez Indians and members of all three confederacies rushed to the aid of the French in this time of danger. Initially, the Natchitoches tribe wanted to attack the Natchez, but being greatly outnumbered, they retired and abandoned their village. Reinforcements from the Hasinai and Kadohadacho confederacies allowed the besieged forces to counterattack successfully, however, and thus ended the Natchez threat. The Caddos clearly recognized their dependence upon French firearms and were willing to take up arms against anyone—including the Spanish—who threatened to disrupt the ties they had established with the French.[54]

In 1729, the viceroy of New Spain accepted the recommendations of Rivera and issued a decree calling for the abolition of the presidio near the Hainai village and the reduction of the number of troops stationed at Los Adaes. In response, the Querétaran missionaries protested to the viceroy and claimed that without the protection of the soldiers, the Hasinais "would become more and more insolent and would desecrate the temples, sacred vessels and sacraments." If the presidio was not to be reestablished, the priests asked permission to relocate the missions so their efforts would not be wasted. The viceroy sustained Rivera's report, and the three Querétaran missions left the Hasinai country for San Antonio in 1731. Only the mission run by the Franciscan fathers of Zacatecas—located near the Nacogdoches village—remained among the Hasinais, along with the two missions for the Ais and the Adaes.[55] Thus, after five decades of dealing with the Europeans, the Caddo confederacies finally succeeded in achieving their goal of minimizing the Spanish influence in their country while increasing the volume of trade with the French, and for the next three decades, the Caddos were free to reap the benefits of their accomplishment.

Chapter 4

The Caddos between Two Empires, 1731–67

No Caudodachos, Nacodoches, San Pedro, or Texas is to be seen who does not wear his mirror, belt of fringes, epaulets, and breechclout—all French goods. And now for the winter, they are giving them blankets, breechclouts, powder and shot. Hence these nations say: "The Spaniards offer fair words; the French, fair words and presents."

They give the captains belts with galloons, coats of red cloth with the same, and ruffled shirts. Thus they came to see me at the mission of Nacodoches, saying to me: "Frenchman this," and "Frenchman that."

—Governor Jacinto de Barrios y Jáuregui, November 8, 1751[1]

Next day we were joined by a party of [Nabedaches] on horseback, who were eager to display with much ostentation the swiftness and agility of their horses, as well as their own skill and dexterity in the art of riding; and it is but doing them justice to say, that the most noble and graceful object I have ever seen was one of those savages mounted and running at full speed. The broad Herculean trunk of his body, his gun leaning over the left arm, and his plaid or blanket thrown carelessly across his naked shoulders, and streaming in the wind, was such an appearance as I could only compare to some of the finest equestrian statues of antiquity.

—Pierre Marie De Pages, 1767[2]

THE PERIOD BETWEEN THE REMOVAL of the three Querétaran missions from East Texas and the French transferal of Louisiana to Spain was the era in which the Caddos most benefited from direct contact with Euro-Americans. Only a few Spaniards were left in East Texas, and French goods flowed freely into the Caddo villages. The Hasinais, nominally subjects of Spain, were strong enough to force the Spanish to allow this trade without disruption. Easy access to French goods also enhanced the Caddos' position relative to the other tribes of Texas, and they assumed a leading role in the rapidly changing diplomacy of the region.

Nevertheless, there were still drawbacks to the French and Spanish presence. Caddo crafters abandoned their traditional methods, and the tribe became dangerously dependent upon European metal goods. Although both the European weapons and the French alliance provided the Caddos great protection from their enemies, the tribe's population continued to decline because of disease. The Caddo confederacies endured these troubles, however, and the middle period of the eighteenth century can be considered the golden age in the tribe's relations with Euro-Americans.

Following the removal of the Querétaran missions and the Spanish presidio in 1731, the French influence among the Caddos reached its zenith. The Nassonite Post among the Kadohadacho confederacy was strengthened by the arrival of a few French families who settled there and constructed a flour mill. This provided the Kadohadachos even more protection from their Chickasaw enemies. At the suggestion of the French, the Yatasis (who had earlier split and joined both the Kadohadachos and the Natchitoches) returned to their village between the two tribes on the Red River. Here the French established another important trading station that allowed them to circumvent the Spanish presidio at Los Adaes and trade with the Hasinais. Surveying the situation in 1744, Texas governor Tomás Felipe Winthuisen reported that in case of war, Los Adaes would be lost not because of the French, but because the Hasinais "would join them in a moment and serve them constantly and faithfully."[3]

The death of Saint-Denis in June, 1744, did not disturb the alliance between the Caddos and the French. Saint-Denis's son proved to be just as adept and influential as his father and was "so revered and obeyed" by the Indians that one of the Spanish officers at Los Adaes was "convinced that they would be willing to give their lives for him in any crisis." This same officer claimed that the younger Saint-Denis distributed goods to the Hasinais "at will," a statement confirmed by the commandant of Presidio de la Bahía, Joaquín de Orobio Basterra. When Basterra visited the Nabedaches in 1746, he noted that all the Nabedache warriors had French rifles, powder flasks, and bullet sacks and were wearing white shirts and capes of fine scarlet. The Nabedache caddi told Basterra that the French from Natchitoches brought them everything they needed by way of the Kadohadachos.[4]

The trade that was maintained between the French and the Caddos gradually transformed the material culture of the tribe. By the mid-eighteenth century, the Caddos had almost completely forsaken their traditional crafts in favor of European-manufactured goods. The items procured by the Caddos to trade with the French—buffalo skins, deer chamois, and bear's fat—were articles traditionally obtained for their own use. In addition to these three staple items, the Caddos supplied the

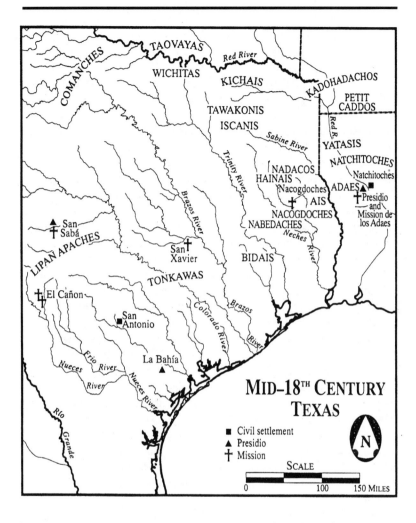

MID-18TH CENTURY
TEXAS

■ Civil settlement
▲ Presidio
✝ Mission

SCALE

0   100   150 MILES

French with surplus corn, horses, mules, and Indian slaves.[5]

In return for these goods, the French supplied the Caddos with a wide variety of items affecting all aspects of tribal life, though weapons were the most important articles the Caddos received. Rifles, powder, and balls allowed the tribe to hunt more efficiently and enhanced its military proficiency as well. In addition to guns and ammunition, the French supplied the Caddos with steel hatchets, tomahawks, and hunting and pocket knives.[6] With the acquisition of these tools of war, the Caddos gradually became dependent upon European firearms, and in 1768, Father Gaspar de Solís noted that all Hasinai men were armed with guns they managed "with great skill"; rarely did he see a warrior with a bow and arrow. In 1790, the commander at Natchitoches, Louis de Blanc, went so far as to declare that the Caddos had forgotten the use of the bow and arrow and were desperate to acquire European weapons. Although de Blanc's claim was an exaggeration (the tribe still did use bow and arrows), it is true that without European guns, the Caddos would have been at an extreme disadvantage relative to their well-armed enemies.[7]

The Caddos also became dependent on European shirts, cloth, and blankets; tools such as scissors, awls, screws, and flints for fire became necessities as well. Cosmetic goods, beads, combs, vermilion, mirrors, copper bracelets, and strips of scarlet were all vanity items the French kept readily on hand to supply the natives, who greatly desired them. By the mid-eighteenth century, life without the European goods had become unimaginable to the Caddos.[8]

Although trade with the French benefited the Caddos materially, close contact with Euro-Americans continued to adversely affect the tribe. Unlike the previous epidemics that had so ravaged the Caddo confederacies, disease in the middle period of the eighteenth century was a subtle constant that gradually reduced their numbers. In 1750, the Zacatecan missionaries among the Hasinais reported that almost every year outbreaks of colds, fever, measles, and smallpox occurred. Eighteen years later another priest claimed that the Hasinais "frequently suffer" from disease, "which makes them horrible to the sight and filthy."[9]

Certainly, sickness was also a problem among the Kadohadacho and Natchitoches confederacies since they, like the Hasinais, experienced population declines in this period. The Kadohadachos suffered the least, however, and their numbers fell from about 1,000 members in 1721 to 750 by 1773. In comparison, the Hasinai confederacy lost nearly a third of their people as the population dropped from 1,500 to around 1,000 members. By 1770, the population of the Natchitoches stood at just 100, while the Yatasis had perhaps 25 more members than their kin downstream.[10]

The Caddo confederacies were able to overcome the terrible losses and remain strong through consolidation. The Hasinai confederacy declined from eight to four tribes; on the western boundary of the Hasinai country, the Nabedaches absorbed their neighbors, the Neches and the Naconos. In the center of the region, only the Hainais and the Nacogdoches remained, while the Nabitis disappeared. By the 1750s the Nacaos on the eastern boundary had vanished, and the Nasonis were well on their way to merging with the Nadacos, a process completed a decade later.[11]

The same streamlining process also took place in the other confederacies. The Kadohadachos were reduced by two tribes, leaving only the Kadohadacho proper and a smaller branch, which the French called the Petit Caddos. The Doustionis merged into the Natchitoches tribe and, as mentioned above, the Yatasis reformed themselves as an independent tribe who lived halfway between the Natchitoches and the Petit Caddos on the Red River.[12]

Despite the great changes to the Caddo world brought by European trade and disease, the social and political structure of the tribe remained intact. Efficient, disciplined government was still provided by the *caddi* and his officers, and the elite class continued to command as much respect as before. The Franciscans at Mission Nacogdoches reported in 1750 that "in matters of counsel [the Hasinai men] give their vote in meetings where a leader presides. They pointed him out for us and . . . they call him caddi." Another priest claimed that all the Hasinai *caddices* were "handsome, brave, and strong" and among the most "valiant" men of their nation. The strong leadership provided by the *caddices* of both the Hasinai and the Kadohadacho tribes allowed them to take full advantage of their easy access to French goods.[13]

The drive to obtain European trade goods, however, caused the Caddo tribes to make a major change in the structure of their religion: the discontinuance of the position of *xinesi*. Since this process occurred gradually and with little fanfare, European observers failed even to take note of his absence; the two most informative reports on Caddo religion—written by Zacatecan missionaries in 1749 and 1750—contain no accounts pertaining to the *xinesi*, the fire temple, or the *coninisi*; thus, it seems likely that the office had been discontinued for some time by then.[14]

Why then would the Caddos eliminate such an important religious figure? Most likely, the motivation can be found in their determination to obtain European goods. Increasingly, the men spent a greater amount of time hunting for furs and rounding up horses and cattle, while the women spent more time dressing the pelts. Also, as the area became militarized—with all the tribes depending upon French arms and other goods—the Caddos' activities in diplomacy and warfare increased dramatically. The Caddo confederacies no longer had the time or inclination to support the position of the *xinesi* and its pomp and formal ceremony.[15]

Despite the absence of the *xinesi* the Caddo tribes (according to the Zacatecan missionaries) continued to be "devoted to the religion of their elders as [they are] in observing all the customs which . . . have been left to them by their ancestors." The priests complained that the tribe still worshipped Ahahayo and "weren't lacking for these miserable ones," the *connas* who continued to draw the tribe away from Christianity. As before, one priest concluded that it would be "impossible (by human means) to force them . . . to change their ways of living from day by day," for any pressure on the part of the missionaries would only cause the Hasinais to become violent.[16]

Thus, the Zacatecan mission among the Nacogdoches tribe remained unsuccessful. In August, 1744, Governor Winthuisen reported that

Mission Nacogdoches had one priest and two soldiers, "but it does not and never has had one Indian reduced to mission [life]." Although the governor admired the Hasinais for their industriousness, he believed that the tribe was "irreducible to civilization and to subjection to the missions. Since every effort that has been made to this end has failed, it is now considered an impossible undertaking." Nicolás de Lafora visited the mission two decades later and found that the missionary, José Calahorra, "had not one Indian to whom he could minister, nor had there been one during more than the forty years of this mission's existence." In 1768, Father Solís judged, "there is no hope, not even a remote one, of [the natives'] reduction and congregation."[17]

The Hasinais continued to raise food in abundance, and the missionaries recognized that the success of the Hasinai economy hindered conversion. The Hasinais, as well as the Kadohadachos and the Natchitoches, harvested so much corn and other crops that they sold their surplus to the missionaries, the soldiers at Los Adaes, and the French. The Caddos were also so efficient at harvesting the fruits of the forest that, according to one priest, not even "one nut is left on the ground, even though the forest is thick and more than three-fourths are walnut and oak."[18]

While much of the Caddos' strength derived from their great agricultural success, the tribe understood that their access to French goods was the reason they were an important tribe in Texas. French arms not only increased the Caddos' military might, but also gave them the opportunity to provide weapons for the other tribes of Texas who, like the Caddos, were now engaged in a full-scale war with the Lipan Apaches. The most important group the Kadohadachos traded with comprised the four Wichita tribes—the Wichita proper, Taovayas, Tawakonis, and Iscanis—which by 1750, had been forced by the Osages to abandon their villages in the Arkansas River drainage. In order to be near their Kichai and Caddo allies, the Tawakonis and the Iscanis settled in their midst on the upper Sabine River. The Taovayas and the Wichitas settled upstream from the Kadohadachos on the Red River in a strongly fortified village. Both groups got involved in the war against the Apaches, and the Kadohadachos helped the Wichita tribes establish a trading relationship with the French.[19]

Farther upstream from the Wichitas were the fierce Comanches, Shoshonean speakers who had moved into the region in the early eighteenth century and had pushed the Lipan Apaches southeastward into the heart of Texas. Both the Kadohadachos and the Hasinais established ties with the Comanches, since they all counted the Apaches as their common foe. Through the Caddos and the Wichitas, the Comanches were able to receive French guns as well. Both the Comanches and the

Wichitas were stronger and more numerous than the Caddos, but the strong ties of friendship and trade the Caddos shared with the French made these tribes very respectful of them. The influence the Caddos held over the Comanches and the Wichitas would remain a key to their success well into the nineteenth century. All these tribes were feared by the Spanish, who called them the Norteños, or Nations of the North.[20]

The Hasinais catered to the Tonkawan and Atakapan tribes, who lived to their southwest on the lower reaches of the Trinity and Colorado Rivers. These tribes had always viewed the Hasinais with respect but now had further reason to befriend them, since the Hasinais had arms to sell. The Hasinais' close ties with these tribes became apparent to the Spanish in 1745. Hoping to receive protection from the Apache menace, the Tonkawan and Atakapan tribes asked the Spanish priests at San Antonio to establish a mission in their country. Instead, the priests tried to persuade these tribes to move to San Antonio to receive their own mission. The Indians, however, refused to leave their homeland because of its proximity to the Hasinais and their supply of weapons.[21]

Since the Tonkawan and Atakapan tribes refused to relocate, a group of missions was established for them in their homeland on the San Xavier River (now the San Gabriel), where the Hasinais continued to wield great influence. In August, 1750, the Hainai *caddi*, Sanchez Teja, came to the area at the head of a large party of Caddo, Wichita, Ais, and Tonkawa warriors. Not only did Sanchez Teja trade with the mission natives, he also persuaded them to abandon the mission. Throughout the period, then, the smaller tribes to the southwest depended upon an alliance with the Hasinais to secure the arms they needed to defend themselves from the Apaches.[22]

Although the Spanish made a few attempts to end the illicit French trade with the Hasinais, the tribe proved strong enough to force the Spanish not only to allow trade with the French to continue, but to provide them with illegal trade goods as well. The first clash between the Hasinais and the Spanish came in 1750, when the governor at Los Adaes denied Saint-Denis entrance into Texas. In response, the French trader gathered the Hasinai warriors at the Nasoni village, supplied them with the latest model French guns, and informed them of the Spanish activities. The news enraged the Hasinai men and caused the Nacogdoches *caddi*, Chacaiauchia, to go to Mission Nacogdoches with his new gun in tow. With "excessive intrepidity, great audacity, and imponderable pride," he confronted the priest, Fray Calahorra, and demanded to know why the governor of Texas was trying to prevent Saint-Denis from trading with the Hasinais. Further, he told Calahorra that all the Hasinai tribes were angry and "ready to take up arms against the Spaniards in favor of the French to avenge this offense, and that by means of [these arms], they would endeavor to throw the Spaniards out of their lands." The *caddi* then threatened the Spaniard with his gun and was so angry that he would have killed him "if he had not been restrained by the humility and submission" of the priest, who prostrated himself at Chacaiauchia's feet. Although the *caddi* may have been bluffing, the Hasinais' trade with the French continued.[23]

The Hasinais thwarted another Spanish attempt to end the French trade two years later. A new Spanish governor, Jacinto de Barrios y Jáuregui, arrived at Los Adaes and noted that the French had all the Indians of "this province devoted to them" because of the presents and trade goods they provided. On October 30, 1752, the governor ordered an officer at Los Adaes, Don Manuel Antonio de Soto Bermúdez, to go to the Hasinai villages with four soldiers to investigate the French trade. Bermúdez entered the Nacogdoches village and distributed presents to ease the anger of the hostile Chacaiauchia. Bermúdez then traveled northeast to the Nasoni village, where the *tamma* told him that the Nasonis never went to the Spanish capital at Los Adaes because they received all the goods they needed from the French by way of either the Yatasis or the Nadacos. Saint-Denis had even gone so far as to appoint the Nadaco *caddi* as a French official, giving him a military coat, a cane, and a hat in recognition of his high station.[24]

Before Bermúdez could leave for the Nadaco village, a rumor was spread among the Hasinais that a group of Spaniards had left Los Adaes to arrest any Frenchman they might find trading among them. On November 18, the Nadaco *caddi*, "irritated and accompanied by many Indians," came to the Nasoni village, told Bermúdez that he would not allow him to proceed any farther, and forced the Spaniard to return to Los Adaes.[25]

The Nadaco *caddi* then convoked a meeting of the Hasinai warriors in his village. He also called Saint-Denis to the gathering and told him "that in view of the fact that the Spaniards did not want the French to enter and trade in their pueblos, which they so greatly desired, [Saint-Denis] should avail himself the opportunity of becoming lord of these lands, for which purpose they were ready to kill all Spaniards in them." Instead of taking up the Hasinai offer, Saint-Denis restrained the warriors. He told them that he would be very angry with them if they attacked Los Adaes, for these were Spanish lands. He was worried that a war would completely disrupt the profitable local trade, and though he wanted to use the Hasinais to intimidate the Spaniards, he did not wish them to go so far as to throw his formal European ally out of the territory. Saint-Denis's influence proved supreme, since the gathering "seeing their captain angered (for they respect him as such), became quiet" and gave up the notion of a concerted attack upon the Spanish.[26]

In response to these reports, officials in Mexico allowed Governor Barrios y Jáuregui to use his own judgment in deciding a course of action to "prevent inciting the factious Indians and causing a break in the friendly relations that is so important to maintain." Realizing that he was impotent to prevent the Hasinais from trading with the French without endangering the Spanish in East Texas, the governor let the illicit trade continue.[27]

To ease the tense relations in the area, Saint-Denis arranged for some Spaniards to trade with the Hasinais as well. Prompted by the Frenchman, the Nabedache, Nacogdoches, Hainai, Ais, and Adaes headmen came to Los Adaes on September 19, 1755, and told the governor it was essential that the Spaniards provide them with rifles and gunpowder to prevent their trade with the French. On the grounds that "there was no other way of holding these vast nations," Governor Barrios y Jáuregui issued trading licenses to two Spanish settlers despite the fact that trading with the Indians was still forbidden by the crown. Since the two traders obtained their goods from the French at Natchitoches, Saint-Denis incurred no loss. Most important, the Hasinais were assured that their trade with the French would not be disrupted, and in return the Hasinais continued to allow the Spanish to remain in East Texas.[28]

Relations between the Spanish and the Caddos—as well as the other tribes of Texas—worsened when the Apaches and the Spaniards ended their hostilities. By the middle of the 1750s, both the Spanish and the Apaches had become the objects of increased Comanche attacks. The beleaguered Apaches, who had once preyed upon the Spanish, now appealed to them to establish a mission in their country in hopes of gaining protection from their common enemy. In May, 1756, following long discussions and debates, Spanish officials made the fateful decision to comply with the Apache requests and build a mission and presidio for them to the northwest of San Antonio on the San Saba River. The Caddos and their allies strongly opposed the establishment of Mission Santa Cruz de San Sabá—located near present-day Menard, Texas—feeling it would provide the Apaches with a safe refuge from them.[29]

For the next decade, the Caddo tribes played a leading role in the developing tripartite struggle between the Spanish, the Apaches, and the Norteños. The Caddos' first move in this struggle was to join a group of two thousand warriors—mainly Comanches, Wichitas, Kichais, Tonkawas, and Bidais—in an attack upon the mission at San Sabá. This huge war party—half of whom were carrying French guns—gathered near San Sabá on the morning of March 16, 1758. They planned to kill any Apaches gathered at the mission in order to frighten the rest of the tribe from ever returning, but when the native force found that no Apaches were present, they turned on the Spaniards, killed eight of them, and set fire to the mission. Although it seems the Comanches led the attack, the Hainai *caddi*—possibly Sanchez Teja—played an important role in the events leading up to the outbreak of violence.[30]

The attack on Mission San Sabá caused the Spanish to seek retribution against the Norteños. Although there was clear evidence that the Hasinais had been involved in the attack on the San Sabá mission, officials at Mexico City decided that war was unthinkable against these long-time subjects of the Spanish crown. They also realized that the Hasinais' close ties with the French made retaliation impractical. Instead, the Spanish decided to launch a punitive campaign against the Tonkawas and the Wichitas. In August, 1759, an expedition under the command of Diego Ortiz Parrilla set out from San Antonio. It surprised a Tonkawa village on the Brazos River on October 2, and the troops killed 2 people and captured 149 more. They forced the Tonkawas to guide them to the well-defended village of the Taovayas and Wichitas on the Red River. These well-armed tribes outnumbered the Spanish, however, and Parrilla's force could not penetrate their palisaded village, above which flew a French flag. Parrilla was forced to retreat to San Sabá after suffering 52 casualties.[31]

The stage was now set for the Caddos to become peacemakers between the Wichitas and the Spanish. The Caddos recognized that peace was necessary to ensure the flow of French goods up the Red River. Just as their role as mediators in the acquisition of French trade had afforded the Caddos an exalted position in the area, their role as mediators between the Spanish and the Wichitas (together with the Comanches) also ensured them a place of importance.

The Hasinais, however, initially had to be persuaded by the French to accept this role, for the tribe had become very nasty to the priests at Mission Nacogdoches in the aftermath of the destruction of San Sabá. In 1760, Saint Denis and Athanase de Mézières, the commander of the French garrison at Natchitoches, rode to Mission Nacogdoches to calm the Hasinai warriors. The two Frenchmen summoned the tribal leaders and explained that the hostilities with the Spanish must end. In response, the new Hainai *caddi*, Canos, offered peace to Fray Calahorra and "with signs of profound humility" asked the priest to solicit peace on behalf of their friends, the Tawakonis and the rest of the Wichitas. When Calahorra promised to visit the Tawakonis and relay their peace proposals to the governor of Texas, the Hasinai warriors rejoiced and demonstrated their good faith by returning a few stolen horses to the Spanish missionary.[32]

On September 16, 1760, Fray Calahorra set out with eleven men for the Tawakoni and Iscani villages on the Sabine River. To assist the peace negotiations, one hundred Hasinai warriors accompanied him as well. At the Tawakoni village, Calahorra met with the headmen of all the

Wichita bands, and a temporary peace treaty was concluded between the Spanish and the Wichitas. Later, Calahorra wrote to the governor of Texas telling him of the importance of establishing good relations with these tribes and recommended that missions be established in their villages.[33]

Over the next few years the Hasinais continued to mediate the peace between the Spanish and other hostile tribes. In the spring of 1761, the Wichitas abstained from joining in horse raids made by the Tonkawas, Yojuanes, and Mayeyes around San Antonio. Fearing they would be blamed, Taovaya and Tawakoni headmen asked the Hainai *caddi*, Canos, to escort them to Mission Nacogdoches so they could declare their innocence to Fray Calahorra.[34]

The peace between the Spanish and the Norteños was threatened, however, by the Spanish insistence on continuing their alliance with the Apaches. Defensive improvements were made at the San Sabá presidio, and two new missions (El Cañon) had been founded for the Apaches on the Nueces River southwest of San Antonio. In response, the Norteños—Hasinais included—resumed their attacks upon the Lipans, destroying Apache settlements on the Frio and Guadalupe Rivers in addition to killing forty Apache hunters on the Colorado. The Taovayas, however, directly broke the peace with the Spanish in June, 1762, by making several raids on the Spanish herd of horses at Presidio de San Sabá and killing three Spanish soldiers in the process.[35]

The Hasinais again kept the Spanish and the Norteños from going to war. On June 12, 1762, a large group of Norteños fell upon a Spanish pack train headed for San Sabá just outside San Antonio. Four Hainai warriors identified the train as Spanish, however, and persuaded the rest of the group to "check" the attack. They joined the Spanish troops and "communicate[d] with them amicably." For the rest of the summer, the Norteños allowed the monthly supply trains to travel unmolested between San Antonio and San Sabá.[36]

Over the next few years, however, the Taovayas continued to make raids upon the Spanish. Finally in July, 1765, the Taovaya chief, Eyasiquiche, traveled to Mission Nacogdoches to propose peace to Fray Calahorra. Once again the Hasinais were involved in the negotiations as the Spanish priest asked Canos to provide translation,[37] but the establishment of peace with the Wichitas was delayed by the accession of Charles III to the throne of Spain in 1759. The new king desired to implement long-needed reforms in the Spanish empire, and all major decisions (such as abandoning the Apache alliance and making peace with the Norteños) were put on hold until the situation could be further examined.

Spanish policy in Texas was further confounded with the ceding of

Louisiana to Spain in 1762, and the abandonment of North America by the friend and supporter of the Caddo confederacies, France. This development was of the utmost importance for the Caddos, since the entire tribe had become a French client. Caddo access to French weapons had allowed them to maintain an important position in the area despite decimation by disease. Without French goods, support, and friendship, the Caddos now found themselves in a very precarious situation—one that would require them to use all their abilities simply to survive. The French withdrawal from North America suddenly ended the golden age of the Caddos.

Chapter 5

Decline:
The Caddos and
Spain, 1767–1803

The village of San Luiz de Cadodachos, which belongs to this district, is one hundred leagues from the fort of Natchitoches and eighty from the Akensas. Situated on the banks of the Colorado River, it is surrounded by pleasant groves and plains, is endowed with lands of extreme fertility, and abounds in salines and pastures. If to these advantages of the place there be added the great loyalty of its inhabitants and importance of their territory, which with respect to neighboring foreigners, should be considered the master-key of New Spain, it is undoubtedly well worthy of the favor with which the enlightened sagacity of your Lordship is pleased to distinguish it. The cacique, Tinhioüen, [is] a man of talent and of great authority in all of the neighboring bands. . . .
    —Athanase de Mézières, October 29, 1770[1]

The cruel epidemic which last year attacked Bejar, Bucareli, and Nachitos with such fury, and with even greater desolation entered the surrounding villages, appeared to have spent itself, when suddenly it appeared in the remote villages of the Jotars [Yatasis], Quitreis [Kichais], and Nasones, whence it passed to our Tuacanas, Taobayases, and Cadodachos, whose loyalty, as always should be well considered. Any misfortune of nations so adorned with such good qualities should be felt as our own. The number of persons of both sexes who have perished among these last exceeds three hundred. But notwithstanding such bad news, I have heard that their harvests have been very abundant, and that they have resigned themselves like civilized people.
    —Athanase de Mézières, November 15, 1778[2]

The Great Caddo tribe of Indians found itself obliged two years ago to change the location of its village on account of the continual war being waged upon them by the Osage tribe. Being persecuted incessantly by their enemies, these Indians were obliged last month to take refuge in the village of the Little Caddo.
    —Louis de Blanc, March 27, 1790[3]

THE FRENCH ABANDONMENT OF NORTH AMERICA and the Spanish acquisition of Louisiana finally forced the Caddo confederacies to accept a formal alliance with Spain—one which lasted throughout the rest of the century. For a while the Caddos were able to profit from their relationship with the weakening Spanish. However, one hundred years of contact with Euro-Americans finally caught up with the tribe just at the time when they could no longer depend upon the stronger French for support. Once again epidemic disease ravaged the Caddos, and the tribe became a target for their native enemies. Although the Caddos were desperately in need of assistance from their new ally, the Spanish proved incapable of providing the Caddo tribes with either adequate protection or the trade goods they needed for survival. By the time Louisiana was transferred to the United States in 1803, all the Caddo confederacies were eagerly looking toward the young republic to replace the ineffectual Spain as a partner.

Although Louisiana was acquired by Spain in November, 1762, the Spanish, to allow King Charles III to study the colonial situation, moved slowly in taking formal possession of the colony. For a while then, the Caddo confederacies were uncertain how the loss of their French ally would affect them. The period of transition from French to Spanish control of Louisiana was potentially tumultuous, but the Caddos were blessed with a pair of strong *caddices* who were able to lead the tribe through this period in a manner that initially favored the Indians.

The most important Caddo *caddi* during this era was Tinhioüen, the impressive leader of the Kadohadacho tribe. According to Athanase de Mézières, who became lieutenant governor of Natchitoches in 1769, Tinhioüen was "held in very high esteem by all" the tribes of the region. De Mézières himself had great respect for the Kadohadacho *caddi* and claimed "he is lively and vivacious" and that he had "never known a man of his color more witty or keener."[4]

Tinhioüen's tribe continued to reside in their ancient homeland near the bend of the Red River about two hundred miles upstream from Natchitoches. There were perhaps 500 members of the Kadohadacho tribe, 90 of whom were warriors. Tinhioüen also had influence over his downstream kin, the Petit Caddos, whose population stood at 300, including about 60 warriors. The Petit Caddos lived on the Red River nearly 120 miles above Natchitoches. The 125 Yatasis—who lived downstream from the Petit Caddos—also received strong leadership from their two headmen, Houhan and Cocay. Their village stood about halfway between the Petit Caddos and the Natchitoches tribe, whose 100 members resided a few miles up the Red River from the town of the same name. Both these tribes were also strongly influenced by Tinhioüen and the Kadohadachos.[5]

Just as Tinhioüen became the leader of the Red River Caddos, the Hainai *caddi*, Bigotes, who took over in 1769, gained ascendance over two

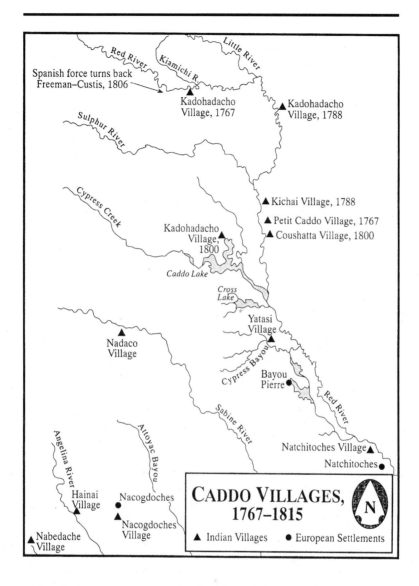

CADDO VILLAGES, 1767–1815

Spanish force turns back Freeman–Custis, 1806

Red River
Little River
Kiamichi R.
Kadohadacho Village, 1767
Kadohadacho Village, 1788
Sulphur River
Cypress Creek
Kichai Village, 1788
Petit Caddo Village, 1767
Coushatta Village, 1800
Kadohadacho Village, 1800
Caddo Lake
Cross Lake
Nadaco Village
Yatasi Village
Cypress Bayou
Bayou Pierre
Red River
Sabine River
Natchitoches Village
Natchitoches
Angelina River
Attoyac Bayou
Hainai Village
Nacogdoches
Nacogdoches Village
Nabedache Village

▲ Indian Villages   ● European Settlements

N

of the three remaining Hasinai tribes, the Nabedaches and the Nacogdoches. De Mézières was struck by the "authority which he [Bigotes] exercises over the neighboring pueblos." Another official at Natchitoches, José de la Peña, felt that Bigotes (Spanish for whiskers) kept his strong intelligence hidden "since he thinks more deeply than some suppose." For a decade Bigotes would prove his intelligence by providing the one thousand members of the Hasinai tribe with skillful leadership. The Nadacos, whose villages were the farthest removed of the Hasinais, retained a degree of independence that would continue to grow throughout the period.[6]

The Caddo tribes did not feel the effect of Spanish rule until after Gov. Antonio de Ulloa's arrival in New Orleans in March, 1766. Luckily for the tribe, the Spaniard did nothing to alter the Indian policy adopted by the French. Ulloa realized that the Spanish method of treating with the natives through missionaries and attempted conversion would not work with tribes accustomed to French trade. To eradicate this trade would only throw the Indians into the hands of aggressive British traders, now poised on the east bank of the Mississippi River. Ulloa kept the natives satisfied by continuing the trade and by employing, in the service of the king of Spain, the same French traders to carry it out. Saint-Denis and de Mézières retained their positions of importance at Natchitoches, and the Caddo confederacies continued to be serviced from there.[7]

The only immediate consequence of the transferal of Louisiana to Spain was increased warfare between the Red River tribes and their ancient enemies, the fierce Osages. Following Spain's acquisition of Louisiana, French traders established themselves illegally on the Arkansas River and supplied the Osages with great numbers of British guns and ammunition smuggled across the Mississippi. To obtain more of these items, the Osages began preying upon the Caddos, the Kichais, and the Wichitas in order to steal horses to trade with the French. According to de Mézières, the Osage onslaught had turned the Red River Valley into a "pitiful theater of outrageous robberies and bloody encounters."[8]

At first, the Kadohadachos attempted to fight back. In 1768, Tinhioüen pursued a band of horse-stealing Osages all the way to the Arkansas River. He found two Osage chiefs at one of the illegal French trading houses and killed them. Two years later, in the summer of 1770, a Kadohadacho headman was murdered by the Osages in retaliation for the previous killings, but Tinhioüen, realizing that the Osages greatly outnumbered his tribe, did not pursue further vengeance this time.[9]

The Osage onslaught also had the effect of driving the Wichitas and the Kichais even farther to the south. The Wichita peace negotiations with the Spanish had never been finalized, so they—along with the Kichais and the Comanches—renewed their plundering of the Spanish settlements of Texas in 1766. Not only did the Norteños steal Spanish horses to recoup their losses from the Osages, they also directly attacked the Spanish soldiers guarding the Apache missions on the Nueces River.[10]

The increased Norteño attacks caused the interim governor of Texas, Hugo Oconor, to take actions that would directly affect the Caddo tribes. Although Texas and Louisiana were now both possessions of Spain, they were administered separately—a situation that soon posed a problem. While

Governor Ulloa had no qualms with allowing the French method of trade to continue within Louisiana, Governor Oconor was determined to stop the illegal commerce with the natives of his province—most important-ly with the Hasinais—being conducted by traders from Louisiana. Oconor, who had been in charge of investigating the smuggling between French Louisiana and East Texas allowed by Texas governors in the past, was certain that the rampaging Norteños were still receiving guns and am-munition from Louisiana through their Caddo allies.[11]

Thus, in December, 1767, Oconor arrested a French trader from Natchi-toches on the road to the Yatasi village. The arrest of the Frenchman alarmed the Caddo tribes since, in light of the increased Osage attacks, they were desperate to prevent their supply of arms and ammunition from being halted by the new Texas governor. In response the Yatasi head-men, Houhan and Cocay, gathered members of the Kadohadacho, Hain-ai, Nacogdoches, Adaes, and Ais tribes at their village to discuss plans for an attack on the Spanish presidio at Los Adaes. The enraged tribes were soon quieted—as they had been many times before—by Saint-De-nis. The Frenchman, now employed by Spain, told them of his opposi-tion to their plans and urged them all to be friendly and peaceful. Once again, the tribes accepted Saint-Denis's advice and quietly returned to their villages.[12]

Saint-Denis brought the incident to the attention of Governor Ulloa, who immediately attempted to dissuade Oconor from carrying out his plan of disrupting trade with tribes who "have been accustomed to it for a long time past." He warned that the result would be "very evil con-sequences," such as a violent uprising against the Spanish, and expressed the concern that the tribes would travel to the "English frontiers to get the things which are withheld from them." Ulloa felt the best way to maintain peace was to provide the natives with presents every time they visited "and to assure them that trade will be kept up in the same way as it has been carried on in the past." Although both governors were soon removed from the scene, their successors ultimately adopted the policy promoted by Ulloa, and the Caddo tribes continued to be supplied from Natchitoches with the trade goods they needed.[13]

The new governors, Alejandro O'Reilly of Louisiana and the Barón de Ripperdá of Texas, realized that peaceful relations with the tribes of the Louisiana-Texas frontier had to be maintained. Spain was too weak and poor to afford war with the tribes—especially when they might ally themselves with the British at any time. Also, since the hostilities with the Wichitas and the Comanches had yet to be resolved, those tribes continued to threaten the Texas frontier. With O'Reilly taking the lead, the governors of the two northern provinces undertook a policy of peace in order to establish Spanish authority over the tribes of Louisiana and the Red River Valley that had acknowledged France and to bar the intrusion and influence of the British from the region.[14]

To put such a policy into effect, Governor O'Reilly called upon the man who was said to have a knowledge of Texas and Louisiana and their native inhabitants "such as no one else possesses," Athanase de Mézières. The French commander informed the Irish governor—both now in the employ of Spain—that he considered the allegiance of the Kadohadachos to be of the utmost importance to any peace plan, since the tribe occupied "the master-key of New Spain." Not only could the Kadohadachos serve as a buffer against British incursion on the northeastern flank of Texas, but their influence over the other Norteños, especially the Wichitas, might help bring about peace with those tribes as well.[15]

Governor O'Reilly accepted de Mézières's estimation of the situation and in January, 1770, gave him approval to open formal relations with the Red River Caddos. To induce the allegiance of the tribes, de Mézières arranged for the Natchitoches, Yatasis, Petit Caddos, and the Kadohadachos to receive annual presents, including clothes, guns, blankets, beads, tools, and jugs of brandy. The latter three tribes were also permitted to have licensed traders at their villages to supply the natives with European goods in return for deer skins, bear fat, and buffalo hides.[16]

In April, 1770, de Mézières gathered the tribes at Natchitoches to establish formal ties with the Spanish. Tinhioüen of the Kadohadachos and Cocay of the Yatasis received the high distinction of being designated medal chiefs by de Mézières, and both "solemnly promised to show the same love and the same respect" for Spain as they had for France. Both ceded to the king of Spain "all proprietorship in the land which they inhabit, [and] have promised him blind fidelity and obedience." Eighty years after first being visited by the Spanish, the Kadohadachos transferred their allegiance from France to Spain.[17]

With the establishment of good relations with the Caddos on the Red River, the Spanish undertook to establish peace with the Norteños. This policy was supported by Tinhioüen and Cocay, and they sent messengers to the hostile bands to alert them to the fact that the "most powerful French and Spanish nations are now united by such close ties that to injure one is to offend the other." Tinhioüen promised de Mézières that he would assemble the principal men of the Comanches, Wichitas, and Kichais at his village in order to achieve peace. The friendly Red River Caddos "greatly interest[ed] themselves in the reestablishment of tranquillity," for they saw that their role as peacemakers offered them an opportunity to strengthen their ties with the Spanish, whom they now depended upon for trade.[18]

Meanwhile the Hasinais, who had been involved in peace negotiations between Spain and the Wichitas following the massacre at San Sabá in

1758, realized that they, like the Kadohadachos, might also gain by reas-suming their previous role as mediators. In June, 1770, the Hainai *caddi*, Bigotes, visited de Mézières in Natchitoches and promised to bring him the head of a tribal member who had killed two French traders and a Spaniard the previous year so de Mézières could nail it to one of the stakes of the fort "as an example" for the rest of the tribes. De Mézières thanked the Hainai *caddi* and promised to give him a Spanish flag and a medal. This pleased Bigotes so much that, "after having broken out in emphatic protestations of gratitude," he told de Mézières that he would visit the Norteños and persuade them to sue for peace.[19]

It was Tinhioüen, though, who first brought together the chiefs of the Taovayas, Iscanis, Tawakonis, and Kichais at his village in Septem-ber, 1770. He sent for de Mézières, who set out from Natchitoches ac-companied by six soldiers. To demonstrate that the remaining French in Louisiana were now subjects of Spain, they added another five Spanish soldiers at Los Adaes to their contingent along with Father Miguel de Santa María y Silva, president of the Zacatecan missions. On their way to the Kadohadacho village, the party passed through the villages of the Adaes, the Yatasis, and the Petit Caddos, where de Mézières reported that they were sheltered and fed with "visible affection" by the natives. The flag of Spain was hoisted at each village, and the headmen of each tribe joined the party as it made its way to the Kadohadacho village for the council arranged by Tinhioüen.[20]

At this meeting de Mézières addressed the headmen of the four Wich-ita tribes that had come to the Kadohadacho village. He told them that their trade had been suspended from Natchitoches because of their at-tack upon San Sabá and the battle with Parrilla in 1759 and made it clear that the French in Louisiana were now subjects of the Spanish king. De Mézières insisted that the tribes "should profit by the good example and inviolable fidelity of the friendly Cadodachos" and also ally them-selves with the Spanish. Both Tinhioüen and Cocay at once seconded the speech with effective arguments "so worthy of their well-known loyalty."[21]

The spokesperson for the Wichitas and the Kichais replied that their discord with the Spanish had arisen out of the Spanish alliance with the Apaches and the establishment of the missions for them at San Sabá and El Cañon. He complained to de Mézières that their former allies, the Comanches, had turned on them because they were now seeking peace with the Spanish. Still, the tribes refused to go to either San Antonio or to Los Adaes to conclude a peace treaty with Texas out of fear of possible Spanish attack. Thus, Tinhioüen's first attempt to negotiate a settlement between the Spanish and the Norteños ended short of success.[22]

In light of the Kadohadacho failure, Bigotes of the Hainais resumed his efforts in the spring of 1771 and visited the Wichitas and the Kichais to persuade them to make peace. A winter of Osage and Comanche attacks helped convince the tribes to accept the Spanish offer, and they gave Bigotes two buffalo skins: a white one to signify that the roads were open and free from blood and one with four crosses painted on it to designate the number of tribes ready to make peace. Bigotes gave the skins to Father Silva and then traveled with the priest to Natchitoches, where he was awarded "liberal presents" by de Mézières. The Frenchman asked Bigotes and a few other members of the Hasinais to lead a Spanish party to the Norteño tribes to request that they come to Natchitoches to formally make peace. Realizing that this would further solidify his standing with the Spanish, Bigotes agreed to de Mézières's request.[23]

The mission was successful, and in September, 1771, Bigotes returned to Natchitoches with four chiefs, one each from the Kichais, Iscanis, Tawakonis, and a branch of the Taovayas tribes. The headmen gathered with de Mézières, the Zacatecan priests, and the commander of the Spanish presidio at Los Adaes and wrapped themselves with the royal banner "as a sign of the union of all and as a token that those who live in La Luisiana" were Spanish as well.[24]

The Norteños excused themselves from traveling to San Antonio to meet with Governor Ripperdá and ratify the treaty there, for they explained that they had been called to go on an expedition against the Osages. Bigotes and forty Hasinai warriors went in their place and were splendidly received by the governor, who clothed Bigotes in a uniform, and gave presents to the other tribesmen. Although the Hasinais had always formally been vassals of Spain, Governor Ripperdá felt that those ties needed to be reinforced and that it was necessary that Bigotes be properly thanked for his services. In a very solemn ceremony, performed in the presence of a portrait of King Charles III, armed troops, and all of the principal personages of San Antonio, Ripperdá commissioned Bigotes as head chief of the Hasinais. He was given the new name of Sauto and, like Tinhioüen and Cocay, was decorated with the royal medal.[25]

Tinhioüen, who had continued to treat with the Norteños, shared in the glory of the moment as well, for in October, 1771, he brought to Natchitoches the chief of another branch of the Taovayas to make peace. Because of his eminence as "great Cacique of Cadodachos," Tinhioüen fixed his mark to the treaty along with the Taovayas chiefs.[26]

Although the Norteños, with Caddo prompting, had agreed to peace with the Spanish, opposition from Oconor—now commandant of the Spanish forces on the entire northern frontier of New Spain—hampered the full implementation of the peace plan. Oconor, whose advice the Spanish Viceroy Antonio María Bucareli y Ursua usually followed, trusted neither the Norteños nor the Frenchman who negotiated the treaties.

He blocked any plan offered by de Mézières and Ripperdá—such as a presidio in the Wichita country or an offensive war against the Apaches— that would have fully cemented peace with the Norteños. Not until after Oconor's removal in 1776 would there be a coordination of Indian policy between officials on the scene and their superiors.[27]

Despite the confusion caused by bureaucratic intransigence, both the Kadohadachos and the Hasinais had profited from their efforts as peacemakers between the Norteños and the Spanish. The Caddo tribes had maintained their trading privileges and firmly established their own friendship with the Spanish. In this manner, the Caddos were able to control the potentially damaging effects of the transfer of Louisiana to Spain and for a time actually profited from it. However, Spanish control of Louisiana (and the absence of French support) meant that they no longer had to be tentative with the Caddos, and now that peace had been established with the Norteños, Spanish officials began to act with a newfound confidence toward the tribe. The Spanish demonstrated this soon after the treaties with the Wichitas were effected by boldly thwarting a possible alliance between the Hasinais and their longtime enemies, the Lipan Apaches.

The Hasinais considered making this revolutionary reversal in diplomacy for a number of reasons. The Spanish peace with the Norteños obviously threatened the Lipan Apaches who had been forced even farther south—to the area around the Nueces, Frio, and Rio Grande rivers—by the Comanches and Wichitas during the 1760s. The desperate Apaches appealed to the Hasinais for peace to obtain weapons with which to defend themselves. Both the Hasinais and the Atakapan Bidais, a small tribe who lived nearby on the Trinity River, had sources that provided them with European guns and ammunition, whereas the Lipans did not. Besides the legal channels of trade established between the Hasinais and the Spanish in Louisiana, the Hasinais and the Bidais were also receiving illicit goods from British traders, who were established along the Gulf Coast of Texas and maintained themselves in the Louisiana town of Opelousas "with audacity."[28]

Sauto (formerly named Bigotes) recognized that peace with the Apaches, coupled with the opportunity to become mediators in the trade with them, would benefit the Hasinais. Peace between the Apaches and the Hasinais, however, was strongly opposed by both the Spanish and Governor Ripperdá. Not only would it jeopardize the peace just established between the Spanish and the Norteños, it would provide the Apaches with weapons with which to attack Spanish settlements in Texas and northern Mexico. The Lipans stole horses, mules, and cattle from the Spanish to obtain the desperately needed guns and ammunition. Thus, Spanish policy continued throughout the rest of the century to thwart any alliance between the Apaches and the tribes of East Texas, especially the Hasinais.[29]

Negotiations began between the Hasinais and the Apaches in late 1771 upon Sauto's return trip from San Antonio and the meeting with Governor Ripperdá. On the road home to East Texas, Sauto was met by Gorgoritos, the chief of the Bidais, and a contingent of about one hundred Apache warriors. The Apache chief proposed a treaty of peace and trade with both the Bidais and the Hasinais. All three tribes met to trade and discuss peace throughout the rest of the winter.[30]

In the spring of 1772, Governor Ripperdá charged de Mézières with the duty of frustrating the proposed alliance between the Hasinais, the Bidais, and the Lipan Apaches. De Mézières went to the Hainai village and, upon finding the Bidai chiefs there, pressured them to declare war against either the Apaches or the Norteños on the grounds that they could not be allies of both. Unnerved by the boldness displayed by the Spanish and unwilling to jeopardize the good relations that had just recently been established, the Hasinais, together with the Bidais, promised not to deal with the Apaches anymore.[31]

It was not until later that summer that the Hasinais were forced to prove their allegiance to Spain. In July, 1772, de Mézières received word from Governor Ripperdá that a large number of Apaches were on their way to the Hasinai country to ratify the treaties of peace and commerce that they had proposed the previous winter. De Mézières sent a message to Sauto and Gorgoritos "urging them not to lose so propitious an occasion to fulfill the promise" they had given him. Further, he told them to "avail themselves of the feigned friendship" with the Apaches and attack them. Sauto, realizing his tribe could not afford enmity with the Spanish, carried out their wishes: when seven Apache chiefs entered his village to offer peace and friendship, Sauto ambushed them, killing four. The other three escaped, and by January, 1773, the rest of the Apaches had made it known throughout Texas they intended to attack the Hasinais to avenge the deaths of their four chiefs.[32]

This came at a most inopportune moment for the Hasinais. In 1772, after a four-year lag, Charles III acted upon the report of the Marqués de Rubí—who had toured the northern provinces of New Spain in 1767–1768—and issued the royal order that led to their reorganization. Among the many changes called for by Charles III was the abandonment of the Spanish effort in East Texas. Now that the French threat from Louisiana was gone, the king saw no need to maintain the capital at Los Adaes, and it was removed to San Antonio. The presidio, as well as the missions under its protection at Nacogdoches, Ais, and Adaes, was also abolished; Spain faced the fact that the missionary effort among the Hasinais and the other tribes had all been unsuccessful and had served only to give

Spain a claim to the country. After the Spanish withdrawal from East Texas, the Hasinais would be left without even the nominal protection the Spanish force had provided for the first time in fifty years.[33]

On May 18, 1773, Governor Ripperdá received instructions to gather all civilians, soldiers, and missionaries and lead them to San Antonio. Upon hearing this news, Sauto cut short a raid upon the Osages in order to meet Ripperdá and ask him not to leave. Sauto knew that the Apaches were planning a revenge attack, and he wanted the protection the Spanish soldiers had provided. Sauto's meeting with Ripperdá was fruitless, and the governor and the inhabitants of Los Adaes departed in late June, passing through the Hasinai country on the way to San Antonio. Once again Sauto pleaded with Ripperdá to stay and further declared he would go to San Antonio to ask that the Spanish and the priests be allowed to return to his country.[34]

Luckily for the Hasinais, the Apaches did not retaliate, and the Spanish shortly returned to the region—partly as a result of Hasinai efforts. At this time a group of civilians who had lived at Los Adaes petitioned the governor of Texas to allow them to return to East Texas. Recognizing the lack of Spanish settlements between San Antonio and Natchitoches to guard against the intrusion of French and British contraband traders, Governor Ripperdá allowed the two most prominent citizens of Los Adaes, Gil Ybarbo and Gil Flores, to travel to Mexico City in December, 1773, to convince Viceroy Bucareli in person. Texita, one of the Hainai *canahas*, accompanied Ybarbo and Flores on their trip. The viceroy was very impressed by the "intelligent and capable" Texita and invested him with the uniform and baton of a captain. Texita's friendly meeting with Bucareli certainly helped convince him—despite Oconor's disapproval—to allow Ybarbo and Flores to lead a party of settlers to the Trinity River, where they established the town of Bucareli about thirty miles west of the Hasinais.[35]

Although it was illegal, the Hasinais and the other tribes of the area carried on a trade with the Bucareli settlers, exchanging furs and horses for European goods. The Hasinais also received presents from Bucareli, and a well-intentioned friendship was established between the two parties. It was short-lived, however, since Comanche raids and the flooding of the Trinity River forced the settlers of Bucareli to flee in the spring of 1779. They went to the site of the abandoned mission among the Hasinais, where they established the civil community of Nacogdoches.[36]

By this time the Provincias Internas—a new administrative unit designed to govern all the northern provinces except for Louisiana—had been organized, and among other policies, the new commandant general, Theodoro de Croix, was officially in favor of the reoccupation of East Texas. Croix appointed Domingo Cabello to be the new governor of Texas, and both men allowed the settlers to remain at Nacogdoches, since it was felt that to force them to return to San Antonio would "be prejudicial . . . to [the cultivation] of the friendship of the Tejas and other allied tribes."[37]

Croix also agreed to one of Ripperdá's long-standing requests—which had been opposed by the now-removed Oconor—of supplying the natives of his province with trade from Texas rather than from Natchitoches. Croix appointed Ybarbo lieutenant general of Nacogdoches and ordered him to establish a trading house. A Spaniard, José María Armán, was named legal trader for all the native tribes of East Texas, including the Hasinais. Though originally established as a mission dedicated to converting the Hasinais to Christianity, in the late eighteenth century Nacogdoches became a trading post dedicated to maintaining the allegiance of all the Texas natives through the method that had proven so successful for the French.[38]

Unfortunately for the Caddos, by the time the Spanish of Texas had adopted French trade practices, disaster had already struck the tribe. In the summer and fall of 1777, and in the following year as well, all the tribes of East Texas were wracked by a "cruel epidemic," the worst since the outbreaks of disease in the 1690s. As with the earlier epidemics, the sickness was transmitted by the Euro-Americans; thus, those tribes closest to the Spanish suffered the most. Disease first struck the settlement at Bucareli in early 1777, and seventeen people perished before it spread to the nearby Bidai villages. More than half of the two hundred Bidai warriors were killed, including their chief, Gorgoritos.[39]

By that summer the epidemic had reached the Hasinai tribes, and Sauto and the Nabedache *caddi* both succumbed to the disease in August. The sickness raged throughout the fall, killing three hundred tribal members and seriously disrupting the Hasinai lines of succession, since there was a lack of heirs for the position of *caddi*. The *canahas* of the Nabedaches and the Hainais asked de Mézières to name a chief for them but he declined, claiming it was the prerogative of the governor of Texas. The Hasinais continued to be plagued by outbreaks of sickness as three *canahas*, acting as chiefs, died in the following five years. The disease caused the Nadacos to relocate farther away from the Spanish settlement at Nacogdoches, and by 1788, they had completed the move northward from the upper reaches of the Angelina River to the waters of the Sabine.[40]

The Yatasis and the Natchitoches were even harder hit by the epidemic than the Hasinai tribe. Their villages were so ravaged by the sickness in the fall of 1777 that it became uncertain whether the two tribes would survive. By 1787, their numbers had declined so much that the commander of the post at Natchitoches remarked that they did not "deserve to be included any longer among the recipients of presents."

Five years later only two Yatasi families remained, and by the beginning of the nineteenth century, the total population of the Yatasis and the Natchitoches had fallen to only sixty-four.[41]

The Kadohadacho confederacy—the farthest removed from the whites—was not affected by the epidemic of 1777. In the fall of 1778, however, the sickness suddenly appeared in the nearby villages of the Nadacos and the Kichais and spread to the Kadohadachos and the Petit Caddos. Tinhioüen, the able *caddi* of the Kadohadachos, survived the disease but witnessed the deaths of three hundred tribal members. De Mézières, who lost his own wife and children in the epidemic, sympathized with the Kadohadachos, feeling "that any misfortune of nations so adorned with such good qualities should be felt as our own." He reported that the Kadohadacho harvest for the year had been good and that they had "resigned themselves like civilized people."[42]

The epidemics of 1777–78 seriously altered the Caddo-Spanish alliance by increasing the Caddos' dependence upon the Spanish at a time when Spain's weakness in America became evident. Pressures increased upon the Caddos from all sides during the final two decades of the eighteenth century, and Spain proved unable to provide the Caddos with the guidance, arms, or military protection they desperately needed in their fragile state.

The Osages brought the worst pressures upon the Kadohadachos. Following a lull of a few years, they once again resumed full-scale attacks upon the tribe, and in the spring of 1777, the Osages stole a large number of horses from the Kadohadachos and killed five men and two women. Although Tinhioüen retaliated later that summer by slaying five Osages who had just robbed a group of French traders on the Arkansas River, de Mézières felt that repeated attacks by the Osages on the Kadohadachos "unquestionably [promise] the total destruction of this commendable nation."[43]

As the tribe continued to be weakened by warfare with the Osages, a faction emerged among the Kadohadachos in favor of abandoning their village on the Red River and moving downstream to join the Petit Caddos. In the spring of 1779, Tinhioüen announced to de Mézières that he wished to travel to New Orleans with his son, Bicheda, and three principal men to discuss his tribe's precarious situation with the new governor of Louisiana, Bernardo de Gálvez. Unfamiliar with the situation along the Red River, Gálvez sought the counsel of de Mézières, and the Frenchman informed the governor that the Kadohadachos provided a barrier against the Osages and that the Spanish owed "the love and respect of the surrounding villages" to the great influence of the tribe, especially Tinhioüen. De Mézières feared that their relocation would leave the country exposed to foreign invasion and would cause the nearby tribes to lose confidence in the Spanish. Since the Kadohadachos occupied "one of the most important keys to the western country," de Mézières asked Gálvez to greet the party with "dignity [and] spectacle" in his most formal gubernatorial attire so as to "make a great impression on their eyes."[44]

Gálvez did not disappoint de Mézières, for upon Tinhioüen's arrival at New Orleans, the governor received the *caddi* with "all the affection and kindness merited by the fidelity [and] love" the tribe had shown for the Spanish. Gálvez decorated Tinhioüen with a large medal and showered him with presents "of considerable importance." Through this warm reception, Gálvez successfully convinced Tinhioüen to keep the Kadohadachos at their traditional village.[45]

The war with the Osages, however, continued to rage. The Kadohadachos lost 160 horses to the Osages in the winter of 1781, and the problem was exacerbated by Spain's inability to supply the tribe with weapons due to the Spanish involvement in the war against Great Britain by the United States and France. Short of powder and bullets, the Kadohadachos were powerless to retaliate against the Osage attacks and could not even hunt out of fear of their enemy. In September, 1782, a Hasinai man and woman arrived at San Antonio and reported that the Kadohadachos had come to his tribe and asked them to make war on the Osages, "who were harassing them a great deal." Nothing, however, came of the war proposal.[46]

Finally, in 1785, the new governor of Louisiana, Estevan Miró, mediated a peace between the Osages and the Kadohadachos. In May, he had the headmen of both tribes come to New Orleans, where he held a formal conference with them in the presence of all the officers who were stationed there. Miró opened the meeting by imploring them both to make peace. The Osage chief, Brucaiguais, hoping to receive a Spanish trader for his village, immediately agreed to Miró's request, but Tinhioüen balked, for he knew "the perfidy and bad faith of his enemies and this made him believe that they would not observe it." With "great fervor," Brucaiguais expressed his desire to maintain the peace and told Tinhioüen that his own father had been killed by the Kadohadachos "almost on the doorstep" of Tinhioüen's house. Nevertheless, he extended his "open hand to receive" Tinhioüen's. The Kadohadacho *caddi* then arose and took Brucaiguais' hand "saying that he had torn from his heart all the hate which he held against" the Osages. The two chiefs embraced, peace was made, and to cement the agreement, Governor Miró gave them each medals.[47]

Before the year was out, however, Tinhioüen's hesitancy at accepting peace with the Osages was proven prophetic. In December, 1785, a band of Kadohadacho hunters was attacked by the Osages; in addition to having their horses and furs stolen, two Kadohadachos were killed and two were wounded. The Osages also harassed the Kichais—close allies of the Kadohadachos—at a village they had recently established on the Red River between the Kadohadachos and the Petit Caddos. Once again, the Spanish proved their inadequacy in protecting the Kadohadachos. Although Miró felt that the Osages needed to be reprimanded for the attacks, he feared that depriving them of trade would only encourage them to deal with the Anglo Americans who—following the Revolutionary War— were now established on the east bank of the Mississippi River. If not with the Americans, the Osages might turn to the British and their trading station at Michilmackinac on the Great Lakes. Thus, the Spanish governor refused to take action against the Osages in 1785.[48]

When Osage attacks continued throughout 1786 and 1787, the Spanish discussed the idea of supplying the Kadohadachos as well as the Quapaws on the Arkansas River with enough arms to allow them to attack the Osages. The commander of the post at Natchitoches, Louis de Blanc, reported that the Hasinais, as well as the Taovayas and the Tawakonis were prepared to wage war upon the Osages at the request of the "great chief of the Caddo and that of the [Quapaw]."[49]

Although the order was given to supply the Kadohadachos and their allies with arms and ammunition, the tribe did not attack the Osages. In early September, 1787, the Kadohadachos and the Petit Caddos came to Natchitoches to meet with José de la Peña, another Spanish official stationed there. When the Spaniard berated the tribe for failing to launch the proposed attack upon the Osages, Tinhioüen explained that "at present it would be impossible for him to attack the Osages because the number of his nation is very inferior to theirs." The *caddi*, however, promised to try to do them as much harm as possible.[50]

Whatever harm he did to the Osages proved to be ineffectual, for the following year, the Kadohadachos gave in to Osage pressure and moved their village downstream nearly halfway between the old village and the Petit Caddos. At the same time, the Kichais threatened to leave the area and move to the Gulf Coast. Both Kadohadacho tribes strongly opposed the Kichais' relocation, for they would be losing a valuable ally against the Osages. In response, Tinhioüen, along with the leaders of the Petit Caddos, led a party of Kichai headmen down to Natchitoches in August, 1788, where the Spanish officials helped convince the Kichais to remain in the area. The two Caddo tribes persuaded the Kichais to move their village to a site on the Red River about twenty miles above the Petit Caddos by consenting to give the Kichais their annual gifts for the present year.[51]

Convincing the Kichais to remain on the Red River proved to be the final official act of the great Kadohadacho *caddi*. Tinhioüen passed away in the summer of 1789, after providing the tribe with firm and steady leadership through twenty years of great hardship and change. On September 30, 1789, the Spanish held a formal ceremony at Natchitoches to recognize Bicheda as the Kadohadacho *caddi*. Bicheda was given a large medal, a uniform, a banner, and thirty jugs of brandy to celebrate his appointment.[52]

Unfortunately, Bicheda proved unable to stem the tide of decline that continued throughout the rest of the century. In February, 1790, only five months after becoming the Kadohadacho *caddi*, Bicheda moved his tribe downstream again to take refuge in the village of the Petit Caddos, since they were "being persecuted incessantly by their enemies," the Osages. After a century of contact with the Euro-Americans, the four tribes of the Kadohadacho confederacy were finally reduced to one.[53]

The years between the epidemics of 1777–78 and the turn of the century were also very difficult for the tribes of the Hasinai confederacy. The devastating epidemic of 1777 killed both Sauto and the Nabedache *caddi*, leaving the Hasinai tribes devoid of effective leadership. Texita, the *canaha* who had received the accoutrements of a captain from Viceroy Bucareli in 1774, assumed the position of Hainai chief in the absence of a clear successor to Sauto.

Chief among the problems facing the Hasinais was the matter of trade. Although the Spanish had finally allowed a trader to be stationed at Nacogdoches, José María Armán fell rapidly into debt and was unable to keep the Hasinais (and the other tribes of the region) adequately supplied with Euro-American goods. As they had in the past, the Hasinais continued their quasi-legal trade with French merchants from Natchitoches, which also failed to provide the tribe with a satisfactory amount of the necessary items for survival. Thus, the Hasinais (along with the other East Texas tribes) were again tempted to make peace with the Lipan Apaches in order to exploit another profitable trading avenue. As the Spanish and the Norteños strengthened their alliance, the Apaches became increasingly desperate for munitions. They stepped up their raids on the Spanish ranches to acquire horses and mules to sell for guns, but since they had no access to firearms, they had to convince the tribes of East Texas to be their intermediaries with the illicit traders at Opelousas and other coastal towns. Weakened by disease and unable to acquire adequate trade from the Spanish, the Hasinais became increasingly susceptible to the entreaties of the Apaches.

Peaceful trade with the Lipans, however, could prove to be highly dangerous for the Hasinais. The Spanish of Texas, who were victimized by the Apache raids, obviously were wholly opposed to the association. Throughout 1778 and 1779, Spanish correspondence is replete with reports of a possible alliance between the Hasinais, the Bidais, and the Apaches. In both years Commandant General Croix instructed the governor of Texas to "adopt provisions for the attainment of separating the Lipans from the Tejas and the Bidais." Croix was interested in thwarting the Hasinai-Apache friendship because he had reversed past policy in 1778 and given his wholehearted support to an offensive campaign— in conjunction with the Norteños—against the Apaches. Thus, the Hasinais, bereft of effective leadership, hesitated to make an alliance with the Lipans, agreeing instead to join an army of Norteños being formed against the Apaches by de Mézières in the summer of 1779.[54]

On August 16, 1779, the new Hainai chief, Texita, arrived in San Antonio with five warriors to meet with Governor Cabello and await the arrival of de Mézières and the Norteños. Texita and his men remained in San Antonio for a few days, during which time he held a series of talks with Cabello. Texita strongly emphasized the shortage of traders among all the tribes of East Texas; he "begged [Cabello] in all earnestness" to provide the tribes with traders "for they lacked many things." While conferring with Texita on August 21, Cabello received a message that six hundred Apaches were on their way to San Antonio to meet him. Realizing the "disastrous results that could ensue" should the Apaches and the Hainais meet, Cabello persuaded Texita and his men to leave by providing presents and an escort of seven soldiers. When the Lipans arrived at San Antonio only a few hours later, they expressed their regret at not meeting the Hainai representatives, for they wanted to be friends. As a show of good faith, the Apaches had brought four Hainai captives to be returned to the tribe. For the time being, though, the Spanish were successful in keeping the two tribes apart.[55]

The Apaches approached the Hasinais once again the following year in an attempt to make peace; the Hasinais' lack of leadership caused them to be unsure of what course to follow. De Mézières, who for nearly two decades had counseled the tribe toward peace with the Spanish and hostility to the Apaches, died in November, 1779. Texita also passed away the following summer, leaving no clear successor to the position of Hainai *caddi*. In desperation, three Hainai men and a woman came to San Antonio in August, 1780, to ask Governor Cabello to appoint a new chief for the tribe. The governor refused on the grounds that the entire tribe must be present for such an appointment to be binding.[56]

Cabello then persuaded the Hainai embassy to accompany him to Presidio de la Bahía, the Spanish fort on the lower San Antonio River. While they were at the presidio, a group of Apaches arrived "and made great efforts" to talk to the Hainais. Cabello refused to allow the Apaches inside the gate of the fort, but the Lipans shouted over the walls that they would give the Hainais horses, guns, and even women in exchange for an alliance. Cabello convinced the Hainais not to join the Apaches by once again handing out presents, including horses for the leader of the group and the woman.[57]

However, Cabello's success was short-lived, and in 1782, the alliance between the Apaches and the Hasinais was finally cemented. In September, a Hainai man and woman arrived at San Antonio and stayed with the governor for a few days. It was not until after their departure that Cabello discovered that the woman had been a Lipan Apache and that the couple had gone on to see her tribe in order to begin the process of arranging a peace.[58]

Two months later in November, 1782, the Apaches secured a settlement with the tribes of East Texas, including the Hasinais. A huge trade fair was held on the Guadalupe River, at which the Apaches traded 1,000 Spanish horses to a group of Tonkawas, Hasinais, Bidais, and others in return for 270 guns. The fair was intended to last for nearly a month but was cut short by a Norteño war party that attacked a group of Lipans and Tonkawas on the nearby Colorado River. The Apaches retreated to the west with their new firearms, while the East Texas tribes traveled to Louisiana to sell the Spanish horses. Nevertheless, this trade between the tribes of East Texas and the Apaches would flourish for the next four years.[59]

Spanish officials were unsure as to what course to take to undermine the East Texas natives' alliance with the Apaches. In January, 1783, Governor Cabello proposed the East Texas tribes be denied the right to trade in Nacogdoches or in the towns along the coast. Commandant General Croix, however, felt that these tribes could be better controlled by providing a present for each nation as a whole and a special present for each chief. This plan was adopted in September, 1783, and arrangements were made for a warehouse to be built in Nacogdoches to store the presents. Now the Hasinais could both trade and receive annual gifts from a site in their midst, rather than having to travel to Natchitoches for presents.[60]

At the same time this decision was being made by the Spanish, a *caddi* finally assumed the position of leader of the Hainais, and in September, 1783, thirty-one Hainai men and three women arrived at the capital so that Governor Cabello could formally recognize the new leader. The *caddi* claimed that he was the brother of Sauto and had a letter from Gil Ybarbo at Nacogdoches that assured the governor of his "good circumstances." Cabello's interpreter confirmed that he had been through the Hainai village many times and believed that the native was entitled to be *caddi*. Governor Cabello accepted these recommendations and named the man Balthazar Bigotes in a formal ceremony. He then presented him with a complete uniform, a baton, a flag, and a patent. Each member of the tribe received a small gift, and the governor then presented the new *caddi* with a horse from his own personal stable.[61]

Following the ceremony Cabello asked Balthazar Bigotes to refuse any communication with the Apaches. The new *caddi*, however, completely disregarded the governor's request and joined a group of Lipans just outside of San Antonio. They all headed toward the presidio at La Bahía, where a larger Lipan contingent awaited them. From there, the Hainais and Lipans made their way to the Guadalupe, where they held yet another trading session with the Tonkawas.[62]

The Hasinais continued the profitable trade with the Apaches through 1784. In response, Governor Cabello ordered Ybarbo and Armán to warn the Hasinais, Tonkawas, and the lesser tribes not to trade or communicate with the Apaches or face forfeiture of their annual presents. In addition, the legal traders that had been provided for them would be removed. Cabello said that Balthazar Bigotes should be informed "how very angry I am with him and his nation for the frequency [of contact] they have with the Apaches." Nevertheless, the Hainai *caddi* disregarded Governor Cabello's wishes, and the trade continued. The Kadohadachos, recognizing the great profits to be made, began bartering with the Lipans as well.[63]

The Caddo tribes, however, were too weak to stand up to the determined Spanish for long. In the summer of 1784, the Spanish assassinated the pro-Apache Tonkawa chief, El Mocho, while he visited La Bahía. Within two years they had succeeded in turning the Tonkawas against the Lipans, leaving the Hasinais as the only important Texas tribe still dealing with the Apaches. The Hasinais were further isolated in 1786, when the Spanish finally negotiated a lasting, general peace with the Comanches while concurrently strengthening their ties with the Wichitas. The Spanish were now prepared to supply those powerful tribes with all the necessary arms to pacify the Apaches in Texas.[64]

In 1786, Governor Cabello, fully assured of Norteño support, took direct steps to end the Hasinai trade with the Apaches. Realizing that the Hasinais were "not capable of causing us any worry, because their forces are so few," Cabello withheld the tribe's annual present. The Texas governor also intimidated the Hasinais by threatening to reveal to the Comanches that the Apaches were being supplied by them. This threat, coupled with a few successful Norteño campaigns against the Apaches, finally ended the Hasinai alliance with the Lipans.[65]

Now the Hasinais as well as the Kadohadachos were at the mercy of the Spanish, who throughout the final decade of the eighteenth century proved incapable of supplying them with the goods they needed. Armán, the official trader at Nacogdoches, had fallen deeply into debt and was unable to acquire items for the tribes of East Texas. To make matters worse, Governor Miró announced in 1788 that trade with Texas was prohibited from Louisiana and refused to issue passports for that province. As a result, the French traders from Natchitoches could not compensate for Armán's ineffectualness, and the Hasinais began to feel the pinch of Spain's inability to provide them with trade.[66]

The Hasinais fully realized this in 1789, when a group of warriors sent to collect their annual present, which had been reinstated two years before, arrived in Nacogdoches only to find nothing for them. The group continued to San Antonio, where Acting Gov. Rafael Martínez Pacheco informed them that because of a severe drought, none of the gifts requested for them had arrived. Pacheco then gave the Hasinai warriors all that he had available "so that they might leave contented."[67]

In January, 1790, another group of Hasinai warriors traveled to Natchitoches to ask Commandant de Blanc for a trader and supplies. He had nothing to give them, so he directed them back to their villages after providing them with a meal. De Blanc reported that since the tribe had forgotten the use of the bow and arrow, they "are reduced to necessity." Hasinai warriors returned to Natchitoches again in September, 1790, only to be turned away once more by de Blanc, who still had nothing to give them. He recognized the danger in this, for he reported the natives "seemed disposed for an uprising," and he feared "that in a short time there will be a fatal revolution."[68]

The Kadohadachos were also adversely affected by the lack of Spanish trade and looked toward other avenues to procure the items they needed. In 1787, Governor Miró had ordered the licensed trader for the Kadohadacho village, Louis Leblanc, to remain in Natchitoches and not barter with the tribe until he paid off his debts. This had forced the Kadohadachos to turn to Louis Lepinet, a Frenchman who had set up an illegal trading post on the Ouachita River to the east of their village. Commandant de Blanc, fearful that the Spanish of Louisiana would lose their influence over the Kadohadachos due to Lepinet's illegal trade, ordered Natchitoches traders to go upstream to the Kadohadacho villages and reopen legal commerce. The Natchitoches traders, however, were unable to recapture the Kadohadacho commerce because of the competition from Anglo Americans, who were filtering across the Mississippi River to barter.[69]

Although the Kadohadachos were receiving illicit trade items, they could not overcome the Osage attacks. In 1792, in response to the continued onslaught, the new governor of Louisiana, the Barón de Carondelet, boldly put forth a plan to arm all the allied Indian nations—including the Kadohadachos—and surround the Osages so as to "finish them once and for all." In preparation, Carondelet commanded the lieutenant governor of Spanish Illinois, Zénon Trudeau, to cut off the Osage trade from St. Louis.[70]

This plan, like so many previous Spanish attempts to make war on the Osages, failed to be implemented. The Osage trade was eventually resumed, and the tribe once more fell upon the weakened Kadohadachos. Finally, in 1800, the Kadohadachos were forced to relocate their village, and this time they took refuge on Caddo Lake, about thirty-five miles west of the main branch of the Red River. The Spanish inability to check the Osage onslaught had caused the Kadohadachos to move their villages three times in twelve years—a factor that would make the tribe very receptive to the acquisition of Louisiana by the United States in 1803.[71]

The Spanish of Texas did not respond to the threat caused by Anglo-American traders until the year before the Kadohadachos moved to Caddo Lake. In 1799, Armán's license to trade with the natives of East Texas was revoked and was recommissioned to the firm of Barr and Davenport. The Hasinai tribes received two traders who initially supplied them with goods on credit. These traders were soon forced to quit, however, since the Hasinais never paid them back in full. To keep the tribe away from the Anglo Americans, Barr and Davenport directly gave the Nacogdoches *caddi*, Cabezon (Big Head), goods on credit. Cabezon was expected to distribute the supplies to the various tribes and to collect payment. The Hasinais never fully repaid Barr and Davenport, either, and when the United States acquired Louisiana in 1803, payment stopped altogether as the tribe went to Natchitoches to trade with the Anglo Americans.[72]

By the late eighteenth century, more than one hundred years of contact with Euro-Americans had proven disastrous for the Caddos. The tribe had welcomed with open arms the Euro-Americans and their advanced metal goods in the belief that they could only enhance the Caddos' already strong position in the area. However, the other aspects of Euro-American contact—disease and increased warfare with stronger tribes—had crippled the Caddos, leaving them only a shadow of their former selves. Since the Caddos could not turn back the clock and regain their former strength and independence, they looked instead to the next empire willing to provide them with support—the United States.

Chapter 6

Resurgence: The Caddos and the Louisiana-Texas Frontier, 1803–15

Your words resemble the words my forefathers have told me they used to receive from the French in ancient times. My ancestors from Chief to Chief were always well pleased with the French: they were well received and well treated by them when they met to hold talks together, and we can now say the same of you, our new friends.

If your nation has purchased what the French formerly possessed, you have purchased the country that we occupy, and we regard you in the same light as we did them.

— Kadohadacho *caddi* Dehahuit to Gov. William C. C. Claiborne,
Territory of Louisiana, United States of America,
September 5, 1806[1]

ALTHOUGH THE LATTER QUARTER of the eighteenth century had been particularly hard on the Caddo tribes, the acquisition of Louisiana by the United States in 1803 afforded them an opportunity to regain the status they had enjoyed prior to 1763.[2] As they had a century before, the Caddo tribes found themselves at the convergence of empire, this time at the center of an international boundary dispute between Spain and the United States that stemmed from the French reacquisition of Louisiana in 1800. Three years later, Napoleon sold the huge expanse of territory to the United States without defining its borders. Thus, the boundary between Louisiana and Texas became subject to various interpretations, the most extreme being that of Pres. Thomas Jefferson, who held that the border was now the Rio Grande. Understandably, the Spanish scoffed at this claim, interpreting the line as being just a few miles west of the Red

River, where it had been when France controlled Louisiana before 1763.[3]

Since the border situation was so tenuous, the allegiance of the native tribes along the border, most importantly that of the Caddos, was understood to be crucial in any boundary determination. The Kadohadachos especially were central to this dispute, for the United States felt that tribes formerly subject to France were now under the jurisdiction of a new "father." Thus, both the United States and Spain claimed the allegiance of the tribe in an attempt to define the border more clearly. In addition, it was understood that in case of war, which was fully expected by both sides, native allies might make the difference. Because of the great influence they had over the rest of the Caddos, the Wichitas, and other tribes in the area, the Kadohadachos were courted by both the United States and Spain. Recognizing the situation, the new Kadohadacho *caddi*, Dehahuit, expertly played the two powers against one another and was able to obtain conditions favorable to the Kadohadachos' well-being and preeminence in the area.

The Kadohadachos' emerging dominance over the Caddos is one of the most important trends of this period. They were by far the largest of the Caddo tribes, consisting of between five and six hundred people and including about one hundred warriors. Dr. John Sibley, who became the U.S. Indian agent for the area, expressed his belief that the Kadohadacho warriors were "looked upon somewhat like Knights of Malta, or some distinguished military order." The Kadohadachos were predominant over the Caddo tribes, "who look up to them as fathers, visit and intermarry among them, and join them in all their wars."[4]

An important reason the Kadohadachos had become so powerful is that, unlike the Hasinai tribes, they had kept the office of the *caddi* intact and in the hands of a few long-lived, capable individuals. While many Hasinai leaders had met with untimely deaths in the last years of the eighteenth century, the Kadohadachos had had only two *caddices*, Tinhioüen and Bicheda, from 1770 to 1800. Dehahuit became the Kadohadacho *caddi* in 1800, following yet another smallpox epidemic that most likely killed his predecessor; the new *caddi*, however, enjoyed Tinhioüen's longevity and continued in his office until 1833. Dehahuit, "whom nearly all the friendly nations recognize as superior," was described by Sibley as being "a very fine looking man" who was a "remarkabley [sic] shrewd and sensible fellow." Under his leadership the Kadohadachos had a decided influence over the rest of the Caddo tribes as well as other tribes in the area; Sibley believed that Dehahuit could gather as many as five hundred warriors from various tribes under his command by virtue of his important position.[5]

Among the tribes influenced by the Kadohadachos were the Yatasis and the Natchitoches, both of whom were in decline. The Yatasis lived on Bayou Pierre, fifty miles above the town of Natchitoches near a few French families and a Spanish guard of eight men, and the Natchitoches resided twenty-five miles downstream. The Natchitoches village was located only five miles above Compti, the highest white settlement on the Red River; as a result, Sibley feared the Natchitoches were "gradually wasting away" from smallpox. In 1805, only twelve men and eighteen women remained of the Natchitoches, and the Yatasis consisted of eight men and twenty-five women. The Natchitoches were respected by the French settlers, and the two groups intermarried. Although they spoke French, they continued to preserve their "Indian dress and habits," and this reflects an important feature of all the Caddo tribes throughout this period: their ability to maintain native culture and native leadership despite close contact with Euro-Americans.[6]

Although the other Caddo tribes fell prey to disease as well, they still remained strong and important groups. They were affected by the smallpox epidemic of 1800, which was followed by an outbreak of the measles three years later. The Hainai *caddi*, Balthazar Bigotes, died during one of these plagues and was replaced by a more ineffectual leader called Blanco (White). The three remaining Hasinai tribes—the Hainais, Nabedaches, and Nacogdoches—continued to live in their traditional villages on the Angelina and Neches Rivers "in great amity" with the Kadohadachos. The Hainais had a population of about 150 people, as did the Nabedaches. Together, the two tribes could field about 50 to 75 warriors. The Nacogdoches were estimated to have a population of 150, 40 of whom were young men.[7]

The Nadacos continued their drift away from the Hasinai tribes. They moved their village closer to the Kadohadachos, residing southwest of them on the Sabine River. They considered "themselves the same" as the Kadohadachos "with whom they intermarry, and are occasionally visiting each other in the greatest harmony." About 200 or so Nadacos remained, 30 to 40 being warriors.[8]

The Kadohadachos also had an influence over other tribes in the region who were not members of the Caddo confederacies. The Adaes and the Ais were particularly hard hit by disease and drunkenness. The Ais were "almost extinct as a nation." As time went on, they scattered and intermarried with the other Caddo tribes. Although the Kichais had moved their village westward from the Red River to the Trinity River, they still maintained strong ties with the Kadohadachos. They could field about 60 warriors and intermarried with the Kadohadachos, with whom they lived "together in much harmony." The Wichita tribes remained the most important group with whom the Kadohadachos associated. The Taovayas and the Wichitas continued to live in their fortified villages on the Red River nearly eight hundred miles above Natchitoches by water.

Together they could field about 400 warriors out of a total population of 1,200 people. The other Wichita tribe, the Tawakonis, had close to 600 people in their village on the Trinity River, 150 of whom were warriors. The Wichitas, especially the Taovayas, were important because of their strategic position on the Red River; any attempt to follow the Red to its source, travel to Santa Fe, or meet with the powerful Comanches would have to go through them.[9]

The Kadohadachos also influenced emigrant tribes from the southeast that had begun to arrive on the Louisiana-Texas frontier in the late eighteenth century. Mainly these were small tribes, such as the Apalaches, Pascagoulas, and Biloxis, who settled on the Red River south of Natchitoches. Two emigrant Creek tribes—the Alabamas and the Coushattas—settled much closer to the Kadohadachos. One part of the amalgamated Alabama-Coushatta tribe, consisting of nearly 600 people, lived on the Sabine River about eighty miles southwest of Natchitoches; another six or eight families of the Coushatta tribe had received permission from Dehahuit to settle on the Red River only about thirty-five miles from the Kadohadacho village. Between them, the Alabama-Coushatta could field about 150 warriors. They were all friendly to the stronger, more established Kadohadachos and were thus welcomed by Dehahuit and his men.[10]

One reason the Kadohadachos were glad to accept these tribes into the area was because they could be used as allies against the Osages. While Osage attacks on the Kadohadachos had abated since the tribe had moved south to Caddo Lake, the threat still existed. In January, 1807, a party of Kadohadacho hunters was attacked by the Osages on their return from the Wichitas and robbed of seventy-two horses. A group of Alabamas and Apalaches came across the Osage bandits a few days later and attacked them, killing five and recovering most of the stolen horses. When the Alabamas and the Apalaches arrived at the Coushatta village with the good news, a victory dance was held there for all the tribes allied against the Osages. Two years later, in 1809, Sibley reported that the Alabamas and the Coushattas were settling on the lands of the Kadohadachos. Dehahuit had "no objection to those Indians remaining there so long as they behave well," for he "calculate[d] on the benefit of their assistance against their common enemy," the Osages.[11]

However, one emigrant tribe from east of the Mississippi River, the Choctaws, did give the Kadohadachos and their allies cause for complaint. One Choctaw village, consisting of 30 warriors, settled to the east of the Kadohadachos on the Ouachita River; another 50 Choctaw warriors lived south of Natchitoches in the Opelousas district. In addition, "rambling [Choctaw] hunting parties" often made sorties into Louisiana and were "at war with the Caddoques, and liked by neither red nor white

People." While not as dangerous as the Osages, the Choctaws were able to cause the Caddo tribes much grief.[12]

The Caddos, by remaining strong both culturally and numerically, maintained themselves as the most influential tribe along the border disputed by Spain and the United States. Nevertheless, the tribe still depended on trade goods and actively pursued an alliance with whichever country could provide them with an ample amount of these necessary items. From the onset, both the United States and Spain understood that trade with the region's natives would be crucial in winning their favor. Sibley asserted that "whoever furnishes the Indians the Best and Most Satisfactory trade can always control their Politicks." Manuel María de Salcedo, one of the governors of Texas during this period, felt that it was necessary for Spain to establish commercial houses in order to more efficiently supply trade for the natives. In this way, the Spanish "would be able to get out of [the Indians] anything [the Spanish] proposed to do because the Indians develop and behave like those who trade with them according to the degree of recognized utility, convenience, and advantages that are presented to them."[13]

The courting of the Kadohadachos began soon after the acquisition of Louisiana by the United States. Americans on the scene were quick to realize the influential position of the Kadohadachos and took measures designed to win the tribe's allegiance. In September, 1803, Daniel Clark, an Irishman who had been living in New Orleans since 1786, sent Secretary of State James Madison a report concerning the tribes of Louisiana. Clark alerted Madison to the importance of the Kadohadachos and the possibilities of an alliance, stating that "they are the friends of the whites and are esteemed the bravest and most Generous of all the Nations in the vast country."[14]

Dehahuit understood the possibilities offered by the American acquisition of Louisiana and made a number of trips to Natchitoches in the fall of 1803 to meet with John Sibley. The doctor impressed Dehahuit by informing him that President Jefferson knew of his tribe, and Sibley promised the *caddi* that the Americans would give the tribe good prices for their furs and provide them with a blacksmith to repair their guns. Dehahuit was pleased and told Sibley that if an area of land was marked out exclusively for his tribe, he would allow the Americans to claim the rest. Certainly, before the end of 1803, the Kadohadachos and the United States were well on their way to establishing friendly relations.[15]

The reports from Louisiana about the significance of the Kadohadachos were soon acknowledged by the officials appointed to govern the newly acquired territory. On February 25, 1804, the governor of the territory of Orleans, William C. C. Claiborne, sent orders to Capt. Edward

Turner, the civil commandant of the District of Natchitoches, informing him of the importance of the Kadohadachos and the Wichitas and instructed him to "receive these people with friendly attention and have regard for their interest."[16]

The first step taken by Turner to gain the friendship of the Kadohadachos was to arrange, with the assistance of Doctor Sibley, a peace treaty with the Choctaws. On May 17, 1804, representatives of both tribes arrived in Natchitoches and agreed to lay down their weapons and establish peace. Both tribes also agreed that, in case one tribe did take up arms against the other, the victimized party would seek retribution through the mediation of agents of the United States rather than obtaining revenge through bloodshed. Whereas the Spanish had been unable to assist the Kadohadachos in their battles with other tribes, the Americans quickly impressed upon the Indians their willingness to put an end to tribal warfare.[17]

In response to the measures taken by the United States, Spanish officials in Texas took actions designed to retain their Native American subjects. The Spanish commander at Nacogdoches, José Joaquin Ugarte, grasped the importance of providing the natives with trade; in a letter to Texas Gov. Juan Bautista de Elguezábal, he stressed the necessity of supplying the tribes with clothing and ammunition in order to avoid conflict with them and to keep their friendship. The commandant of the Provincias Internas, Nemesio Salcedo, also realized the importance of the allegiance with the native tribes of Texas. In May, 1804, he instructed Governor Elguezábal to "try all peaceable means to see that [the transfer of Louisiana] does not influence the Indian tribes to change the peaceable relations they have hitherto maintained with us." Elguezábal was ordered to "take pains to encourage their loyalty and good will."[18]

Although Spanish officials were sure that the Hasinais were their rightful subjects, they were confused about the status of the Kadohadachos. In the summer of 1804, Governor Elguezábal noted that five American traders traveled upstream from Natchitoches and visited both the Kadohadachos and the Wichitas. Elguezábal allowed them to pass in the belief that these tribes resided in Louisiana and were, therefore, subjects of the United States. Commandant Salcedo, however, wholeheartedly disagreed with Elguezábal's opinion and on July 17, 1804, informed the governor of "the unquestionable rights we have to the section occupied by the [Kadohadachos and Wichitas] and you must realize we must preserve and maintain these rights." By the summer of 1804, the boundary dispute between Spain and the United States was beginning to intensify, and the Kadohadachos were directly in the center.[19]

Up to this point, the Kadohadachos had received only promises of trade from the Americans and were waiting to see exactly what benefits they could gain from tying themselves to the United States. Congress had yet to authorize the distribution of presents to the natives of Louisiana, and for a while this handicapped the American effort to win the allegiance of the Kadohadachos. In August, 1804, Dehahuit visited Captain Turner at Natchitoches and was disappointed that his party did not receive a gift. Turner, however, told Dehahuit that the United States would establish an official trading house at Natchitoches "for the purpose of supplying their wants on moderate Terms." Dehahuit "expressed much satisfaction" at hearing this promise, and after Turner gave the group rations, the *caddi* "retired from the Post well pleased."[20]

Nonetheless, the matter of distributing presents to the Kadohadachos was becoming an urgent problem for the Americans. In October, 1804, Dehahuit notified Turner that he was en route to Natchitoches and expected to receive presents. Turner alerted Governor Claiborne of the *caddi's* impending visit and stated that since the "Spaniards are exerting every means to Induce the Indians to be unfriendly . . . it would not be good policy to let him return [to his village] dissatisfied." Governor Claiborne readily understood the importance of distributing presents to the Kadohadachos. Despite being unauthorized to give the natives gifts, the governor assumed full responsibility and permitted Turner "to make Presents to the Chief of the Cadoos [sic] and his principal men," the value of which should not exceed two hundred dollars. When the Kadohadacho party arrived at Natchitoches, Dehahuit and his men were given powder, lead, and tobacco. Now assured that his tribe would receive presents from the Americans, Dehahuit asked Captain Turner for an American flag to fly over his village, for it was "customary to have the Flag of the Nation who claimed his Country in which they lived." Because of the Americans' proven ability to provide the tribe with goods, the Kadohadachos informally recognized them as their new "father" in late 1804.[21]

As a result of the tension on the Louisiana-Texas frontier, President Jefferson procured a part-time Indian agent for the area in December, 1804, and chose John Sibley. This position became permanent the following year. The agent's duties included barring illicit traders from the tribes and making certain that no one settled on their lands; however, Sibley's most important task in relation to the Kadohadachos was to win their allegiance for the United States. For the next decade, Sibley was the most important American on the border vis à vis the natives. He was fair and wise in his dealings with them and always treated the tribes, especially the Kadohadachos, with great respect. Because the friendship of the natives was critical during the first years of Louisiana, an agent who protected their interests was crucial, and in John Sibley, the United States had found the right person.[22]

Upon receiving his appointment, Sibley was instructed by Secretary of War Henry Dearborn to confer with the native tribes, secure their friendship, and inform them that they must break all connections with the Spanish. Sibley, who appreciated trade as a method for gaining the tribes' allegiance, immediately dispatched men up the Red River to barter with the Kadohadachos and the Wichitas. The Spanish unsuccessfully attempted to stop them at their station at Bayou Pierre. The Spanish commander, José Manuel de Castro, wrote to Dehahuit asking him to detain the traders at his village. The Kadohadacho *caddi*, however, refused to comply with this naive request.[23]

A few months later, Castro made a bolder attempt to stop the Kadohadachos' intercourse with the United States. In early 1805, Dehahuit and a few young men were on their way to Natchitoches with furs when they met Castro at Bayou Pierre. Castro warned Dehahuit that if his party should return from Natchitoches with American goods, Castro would confiscate them. This warning angered Dehahuit, who threatened to kill the whole Spanish guard. He told Castro that the road to Natchitoches "had always been theirs, and that if the Spanish prevented them from using it, as their ancestors had always done, he would soon make it a bloody road." Alarmed by Dehahuit's bold stance, Castro allowed the group to pass without incident on their return from Natchitoches.[24]

The Spanish were powerless to prevent the United States from establishing its trade superiority. On May 23, 1805, Sibley received three thousand dollars' worth of merchandise from the government to distribute to the native tribes as presents and trade goods. Secretary Dearborn instructed Sibley to use all means to conciliate the natives, especially "such natives as might, in case of a rupture with Spain, be useful and mischevous [sic] to us." Governor Claiborne, who had a clearer understanding than Secretary Dearborn which tribes this implied, wrote to Sibley in June with some additional words of advice; Claiborne felt that, since the Kadohadachos "manifested a decided influence over the various Tribes of Indians," Sibley should direct his attention "more particularly" to that tribe. The governor had no doubt that Sibley would "be able to render more permanent" the "friendly disposition" of the Kadohadachos. Soon afterward, Claiborne assured President Jefferson that the United States would "experience very little difficulty" with the tribes west of the Mississippi River. Since the Kadohadachos were well-disposed toward the Americans, Claiborne believed "the friendship of the Indians generally may be acquired and preserved."[25]

As soon as Sibley received the merchandise allocated by Congress, he alerted the surrounding tribes of his acquisition. The new Spanish commander at Nacogdoches, Dionisio Valle, noted in June, 1805, that an American trader passed Bayou Pierre on his way from the Wichita and Kadohadacho villages upstream. He reported that it was "openly known that the Caudacho Indians are receiving presents at Natchitoches as subjects of Louisiana," and he had no doubt that the Wichitas were being "stirred up in a similar way."[26]

Not only the Red River tribes were being "stirred up" by the Americans; the Hasinais were as well. Through the Kadohadachos, Sibley had made overtures to the Hasinai tribes, and in June, 1805, twenty-five Hainais appeared at the Spanish post at Nacogdoches hinting "at the offers of presents and prospects of trade" with the Americans. Although Valle advised them that it would be improper to accept these offers, warriors from the Hainai as well as the Nadaco and Nacogdoches tribes visited the American post at Natchitoches in August. Valle blamed the Kadohadachos for this, and he feared "their instigation may lead those tribes to form a friendship and to trade with said Sibley."[27] As France had previously done, the United States was attempting to spread its influence over the tribes of East Texas through trade, and, also as before, the Hasinais were accepting the trade offers from Louisiana.

Prompted by the discovery of a proposed American expedition, Spain's cautious attitude toward the Kadohadachos ended. Led by Maj. Thomas Freeman and Dr. Peter Custis, the expedition was designed by President Jefferson to ascend to the source of the Red River in an attempt to determine the boundary between Louisiana and Texas. In addition, Freeman and Custis were ordered to "court an intercourse with the natives as intensively as you can" and to instruct the tribes that they were no longer subjects of Spain but "henceforth [the United States would] become their fathers and friends."[28] More than any other event, the Freeman-Custis expedition placed the Kadohadachos directly at the center of the conflict between the United States and Spain.

Commandant Salcedo considered the American expedition to be an invasion of Spanish territory and was determined to thwart it. On October 8, 1805, he instructed the new governor of Texas, Antonio Cordero, to post more troops either at Bayou Pierre or the nearby reinstituted fort at Los Adaes in order to "compel withdrawal of the Red River expedition." He stated that this "object must be facilitated by the Indians who live in those districts," for he recognized "the accomplishment of the expedition can be completely obstructed by the allied tribes, provided the [natives] are caused to take interest in this matter through the necessary craftiness and compensations." Obviously, Salcedo understood that the Indian tribes of the region held the key to the Red River, and only through their cooperation could the Spanish successfully arrest the American encroachment.[29]

Throughout the winter of 1805–1806 the Spanish tried in vain to win the allegiance of the surrounding tribes, including the Hasinais.

The commander at Nacogdoches reported in February, 1806, that the "neighboring Indian tribes which have always visited this post are coming here less frequently not so much on account of lack of affection for the Spaniards" but because of the trade advantages and the greater number of presents they received from the Americans at Natchitoches.[30]

This supply of goods was increased in 1806 by the establishment of an official U.S. Indian trading factory at Natchitoches. The federal government had established a system of trading factories in 1795 designed to regulate commerce between Anglo Americans and Indians to make sure the natives were not swindled or given cause to take to the warpath. Like the others, the factory at Natchitoches was charged with supplying the surrounding tribes with guns, ammunition, clothes, utensils, beads, and blankets at fair prices. As in previous days, the Caddo trade was mainly in deer skins, buffalo robes, and bear oil.[31]

By the time Freeman and Custis began the expedition in mid-April, 1806—when they entered the Red River at its mouth with two flat-bottomed boats, a pirogue, twenty-one soldiers, and a black servant—the Caddo tribes had certainly been swayed by the American presents and trade goods. In response to the launch of the Freeman-Custis expedition, the Spanish mounted a troop, commanded by Francisco Viana, to stop the American party by force if necessary. Viana ordered Lieut. Juan Ygnacio Ramón to take the Nacogdoches garrison up the Neches River for training exercises to prepare to meet the Freeman-Custis expedition. Ramón subsequently attempted to enlist the services of one hundred warriors from the Hasinai tribes for battle against the Americans but was forced to admit "that not a single one of them wishes to come."[32]

The Freeman-Custis expedition reached Natchitoches on May 19; the party remained there until June 2, and in the meantime increased their force to forty-seven men and seven boats to defend against the Spanish threat. Six days later, Viana ordered Lieutenant Ramón to intercept the American party at the old Kadohadacho village—far upstream from their new site on Caddo Lake—where the French had established the Nassonite Post early in the eighteenth century. Because of his unfamiliarity with the area and his inability to find any of the promised Hasinai warriors, Lieutenant Ramón hired a Yatasi *canaha* to guide him and his troops to the old Kadohadacho village, but the Yatasi *canaha* took Ramón to the Kadohadachos' present village by mistake. Dehahuit met Ramón, who asked him accusingly if he "loved the Americans." The *caddi* ambiguously answered that "he loved all men; if the Spaniards had come to fight they must not spill blood on his land, as it was the command of his forefathers that white blood should not be spilled on their land." Ramón accepted this vague reply and left the village; Dehahuit then sent him a message stating that when Freeman and Custis arrived, the *caddi* planned to supply the Americans with guides to take the party farther upstream. Yet again, Dehahuit refused to allow the Spanish to dictate policy to the tribe.[33]

Dehahuit immediately followed through on his threat to assist the Americans. Captain Freeman had sent Lucas Talapoon, a French guide and interpreter, ahead from Natchitoches to ask the Kadohadacho *caddi* to meet the party at the Coushatta village on the Red River. Unable to come immediately, Dehahuit sent Talapoon and a Kadohadacho courier to the Coushatta village—which stood nineteen miles above the natural logjam known as the Red River raft—to inform the Americans both of the presence of Ramón's troops near his village and their intention of stopping the expedition by force. After two weeks of struggling with the Red River raft, Freeman and Custis finally reached open water on June 24. Upon receiving Dehahuit's message, Major Freeman sent the courier back to ask the *caddi* to meet the Americans at the Coushatta village.[34]

On July 1, Dehahuit and forty Kadohadacho warriors arrived on the bank of the Red River opposite the Coushatta village and fired their guns in a salute that was returned by the Americans on the other side. As the natives crossed the river, the members of the American expedition drew themselves up in single file to receive the Kadohadachos "with marked attention." As Dehahuit entered the camp, another salute was fired "with which he seemed well pleased; observing to the Coushatta Chief that he never had been so respectfully received by any people before."[35]

The Americans clarified the objective of their mission to the Kadohadachos, telling them that France had sold Louisiana and that "henceforward the People of the United States would be their fathers and friends and would protect them and supply their wants." Dehahuit readily agreed to this, replying that he would now look to the Americans for "protection and support." He said that, although he had no complaints to make against either the Spanish or the French, the Kadohadachos now had an "American father, and in the two years he had known the Americans he liked them also for they too had treated his people well." He was especially pleased by the way the members of the expedition were "treating him with a respect and candor which the Spaniards did not evince in their conduct." Dehahuit added that he wanted them to proceed and meet his neighbors, the Wichitas, who would also be glad to see the Americans.[36]

Freeman celebrated this successful meeting by distributing food and liquor to the Kadohadacho warriors. After toasting their alliance, the Americans fell into single file in order to allow each native warrior to shake their hands; the Kadohadachos were impressed with their new friends, and the principal warrior told the American sergeant that "he was glad to see his new brothers had the faces of men, and looked like men and warriors . . . let us hold fast, and be friends forever."[37] The warm reception the American expedition provided the Kadohadachos at the Coushatta village firmly cemented the good relations the two parties would enjoy for the next decade. In light of the actions subsequently taken by the Spanish, the friendliness of the Americans was certainly magnified in the eyes of the tribe.

The next day Dehahuit informed Major Freeman that more Spanish soldiers were en route from Nacogdoches to intercept the Americans "and drive them back or take them prisoners." Dehahuit promised the major he would send messengers from his village to update information concerning the Spanish troops; he also ordered three other tribesmen to remain with the expedition as "guides, spies, or messengers."[38]

In the meantime, Commandant Salcedo ordered about one thousand troops under the command of Lieut. Col. Simon Herrera to meet Lieutenant Ramón's force at the Kadohadacho village and then proceed to their old village upstream to intercept the American expedition. After arriving at Nacogdoches on July 15, the Spanish force commanded by Herrera set out for the Kadohadacho village. Upon his entrance, Herrera informed Dehahuit that his village was on Spanish soil and that he would have to move eastward if he planned to continue to display the American flag. When the *caddi* hesitated, the Spanish troops boldly cut down the flagstaff. The soldiers then taunted Dehahuit by telling him that they were going after the Americans "whom they would serve in the same manner, and if resistance was made, either kill them, or carry them off prisoners, in irons." The insulting actions of the Spanish force caused some of the Kadohadacho warriors to take up arms, but they were quieted by Dehahuit's cooler head. If the *caddi* had had any doubts about allying his tribe with the Americans, Herrera's visit had most certainly put these to rest.[39]

Following Herrera's departure from his village, Dehahuit immediately dispatched three Kadohadacho messengers to find the Americans on the Red River. They met Freeman and Custis high above the Coushatta village on July 26, informed the party of the incident at their village, and told them that the Spanish planned to intercept them with one thousand troops. Three days later the Americans were met by the overwhelming Spanish force, and the expedition was obliged to retreat. On August 23, Freeman and Custis reached Natchitoches and informed Governor Claiborne of their fate.[40]

The party's return initiated an exchange of letters between Claiborne and Herrera that presented both the Spanish and American claims concerning the Kadohadachos. On August 26, Governor Claiborne protested the fact that the Spanish troops had stopped the American expedition on American soil. By chopping down the American flag in the

Kadohadacho village, in his opinion the Spanish had committed "another outrage." Claiborne further argued that while Louisiana had belonged to France, the Kadohadacho tribe had been "under the protection of the French Government . . . hence it follows Sir, that the cession of Louisiana to the United States . . . is sufficient authority for the display of the American Flag in the Caddo Village." Lieutenant Colonel Herrera, in answering Governor Claiborne two days later, agreed that the United States possessed Louisiana but asserted that the "Cado [sic] nation is not upon [Louisiana] and on the Contrary the place which they inhabit is very far from it and belongs to Spain." In this way, Herrera justified the removal of the American flag.[41]

Ultimately, the matter was left unresolved, and war was averted by the signing of the "Neutral Ground Agreement" on November 1, 1806, by Spain and the United States. This document remained in force until 1821 and established a neutral strip between Louisiana and Texas, which, though claimed by both countries, remained ungoverned and unoccupied. The Kadohadacho village fell within this neutral ground, and, thus, both countries continued to claim the tribe as subjects—a situation that proved most profitable for the tribe.[42]

The Freeman-Custis expedition and Spain's reaction, however, served only to propel the Kadohadachos further toward the Americans; two weeks after the expedition was repelled, Dehahuit and a delegation of fourteen warriors were received in Natchitoches by Governor Claiborne, army officers, and leading citizens. The governor asserted to the *caddi* that the Kadohadachos were now subjects of the United States and asked that he let his "people hold the Americans by the hand with sincerity and Friendship, and the Chain of peace will be bright and strong; our children will smoke together, and the path will never be colored with blood." After smoking the ceremonial pipe, Dehahuit told Governor Claiborne the Americans were his "new friends," and he affirmed Claiborne's claim of jurisdiction by stating, "If your nation has purchased what the French formerly possessed, you have purchased the country that we occupy and we regard you in the same light as we did them."[43]

Although the United States had formally won over the Kadohadachos, Doctor Sibley did not take the alliance for granted and continued to display friendship to the tribe. For instance, in January, 1807, when Dehahuit's house caught fire and destroyed his family's corn supply, Sibley ordered twenty-three barrels of flour to be distributed to the Kadohadachos as compensation. One month later a party of Kadohadachos arrived in Natchitoches to trade the furs they had acquired during their annual winter hunt. Sibley gave them a warm welcome and presented a hat and a blue half-regimental frock coat to Cut Finger, "a particular friend and Companion" of Dehahuit, in return for his being "friendly and attentive" to Major Freeman's party.[44]

Dehahuit arrived in Natchitoches on April 14 with fifteen men and pirogues loaded with skins to trade. Sibley impressed the Kadohadacho *caddi* by presenting him with a scarlet regimental coat trimmed with black velvet and white plated buttons. The American agent gave the son of another Kadohadacho principal a blue half-regimental coat trimmed with scarlet and white linen. All this largess touched Dehahuit and his men and assured the Kadohadachos that they had been correct in siding with the United States.[45]

Soon after Dehahuit's trip to Natchitoches, the Kadohadachos called upon their "father" to provide them with something more than just presents. On May 5, 1807, Dehahuit sent three messengers to Natchitoches to inform Sibley that a party of Choctaws had crossed the Sabine River and murdered two Nadaco women. Dehahuit insisted the Nadacos were "under his protection" and demanded that Sibley fulfill the stipulations of the treaty with the Choctaws that had been agreed to in May, 1804. Dehahuit, in his capacity as the Kadohadacho *caddi*, now claimed jurisdiction over each confederacy in his official dealings with the Euro-Americans.[46]

Sibley accepted Dehahuit's claim and sent messengers to order the Choctaw headmen to come to Natchitoches "for the purpose of concerning Measures to give to the Caddo Chief the satisfaction he demanded." Upon their arrival in Natchitoches, Sibley berated the Choctaws for breaking the peace and convinced them to send a peace delegation to the Kadohadacho *caddi*. Subsequent to the murder of the two Nadaco women, the Nadaco *caddi* had held an assembly in which he had convinced the Hasinais to join him in a campaign against the Choctaws. As a result, Dehahuit was absent when the Choctaw delegation arrived at the Kadohadacho village because he had gone to Texas to pacify the Hasinai tribes.[47]

Dehahuit successfully assuaged them by arranging that they, along with a group of Kichais, Wichitas, and Comanches, would travel to Louisiana for a grand council with Sibley. On August 10, Sibley welcomed three hundred Indians to his post and distributed a great number of presents. After smoking the peace pipe, Sibley informed them that, although Louisiana had been transferred to the United States, the boundary between Louisiana and Texas remained undefined. Sibley confirmed that the natives could be friends with both the Spanish and the Americans, and he invited the tribes to trade at Natchitoches and accept American traders in their villages regardless of which side of the border they lived on.[48]

Following Sibley's speech the Tawakoni, Kichai, and Comanche chiefs all expressed gratitude for his welcoming words. Then Dehahuit rose and informed Sibley that he had told the western tribes many good things about the agent at Natchitoches, and the *caddi* expressed "great Satisfaction" with the warm welcome that Sibley had given his native allies. The grand council of 1807 proved mutually beneficial to the United States and the Kadohadachos, and with the aid of Dehahuit, Sibley succeeded in extending his country's influence well into Spanish Texas; likewise, Sibley's graciousness only added to the esteem of the Kadohadacho *caddi*.[49]

Brimming with confidence over the success of the council, Dehahuit pressed Sibley about the outstanding problem with the Choctaws, who had failed to show up for the meeting. The *caddi* placed all responsibility upon the shoulders of the American agent, for he felt that the peace between the Kadohadachos and the Choctaws had been carried out only at the instigation of the United States. Dehahuit demanded that Sibley force the Choctaws to make restitution as called for in the treaty, warning that the allied tribes had come to Natchitoches to see "whether the treaty is to be fulfilled or not."[50]

Dehahuit also pressed Sibley about Anglo-American incursions into his territory. In August, 1807, Sibley noted that a "banditti of thieves" had assembled together and formed a camp in the Neutral Ground between Louisiana and Texas "for the purpose of committing outrages with impunity," mainly in the form of horse theft, upon both the whites and the natives. The Kadohadachos complained to Sibley about these thieves and warned that, if he did not do anything about them, they would kill them. Although Sibley did ultimately break up the bandit camp, he believed that his actions had provided the Kadohadachos with only temporary relief.[51]

Despite the strong ties with the Americans, the Kadohadachos and the Hasinai tribes continued to have casual contacts with the Spanish in Texas, who still considered both tribes as subjects. When the Hasinai tribes returned to their villages after the Natchitoches council in September, 1807, Blanco, the Hainai *caddi*, was reprimanded by the Spanish commander at Nacogdoches for having gone to a foreign country. Blanco apologized to Viana, blamed the Kadohadacho *caddi*, and promised not to leave without informing him.[52]

Although the Kadohadachos were held responsible for leading the Hasinais to Natchitoches, the channels between the Spanish and the tribe were reopened once the furor over the Freeman-Custis expedition had died down. In November, 1807, the Spanish commander at Nacogdoches welcomed Dehahuit and twelve Kadohadacho warriors, who remained for a week and received food, brandy, tobacco, and a shirt. Two months later, another Kadohadacho party stopped in Nacogdoches on the return from their winter hunt; this time they received gifts including scissors, awls, mirrors, combs, beads, and vermilion.[53]

The close ties between the Hasinai tribes and the Spanish were demonstrated in the summer of 1809. Blanco died without a clear successor in June, and immediately afterward tribal members petitioned Governor Salcedo of Texas to appoint a chief for them. This *canaha* appointee (who remains nameless in the records) died three years later, and once again the tribe asked Spanish officials to recognize a new leader.[54] Later in the summer of 1809, Dehahuit represented the Nadacos and the Nacogdoches before Governor Salcedo—just as he had previously done for his allies with the Americans. In August, the *caddices* of the two tribes traveled to San Antonio with the Kadohadacho *caddi*, "the most important of his nation," to make Salcedo realize the necessity of providing the Hasinais with a trader. The governor acknowledged the Kadohadachos' request on behalf of their kin, and he authorized Marcel Soto to establish a trading post in the area.[55]

Soto's post, however, was unable to furnish the Hasinais with adequate trade, in part because the following year Texas was thrown into turmoil by the Hidalgo revolt in Mexico, which sparked a call for independence from Spain. In Texas this resulted in a military struggle between the royalist forces and the so-called republican revolutionaries, and the practice of American filibusters continually crossing the border from Louisiana to aid the republicans complicated the frontier situation. The Caddo tribes again found themselves at the center of a Euro-American conflict—as both the royalists and the republicans sought to win the alliance of the border natives. Dehahuit again expertly manipulated the situation to benefit his tribe.

The chaotic situation caused Sibley to take steps to ensure the loyalty of the tribes along the border. Sibley believed the Kadohadacho *caddi* to be "a man of more importance than any other ten chiefs on this side of the Mississippi" and, thus, primarily focused his efforts on Dehahuit. Sibley frequently had long, friendly conversations "with this man who has a strong mind" in which the world situation and its effects on Texas were discussed. Sibley never seriously doubted the chief's fidelity to the United States and stated that Dehahuit "never withdrew . . . his particular Confidence and friendship."[56]

By the end of 1811, the struggle had greatly intensified in Texas, inducing Sibley to "pay particular attention to those tribes who might be affected by that State of things, the Panis [Wichitas] and Caddos particularly." Dehahuit used his prestigious rank to counsel the Wichitas; half the Taovayas had joined the Comanches who wished to enter the fray, and the other half had joined the peaceful Tawakonis. Dehahuit "was using his interest among them (which is great) to persuade the [Taovayas] to live together as usual."[57] For the next few years, as the situation heated up along the Louisiana-Texas frontier, this role as counselor and emissary to the Texas tribes was the most important one Dehahuit and the Kadohadachos would play.

In 1812, the largest of the filibustering expeditions, headed by Bernardo Gutierrez and William Magee, respectively a Mexican revolutionary and a former American Army lieutenant, crossed into Texas from Louisiana. In response, the Spanish royalists increased their efforts to induce the tribes of Texas to fight on their side. In May, 1812, Dehahuit informed Sibley of the royalist overtures, and the American agent counseled him "to have nothing to do in their dispute." He furthermore asked Dehahuit to convey his advice to the Texan tribes and expected that "this communicated from the Caddo chief will be conclusive."[58]

A month later the United States declared war on Great Britain, beginning the War of 1812. Along the Texas-Louisiana border, it was fully expected that the war would extend to a struggle with Spain as well and that an official American invasion of Texas would result. This only intensified both Spanish and American attempts to win the allegiance of the border tribes. In July, the Spanish royalists sent an agent to the Kadohadacho village to persuade Dehahuit to visit Texas and to join their forces. The *caddi* faithfully informed Sibley of this invitation but, nevertheless, traveled to Nacogdoches to receive presents from the Spanish. He then went on to San Antonio with Marcel Soto and met with Governor Salcedo. Dehahuit made no firm commitments to Salcedo, for when he visited Natchitoches later in the summer with the Nadaco *caddi*, Sibley found them both "unshaken in their Amity and attachment to the U.S."[59]

Sibley then asked Dehahuit to undertake a mission to inform the Texas tribes that any invading American troops "would not enter as enemies of any Red people" or Creoles. Sibley enjoined the natives to be neutral; he felt sure the tribes would heed his advice because he was "personally well acquainted with all the Chiefs and leading Men amongst and the Caddo chief himself being the Bearer who is my particular friend, they will certainly Receive my tokens and Smoke my tobacco." Dehahuit complied, and he was received with great respect by the tribes he visited since "he was regarded as a messenger of peace from heaven." Dehahuit even convinced a group of Comanches to break their promise to join the Spanish royalists. The *caddi* returned to Natchitoches in February, 1813, and told Sibley that the natives would remain neutral; but if the United States was attacked, they would join the Americans and fight "as long as there was a Warrior remaining."[60]

The pressures on the Kadohadachos continued to increase. After suffering a number of defeats, the royalist forces in Texas turned the tide and crushed the revolutionaries in the summer of 1813. Many Americans in Natchitoches feared the Spanish would attempt to exact retribution in Louisiana—either by invading or by inciting the tribes. Concurrently, a new threat materialized from east of the Mississippi in the form of the Creek Indians, who were at war with the United States; these hostiles sent emissaries across the river to recruit native allies by arguing that the United States was ultimately inimical to all Indians.

In response to these threats, the Americans held a series of meetings with the Kadohadachos aimed at retaining their friendship. On October 5, 1813, Sibley met with the Kadohadachos, Yatasis, Nadacos, and three emigrant tribes—the Alabamas, Coushattas, and Apalaches—and claimed that many lies were being told by both the Spanish and the Creeks. He implored them not to listen to the Creeks in particular, assuring them that the president "continued his friendly dispostion towards his Red Children, that he wished them all clean Paths, good Crops of Corn, good hunting and happiness."[61]

The Alabama chief answered that he deferred to "his Older Brother the Caddo Chief and would always be advised by him." Dehahuit told Sibley he had heard various reports but had learned to be very cautious in what he believed. He asserted that from the time he "first Took his great Father the President of the United States by the hand," he had always followed a "policy of being kind and friendly to white people." He promised Sibley that if the United States needed assistance, all the warriors under his jurisdiction would enlist. Dehahuit further demonstrated his loyalty to the Americans by suggesting that he personally reiterate Sibley's desire for peace to "all the Tribes to the West Under his Influence as well as his Own Nation." Instead, Sibley requested that Dehahuit travel south and visit the tribes he had not counseled the year before.[62]

Dehahuit returned to Natchitoches a week later to meet with Thomas M. Linnard, the official U.S. trader, who assured the *caddi* that the Creeks and the Spanish were not to be trusted. Linnard reported that Dehahuit expressed "much satisfaction at the information communicated" and promised "he was ready and willing to make common with [the United States] and that our enemies should be his enemies."[63]

The final council with Dehahuit occurred on October 18, when he met with Governor Claiborne at Natchitoches. Claiborne recalled their meeting in 1806 and thanked Dehahuit for "the advice you have given to your own people, and to all red men with whom you have influence, [which is like] that of a father to his children." He noted that the Creeks had already sent war emissaries to the Indians west of the Mississippi but nevertheless hoped "that all these people will look up to you, as an elder Brother, and hold fast your good advice" of not joining the Creeks in their war against the Americans. In order to express his gratitude, Claiborne gave the *caddi* a sword, since "to a Chief, a Man, and a Warrior, nothing could be more acceptable."[64]

The American meetings with Dehahuit in 1813 proved successful, since none of the tribes influenced by the Kadohadachos joined the Creeks. In fact, Dehahuit's counsel had made the tribes more than willing to join the United States in the war that continued against the English. In August, 1814, Nabedache, Hainai, Kichai, and Tawakoni warriors visited Sibley in Natchitoches to proffer their services. Noting that the Kadohadacho *caddi* had "an entire influence over them," Sibley felt that it would be wise to accept their offer in case of a British invasion.[65]

When the threat of a British landing in Louisiana materialized in late 1814, the Americans did entreat the natives to assist them, and under the leadership of the Kadohadachos the tribes proved true to their word. Governor Claiborne quickly alerted Gen. Andrew Jackson, commander of the American forces in New Orleans, to the importance of the Kadohadachos. On October 28, the governor advised Jackson to confer with Dehahuit because he was "the most influential Indian on this side of the River Grande and his friendship, sir, will give much security to the frontier of Louisiana."[66]

Although Jackson was unable to meet with Dehahuit, he nevertheless enlisted the *caddi*'s services. The general gave the order in December asking the Kadohadachos and their allies to be "mustered into the service of the United States." As promised, the natives answered the American call, and 150 warriors arrived at Natchitoches ready to aid their allies. Because it was too late for the force to travel to New Orleans to intercept the British, they were held in readiness at Natchitoches—in case they were needed to secure peace along the Spanish border.[67]

General Jackson's victory over the British at New Orleans on January 8, 1815, ended the War of 1812 as well as the tensions upon the Texas-Louisiana frontier. Although the Kadohadachos and their allies did not actually fight alongside the Americans, they had remained stalwart friends of the young republic and had played a large role in helping the United States secure its southwestern border. The respect given to the Kadohadachos and their *caddi*, Dehahuit, by the Americans helped win the tribe's allegiance. The attention the Kadohadachos received from the United States added to the eminence of the tribe, and the Kadohadachos consolidated their role as leaders of the Caddo tribes of the Louisiana-Texas frontier. In addition, the Caddo tribes, largely thanks to Dehahuit's skillful leadership, obtained an abundance of trade goods from the Americans that the Spanish had previously been unable to provide. Unfortunately for the Caddos, their renewed success would prove short-lived, for the attitude of the United States toward the Caddos—so courteous while the border situation was unsettled—changed once the tensions subsided, becoming increasingly hostile to the tribe that had provided such invaluable assistance in the southwest.

Chapter 7

Disruption of the Caddo World and the Treaty of 1835

My Children: For What do you mourn? Are you not starving in the midst of this land? And do you not travel far from it in quest of food? The game we live on is going further off, and the white man is coming near to us; and is not our condition getting worse daily? Then why lament for the loss of that which yields us nothing but misery? Let us be wise, then, and get all we can for it, and not wait till the white man steals it away, little by little, and then gives us nothing.
—Kadohadacho *caddi* Tarshar to his tribe,
June 26, 1835[1]

DURING THE PERIOD BETWEEN the Louisiana Purchase and the end of the War of 1812, the Caddos profited from the tensions between the United States and Spain and experienced a renaissance. After 1815, however, the Caddos faced new problems in their dealings with Euro-Americans. For the first time, the tribe was pressured by settlers as Anglo-Americans poured into East Texas, diminishing the game and supplying the natives with alcohol. Refugee natives from the East also pressured the Caddos; though these tribes were generally friendly, they ultimately crowded the Caddos and challenged the Kadohadachos' preeminent position in the area. With the border relatively calm, the Kadohadachos were not as important to either Spain (and later Mexico) or the United States as before, and less attention was paid to their needs. As their position weakened throughout the 1820s, the Kadohadachos became a prime candidate for removal in the 1830s, when the official Indian policy of the United States changed dramatically during the administration of Pres. Andrew Jackson.

Following General Jackson's victory at New Orleans in January, 1815, however, the situation continued to appear very promising for the Caddos. The tribe emerged from the War of 1812 in a much stronger position than they had held prior to the Louisiana Purchase. While the Caddos were courted by two Euro-American powers, goods had flowed into their villages; as a result, by 1815 the Caddos developed a thriving culture that borrowed select items from the Euro-Americans, while at the same time maintaining a strong native base.

One Spanish official, Juan Antonio Padilla, visited the Texas tribes in 1819 and noted rather ethnocentrically that the Kadohadachos, "of all Indians, perhaps, are the most civilized." In addition to Euro-American metal goods, horses, and mules—all of which had been vital to the tribe for centuries—the Caddos also adopted the use of domesticated animals like chickens and hogs. To some extent, the Caddos even wore Euro-American–style clothing. In 1828, a Kadohadacho man and woman were painted in watercolor by a Mexican artist, Lino Sánchez y Tapia; both are wearing the clothes of well-dressed Mexican peasants. The Kadohadacho man has on a hat, a cotton pullover shirt, and knee-length breeches. His female companion has her hair tied up in a bun and is wearing a cloth blouse, skirt, and knee-length coat. Since these clothes certainly constituted the "best" attire the Kadohadacho couple owned, it demonstrates how accustomed the tribe had become to Euro-American styles of clothing. Although Padilla was not very impressed with the tribes of Texas, he did believe that the Kadohadachos in particular were "not so dirty nor so ugly [and] they might even pass as handsome."[2]

Despite the Caddos' acculturation in some areas, the tribe continued to maintain the foundations of their original culture. Although a few tribal members spoke French and Spanish, the original Caddoan language was still used. Many of the tribe wore noserings and silver pendants; in addition, some pierced the entire earlobe, "making way for silver rings, bright glass tubes, feathers, and sometimes even dried bird skulls." The Caddo men cut their hair in the traditional manner, with their heads being "completely shaven save for a single crest of hair." The tribes continued to live in their trademark grass houses and raised "large quantities" of vegetables, "which [were] sufficient for their families." The men still hunted bears, buffalo, and deer for skins to sell in Natchitoches in exchange for Euro-American goods.[3]

Orderly government was maintained by the *caddices* of the various tribes, with the Kadohadacho *caddi*, Dehahuit, now recognized as their superior. The Caddo religion remained strong, and the tribe continued to believe in Ahahayo; Padilla reported that the tribe had an "idea of God and confess him to be the author of all creation." The tribe also had dances and religious festivities, often led by the *connas*. In Padilla's eyes, the Caddos persisted in clinging to the "false ideas inherited by their

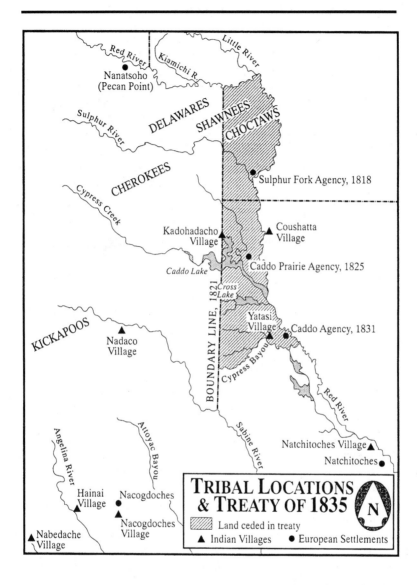

TRIBAL LOCATIONS & TREATY OF 1835

Land ceded in treaty
▲ Indian Villages   ● European Settlements

ancestors"; in other words, the Caddo religion continued to give the tribe necessary sustenance.[4]

The success that the Caddos experienced from 1803 to 1815 allowed the tribe to stem the population decline that had so threatened it in the late eighteenth century. The Kadohadachos numbered about five hundred people and now lived in four villages located to the north of Caddo Lake. The people of the three Hasinai tribes—who continued to reside in their ancestral villages on the Neches and Angelina Rivers—numbered near four hundred, all gradually coalescing behind the leadership of the Hainais. The third Caddo group, the Nadacos, remained on the Sabine River and numbered about two hundred fifty.[5]

The Caddos' overall well-being caused the tribe to be optimistic about diplomatic matters. While the Caddo tribe—led by Dehahuit and the Kadohadachos—had clearly sided with the United States in the southwestern border dispute with Spain, the easing of tensions accompanying the end of the War of 1812 allowed the tribe to resume a position friendly to both powers. With the signing of the Adams-Onís Treaty in February, 1819, the boundary between Louisiana and Texas was finally determined as being the Sabine River from its mouth to 32 degrees longitude, then north to the Red River, and westward along the Red to the 100th meridian. Since the boundary line between the Red and the Sabine was not immediately surveyed, it remained unclear upon which side of the border the Kadohadacho villages lay. Once again, the tribe was afforded the opportunity of treating with both Spain (Mexico after 1821) and the United States.[6]

Dehahuit reopened relations with the Spanish in 1816 by traveling twice to San Antonio to meet with officials. Three years later, Juan Padilla met with the Kadohadachos and noted that the tribe was friendly to the Spanish, "entertaining them in their houses and aiding them in every possible manner." Padilla also reported that the *caddi* of the Kadohadachos held a title and a medaled commission from the Spanish.[7]

While the Spanish in Texas were very receptive to the overtures of the Kadohadachos, the tribe's relationship with the United States went sour after the War of 1812. John Sibley was removed as agent in January, 1815, in part because the citizens around Natchitoches believed that he was more interested in the Kadohadachos' well-being than their own. His successor, Thomas Gales, only lasted until May, 1816, when he was replaced by John Jamison, a man less concerned with the Kadohadachos' problems than Sibley had been.[8]

The most pressing problem the Kadohadachos and Jamison had to deal with was the influx of Anglo Americans into the area. Some of the American settlers were farmers in search of better land, and some of their accounts characterized the Kadohadacho land above the Red River raft as having "very rich and productive" soil well-suited to cotton. One man went so far as to claim that he believed the area not to be "surpassed by any part of the Union." Good land such as that of the Kadohadachos would attract American settlers regardless of the fact that it was native country. Though settlement for agricultural purposes did exist, it was hindered by the fact that the Red River raft prevented easy access to the area by water, making it difficult to get crops to market. Peter Custis had stated in 1806 that if the Red River raft were removed, "this country in a very short time would become the Paradise of America." But not until plans were made to remove it in 1833 did the Kadohadachos' land become a prime target for cotton planters.[9]

As early as 1811, Sibley had reported a "collection of Bad men and Some women" who had settled at Nanatsoho (Pecan Point) on the Red River, upstream from the Kadohadacho village. These intruders had built cabins and planted corn in addition to "doing great mischief Among the Indians." By 1818, there were twelve families at Nanatsoho and twenty others above them at the mouth of the Kiamichi River. The Kadohada-chos repeatedly complained that the whites of these settlements were destroying game "in the most wanton manner," but their agent was pow-erless to dislodge them.[10]

It was not farmers and settlers but illegal traders that gave the Kado-hadachos and the government agents the most trouble. Many of the whites who gravitated to the Louisiana-Texas frontier were individuals seeking trade with the natives and illegally diverting their commerce from the official U.S. trading post at Natchitoches. These illicit traders were able to capture the trade of the Caddos by supplying them with alcohol, an item the tribe increasingly desired. After the turn of the century—and especially following the War of 1812—alcoholism became a serious prob-lem. With the Caddos being pressured from all sides and liquor increas-ingly available, many turned to drink, sometimes trading an entire year's worth of furs for a one-night binge. The *caddices*, as well as the American agents, were helpless to prevent the serious problem of alcohol addiction.

In March, 1817, Jamison reported that "hordes of hunters and licen-tious traders [had] entered the Indian villages and camps on Red River" above Natchitoches. W. A. Trimble, commander of the western section of the 8th Military District, noted that there were five illegal traders at Nanatsoho and three at the mouth of the Kiamichi River who had "tak-en the Indian trade from Natchitoches." They were characterized as be-ing "generally the most unprincipled men," who only practiced "the most degrading and fraudulent impositions" upon the natives by obtaining "skins with whiskey in the most fraudulent traffic."[11]

Dehahuit was very upset at the presence of these traders and pressed Jamison to remove them. In April, 1817, Jamison arranged for a detach-ment of soldiers to accompany him north of Natchitoches to arrest the traders, for he felt that "the disaffection of the Caddo chief . . . has arose from the Want of protection." Jamison hoped that his actions would con-vince Dehahuit and the Kadohadachos that the federal government re-mained committed to protecting the tribe from white incursions "and perhaps restore confidence."[12]

Along with a troop of soldiers commanded by Maj. David Riddle, Jamison traveled from Natchitoches to Nanatsoho and successfully disrupted the illegal trade. Five or six thousand dollars' worth of goods were seized by Jamison, and a few traders were sent to New Orleans for trial. Other traders and white hunters were chased out of the country by Jamison's party. John Fowler, Linnard's successor as official trader at Natchitoches, noted that "the Indians were much pleased" with Jamison's actions.[13]

By the following summer, however, the traders and squatters had returned, though the official trading post and agency had been moved upstream from Natchitoches to the mouth of the Sulphur River. Fowler reported to his superior Thomas McKenney, the superintendent of Indian trade, that men were leaving Natchitoches everyday with pirogues filled with whiskey to barter with the natives. The Kadohadachos complained to the American officials that these traders pursued them "like wolves," cheating them out of their property and destroying the game "in the most wasteful manner." In addition, the drunkenness of the tribal members caused by the illicit trade resulted in the *caddi* losing control of some of his men. Fowler feared a native uprising if the whiskey trade were not halted.[14]

Although a few of the Red River tribes threatened the Americans with a show of force, peace was maintained for the time being. The Kadohadachos were still the most influential tribe in the area, and no action would be taken without their lead. In the summer of 1818 and again that winter, however, Dehahuit and a group of warriors traveled to Texas to hunt, meet with the Hasinais, and receive presents from the Spanish.[15]

In April, 1819, Dehahuit returned from Texas certain that he could count on the Spanish for support. Boldly, the *caddi* angrily informed Fowler that all the lands above the Red River raft were his and threatened that the Kadohadachos would drive away every American. Fowler claimed that Dehahuit's "hatred of americans seems to be invincible." Put off by Dehahuit's "insolence," Fowler believed it would be wise to appoint a "more useful" *caddi* who would be easier for the Americans to control. If this action was not taken, Fowler recommended cutting off the Kadohadachos' presents and refusing to repair their guns. He believed this would cow the tribe, for they would "soon feel the dependence of the Government, which they appear at present to have no idea of." Jamison, who usually understood and was sympathetic to the tribe's problems, agreed with Fowler and felt that Dehahuit should be sent to Washington for he was "vain, and with his vanity ignorant of our resources."[16]

However, cooler and wiser heads at Washington prevailed. Superintendent McKenney held strong beliefs about the possibilities of "civilizing" the natives: he shared the Jeffersonian notion that, with the benevolent guidance and protection of the federal government, the noble savage could turn into the ideal yeoman farmer. He realized that the greatest threat to this process was white intrusion onto native lands and the illegal dispensation of alcohol. Therefore, upon informing the secretary of war of Dehahuit's threatening attitude, McKenney claimed that it was caused by traders who "almost literally drown that country with whiskey." The superintendent proposed that the Americans adopt a vigorous policy of dislodging the traders "and in proportion to rooting them out, would the war spirit of the Caddo chief subside."[17]

McKenney's advice, though, was not fully implemented, and only half-hearted attempts were made to dislodge the illegal traders. As the border with Spain was set, the United States no longer felt the need to win the Kadohadachos' favor. In response to the federal government's neglect, the Kadohadachos and their allies stole the intruders' horses and ran off their hogs. In June, 1820, William Miller, the territorial governor of Arkansas, informed the secretary of war that a native "party of banditti" had been formed on the Red River under the direction of the Kadohadachos, "who are a very considerable tribe." On one occasion, the Kadohadachos stole the settlers' horses, but following a small skirmish a white posse recaptured them.[18]

Despite the hostile attitude of the Kadohadachos, and renewed efforts of the U.S. government to stop them, white incursions onto tribal lands continued. In October, 1823, the Arkansas territorial assembly noted that there were about fifteen hundred whites on the Red River below the mouth of the Kiamichi River near Pecan Point. While most of these settlers were above the Kadohadacho lands, they caused the tribe problems by depleting game and making liquor available to them. In November, 1823, the secretary of war ordered George Gray, Indian agent for the area since 1819, to remove the white intruders immediately. Gray was authorized to "use force if they refuse." His efforts were obviously fruitless, for in the following year Gray was ordered again to force white settlers away from Kadohadacho lands.[19]

In 1821, the United States abandoned the trading factory system and began issuing licenses to independent traders. This only made it more difficult for the agent to regulate trade, and the Kadohadachos continued to be bothered by illegal liquor merchants. In December, 1824, Gray reported that he was having difficulty with the Coushattas and the Kadohadachos, who were selling their horses for whiskey and getting unruly. With all the settlers pouring into the area, Gray was finding it hard to discern the whiskey traders from among the general white population.[20]

In addition to the Anglo-American influx, both the Kadohadachos and the Hasinais were pressured by eastern emigrant tribes—driven from their homes by land-hungry Americans—flooding into Texas and Louisiana. In 1817, Fowler reported that, since the area around the mouth of the Sulphur River abounded in game, the natives were "flocking there" and "constantly increasing by emigration from the eastward." Among these emigrant tribes were an estimated five hundred Choctaws, who had settled their differences with the Caddos, scattered above the Kadohadacho villages. A few hundred Kickapoos—late arrivals from the Old Northwest—also roamed along the upper reaches of the Sabine and Angelina Rivers. The Delawares and the Shawnees formed a village (on the west bank of the Red River sixty miles above Natchitoches) consisting of one hundred natives with "considerably more to come." By 1822, there were at least five hundred Delawares and Shawnees living in Lost Prairie, an area between the Sulphur and Red Rivers; these tribes, particularly the Delawares, would always enjoy good relations with the Caddos.[21]

The most important emigrant tribe to settle near the Caddos was the Cherokees, who had begun to filter across the Mississippi River before the turn of the century. Despite a few early skirmishes, matters remained peaceful between the Caddos and the Cherokees for almost two decades. By 1817, there were perhaps one hundred Cherokees in the area near the mouth of the Little River, where they "had obtained permission from the Caddos to settle."[22]

At first, these tribes were welcomed by the Kadohadachos, and in return they showed their hosts great respect. Fowler noted that the Kadohadachos "[are] the oldest tribe of Indians in this country and are looked up to with a degree of reverence by all the Indians on Red River." Commander Trimble claimed that the Kadohadachos were "considered the mother nation of the country and have a general superintendence over all the tribes in the vicinity." Padilla believed that all the tribes on the Louisiana-Texas frontier recognized the Kadohadacho *caddi* "as a superior."[23]

In addition to the respect they received, the Kadohadachos welcomed the emigrant natives as allies against the ever-hostile Osages. Jamison informed the secretary of war in 1817 that the Kadohadachos, Choctaws, Cherokees, Coushattas, "and all other tribes" were at war with the Osages. At first, the Kadohadachos led many of the war parties against the Osages, but during the winter of 1819–20, another one hundred Cherokees were led by their political chief Duwali (or Bowl, as he was called by the whites) into the Lost Prairie region. The Cherokees soon began to take the lead in forming war parties against the Osages— a sign of the lessening esteem of the Kadohadachos and a portent of things to come. As increasing numbers of the powerful Cherokee tribe continued to settle among both the Kadohadachos and the Hasinais, they threatened the position of the Caddos, and tensions between the tribes increased.[24]

The large numbers of whites and natives settling on their lands, coupled with the deteriorating relations with their American agents, caused the Kadohadachos to consider removing from their homeland to resettle in Spanish Texas near their Hasinai kin. In November, 1820, the tribe sent a message to Governor Martínez informing him of their desire to settle in Texas and adding that they would assist the Spanish in their renewed battles against the Lipan Apaches and the Comanches. The governor and other officials took the matter seriously, and inquiries were made as to how much land the Kadohadachos would need and how they would support themselves. In August, 1821, Dehahuit and eighty-three tribal members traveled to Monterrey to discuss the move with Joaquín de Arredondo, the commandant general of the newly formed Eastern Interior Provinces. The Spaniard offered the Kadohadachos a tract of land southwest of the Hasinais on the Guadalupe River above the road from San Antonio to Nacogdoches.[25]

The Kadohadachos returned to their villages to consider the offer, when events occurred in Mexico that radically altered the situation. On August 21, 1821, Agustín de Iturbide, leader of a plot that had been in the making for the past year, forced the Spanish viceroy to sign the Treaty of Córdoba, which recognized Mexico's independence from Spain. The Spanish ultimately disavowed this agreement and threatened to send troops to reclaim New Spain, and this move caused Iturbide and his ruling junta to seek an alliance with the "Northern Indians"; thus, they turned toward the tribe they still considered to be the most influential on the Louisiana-Texas frontier, the Kadohadachos.

On September 28, 1821, Iturbide sent a letter through Commandant General Arredondo and Governor Martínez to the Kadohadacho *caddi* asking him to gather the chiefs of the Comanche and Lipan Apache tribes—with whom Martínez had arranged a temporary peace—and come visit him in Mexico City. He ordered Arredondo to provide the Kadohadachos with "everything they need or ask for" so that when they returned home, "they would tell the other [tribes] about all the many things they will have seen and admired, and that now we are all brothers [who] may live in peace and tranquility."[26]

Unfortunately for the Kadohadachos, the delivery of Iturbide's invitation to Dehahuit was long delayed. It did not reach Monterey until November 2, and then was not transmitted to the *ayuntamiento* of Bexar until three weeks later. On November 28, four Mexican soldiers set out from San Antonio with the letter, but the poor condition of their horses did not allow them to reach the Kadohadacho village until January, 1822, when they found that Dehahuit was out on his winter hunt. Finally, on January 22, Dehahuit replied to Governor Martínez and informed him that all his people were scattered and that the chiefs of the Lipans and the Comanches could not be found; thus, he would be unable to travel to the capital until spring. In March, Dehahuit sent Martínez yet another letter promising to visit Mexico City in the future.[27]

Ultimately, Dehahuit never did make the trip to Mexico, and in the meantime Richard Fields, the Cherokee war chief—who also handled diplomatic negotiations—took the initiative from the Kadohadachos and began corresponding with Mexican authorities. Because Fields, who was one-eighth Cherokee, could read and write English and Spanish, he had an important advantage over Dehahuit and the Kadohadachos, who always depended on outsiders for their correspondence. Taking advantage of Dehahuit's uncharacteristic hesitation, Fields and twenty-two Cherokees visited San Antonio in November, 1822, and concluded an agreement with the new governor of Texas, José Felix Trespalacios, which gave them official permission to settle in Texas. Realizing that the agreement was not valid without higher approval, Trespalacios sent Fields on to Mexico City to gain an audience with Iturbide. Although the delegation did meet with the new commandant general of the Eastern Interior Provinces, Gaspar López, it was unable to see Iturbide, who was overthrown on March 19, 1823, and replaced by the Mexican Congress.[28]

Despite the fact that the Trespalacios-Fields agreement had not been officially recognized, the Cherokees in Texas acted as if it were in force and took steps to replace the Kadohadachos as the leading tribe of the Louisiana-Texas frontier. In the spring and summer of 1824, the Cherokees formed an alliance with all the emigrant tribes in East Texas. Although the Cherokees failed to conclude a treaty with the Lipans and Comanches, Fields was able to claim that he spoke for the Texan Delawares, Shawnees, and Kickapoos; thus, the Mexican government transferred its attention from the slumbering Kadohadachos to the aggressive Cherokees.[29]

Newly arriving Anglo Americans in Texas also neglected the Caddo tribes in favor of the Cherokees. In March, 1825, the newly formed state of Coahuila and Texas instituted a colonization law that allowed foreigners—Indian tribes as well as whites—to obtain land within its borders. Soon thereafter, the state granted contracts of huge tracts of land in East Texas to three Anglo-American empresarios, individuals who would be responsible for colonizing the area. Two of these grants—one to Haden Edwards and the other to Frost Thorn—included land claimed by the Hasinais and the Cherokees. Eventually, conflict with the Americans over the land grants would draw the Hasinais and the Cherokees together.[30]

For the time being, however, the situation only caused trouble between the Caddos and the Cherokees. Fields complained to the governor of Texas that his tribe was not on friendly terms with the Hasinais "through jealousy that we are settled on their lands." Unfriendliness between the two groups was exacerbated by the attitude the Cherokees took toward the other native tribes of Texas. The Wichita allies of the Caddos—particularly the Tawakonis and the Wacos (formerly the Iscanis)—as well as the Comanches, Lipan Apaches, and Tonkawas began raiding the newly founded Anglo-American settlements almost immediately. In March, 1826, Fields offered the Cherokee services to the Mexican government for war against the hostile tribes, adding that the Cherokees were willing to police the frontier and keep the Kadohadachos, Nacogdoches, and Wacos from attacking the other emigrant tribes. All the native tribes of Texas quickly understood the hostile attitude of the intruding Cherokees.[31]

In part, the Caddos' experience with the Cherokees caused them to have second thoughts about accepting further emigrant tribes on their land. However, in 1825 the U.S. government arranged for the small, friendly Louisiana tribes to congregate upon the Kadohadacho lands above the Red River raft, feeling it would be easier to protect the natives from white incursions if they were concentrated on a well-defined tract of land. In October, 1825, Agent Gray informed Dehahuit of the government's desire; since the tribes had always depended upon the Kadohadachos, the *caddi* replied that he had no objections but also stated that he should receive a small annuity from the United States for assenting to the plan. Gray agreed to the *caddi*'s request and was authorized by McKenney to give Dehahuit fifty dollars a year "as a token of good will . . . and for the offer he has made the bands now in Louisiana to come and join them."[32]

In preparation for this relocation and with the tribe's consent, the boundaries of the Kadohadacho lands were officially delineated for the first time. In the east, the boundary was set at the old, western channel of the Red River, called Bayou Pierre, while the yet-to-be-fixed Mexican border would be the western line. The Sulphur River was the northern boundary and Cypress Bayou the southern.[33]

In addition to the Louisiana bands, the federal government wanted the Quapaws of Arkansas to settle on the Kadohadacho lands. By the early 1820s, the Quapaws were being pressured by both the Osages and the influx of whites. In 1822, the Quapaws expressed interest in selling their lands to the United States to join with the Kadohadachos in claiming they were "influenced in this wish by the solicitude which the Caddos have expressed on the subject."[34]

On January 19, 1825, the Quapaws and the United States entered into an agreement in which the tribe sold its lands to the government and agreed to be "concentrated and confined to the district of country inhabited by the Caddo Indians and form a part of said tribe" within one year. Unfortunately, neither the Quapaws nor the U.S. government had spoken to the Kadohadachos since 1822 about the Quapaw relocation.

Gov. William Izard of the Arkansas territory warned that, although the two tribes had "a tradition of having been allied in some wars . . . they have had no intercourse with each other for a long time, and their languages are totally different."[35]

The attempt to amalgamate the Quapaws with the Kadohadachos was beset with problems from the very beginning. In July, 1825, a small party of Quapaw chiefs visited the country of the Kadohadachos to inspect the land and inform Dehahuit of the imminent arrival of their entire tribe. The uninformed Kadohadachos were surprised by this news, but the *caddi* consented to set aside a piece of land for the Quapaws. When the entire Quapaw tribe arrived in early 1826, however, Dehahuit's eagerness to have the tribe settle on Kadohadacho land quickly soured for the Quapaws numbered 458, almost as many as the Kadohadachos. Dehahuit immediately began to have second thoughts about accepting such a large, independent tribe in his territory. By April, 1826, the Quapaws were threatening the Kadohadachos with war because Dehahuit refused to grant the Quapaws a title to the land on which they resided.[36]

Matters went from bad to worse for the Quapaws. The land on which the Kadohadachos had allowed the tribe to settle was subject to flooding, and their first year's crop was ruined by high water. Dehahuit, fearing there was not enough good land to go around, only allowed the Quapaws to cultivate those lands near the river bottoms or on soil too poor for cultivation. By 1829, some of the Quapaws had returned to Arkansas and petitioned the governor to allow them to resettle on their old lands. Most of the Quapaws were back in Arkansas by 1832 and "adverse to returning" to the Kadohadachos since their inhospitable hosts had "murdered three of them and otherwise maltreates them." The following year, the Quapaws removed to the Indian Territory west of Arkansas that had been set aside for the relocated tribes of the East.[37]

Nonetheless, emigrant tribes continued to arrive in the area, putting extreme pressure on the Caddos. On June 13, 1827, Gray informed the secretary of war of the alarming increase of natives, stating "it appears to be the whirlpool that is sucking within its bosom, the restless and dissatisfied, of all nations and language; parties of broken up tribes are continually pouring in, and it is becoming a receptacle for detached parties from all parts." The Hasinais in Texas were experiencing the same pressures as the Kadohadachos. In 1828, Mexican Gen. Manuel de Mier y Terán headed a commission that traveled through East Texas to gather information preparatory to running the boundary between Louisiana and Texas as called for in the Adams-Onís Treaty of 1821. Although there were a great number of Anglo-American settlements interspersed among the tribes of East Texas, it was the emigrant tribes who raised the ire of the Hasinais. The Hainai and Nadaco *caddices* met with Terán on May

30 as the commission passed near the Neches River; they "expressed great vexation at the admission into this territory of tribes coming from the north and stated if they had more men they would declare war on them."[38]

The increasing pressures in the late 1820s greatly demoralized the Caddo tribes, causing them to turn increasingly to alcohol. In 1828, a licensed trader noted that the Choctaws—hired by whites for commission—were selling liquor to the Kadohadachos within a fourth of a mile from the Indian agency, which had been moved downstream from the mouth of the Sulphur River to be closer to the Kadohadacho and Coushatta villages. The Kadohadachos, who had come to meet Gray in order to receive presents, were too inebriated to conduct any business with the agent "in consequence of the whole nation arriving by some unknown person furnishing them with whiskey." On one occasion, when the agent's interpreter attempted to relieve the natives of liquor, he "was molested and compelled to retreat for Safety."[39]

Not only was alcohol causing the tribal members to become unruly, it was also threatening the agricultural base of the tribe. One of the most important features of the Caddos had been their ability to sustain themselves, no matter how hard they were hit by disease or political misfortune. By the mid-1820s, however, the federal Indian agent was forced to supply the Kadohadachos with food, since their drunkenness and depression caused them to neglect their fields. Game near the Kadohadacho villages was scarce, and the influx of whites and natives forced the tribe to travel even farther west for their winter hunts.[40]

The situation reached crisis proportions following the death of Agent Gray in November, 1828. Thomas Griffith was appointed as his successor but he died before assuming the position, and the Kadohadachos were left without an agent until the summer of 1830. In the interim, the Kadohadachos did not receive either the presents or the rations they had come to depend on, and in desperation they joined with the Hasinais to raid the livestock of the Cherokees, whose population had grown to around five hundred.[41]

In August, 1830, the Cherokees in Texas prepared a retaliatory attack upon the Caddo tribes. The weaker Kadohadachos retreated to their villages and begged the newly arrived agent, Jehiel Brooks, for protection. Brooks distributed powder and lead to the tribesmen so they could defend themselves, informing them that the government would protect them only if they stayed within the boundaries of the United States. In September, the members of the Hasinai tribes visited the Kadohadachos to form a "league for their mutual defense against the more powerful nations in Texas, who threaten them also, alleging that they are under the [Kadohadachos'] influence." Brooks told Dehahuit to dismiss the Hasinais and to remain on his own lands. At the same time, Brooks convinced

Col. Peter Bean—Mexico's Indian agent for Texas—to keep the Cherokees from attacking the Kadohadachos, and the tribe was spared the wrath of the more powerful intruder.[42]

Although Brooks did back the Kadohadachos in this case, his appointment by Pres. Andrew Jackson represented a change in the official Indian policy of the United States. Whereas the federal government had previously attempted to provide the tribes at least nominal protection from white incursion upon their lands, the Jackson administration felt that the removal of the natives would be the most beneficial policy for both the whites—who would receive the Indian land—and the Indians. With the passage of the Indian Removal Act in 1830, Jackson was able to implement his program of buying the natives' land and resettling them west of the Mississippi River where, free from white intruders, the tribes would ideally adopt the techniques of "civilization" that would allow them to survive.[43]

As Jackson's appointee for the position of agent for the Kadohadachos, Brooks shared the president's views on Indian matters. Unlike his predecessors, Brooks was more concerned with removing the Kadohadachos from their ancestral lands than with providing the tribe either protection from whites or the guidance they needed in troubled times. Also unlike his predecessors, Brooks was concerned with individual profit rather than unselfish duty, as his later actions would demonstrate.

Upon assuming his position in the summer of 1830, however, to his credit Brooks immediately provided the tribe with protection and support. After thwarting the Cherokee threat from Texas, Brooks took steps to keep the tribe from starving, since the 1830 corn crop of the Kadohadachos—as well as that of the Hasinais—was destroyed by drought and general neglect. The starving Hainais and Nadacos joined the Kadohadachos in the fall of 1830 and preyed upon the whites' livestock in the Bayou Pierre district.[44]

Since Brooks did not have enough food on hand to feed the combined tribes, he tried unsuccessfully to get the Hasinais to return to Texas. That winter, while the men were on their buffalo hunt, the remaining tribal members—mainly old men, women, and children—were reduced to begging and stealing from the adjacent whites because Brooks had already exhausted his allowance for provisions "in barely preserving these miserable beings from starvation." During an uncommonly severe winter, Brooks was forced to ask the secretary of war for an extra food allowance.[45]

In addition, the Kadohadachos continued to be hounded by illegal whiskey traders. In the summer of 1831, Brooks took steps to end this trade and reported that he was "at last succeeding" in his exertions "to arrest the progress of illicit trade which had been carried on throughout the Indian country to a large extent." Brooks felt that he had "gained the esteem" of the Caddos by supplying them with food and protecting them from both the Cherokees and the illegal traders.[46]

Brooks was greatly mistaken, however, for Dehahuit and the rest of the tribe were very upset with the new agent. In May, 1831, the Kadohadacho *caddi*, with the help of white friends from Natchitoches, addressed a letter to President Jackson in which he declared that he and all the Indians in his vicinity had "lost all confidence in Brooks." Dehahuit demanded a new agent, saying Brooks was "no better than none," since the tribes could "get nothing done by the present agent." Dehahuit's main complaint against Brooks was that he suspected the agent of keeping his fifty dollar annuity, which he had not received for three years. Obviously, Dehahuit did not feel that Brooks had the best interests of the tribe in mind.[47]

Brooks demonstrated his true intentions during his trip to Washington in the winter of 1831–32, when he visited the White House and discussed extinguishing the Kadohadacho title to the land with President Jackson. Both Brooks and Jackson knew that plans were being made for engineer Henry Shreve to remove the Red River raft, and both men realized that if the Red River were cleared for navigation, the pressure on the Kadohadachos to give up their land would be great. In accordance with the new federal policy toward Native Americans, Jackson and Brooks felt it would be best for all parties if the tribe would relinquish their land and remove to the west.[48]

In the spring of 1833, Captain Shreve arrived in Natchitoches to begin the process of removing the Red River raft, a prospect which greatly excited the populace. There ensued an immediate scramble for the Kadohadachos' rich lands, and citizens filed suits in court that stated the tribe had no right to the area they occupied.[49]

At this crucial moment when the Kadohadachos needed strong leadership the most, their esteemed *caddi* Dehahuit died. Bereft of guidance, the Kadohadachos were uncertain as to what action to take in the face of increased hostility from the whites. One tribal faction wanted to name a war chief to lead the tribe in driving off the whites, who continued to settle upon their lands and provide them with illicit whiskey. Brooks, who caught wind of this idea, arranged a meeting with the tribe, and as a show of force, he asked the commander at nearby Fort Jesup to provide him with troops to intimidate the Kadohadachos.[50]

In June, 1833, Brooks met with the tribe and conferred the title of *caddi* upon the choice of the Kadohadachos, Tarshar, "the Wolf." With the support of the troops, Brooks got Tarshar—a much less decisive man than Dehahuit—and the rest of the tribe to revive "pledges and promises of continued good faith to the government and friendship with the white settlers on the frontier." Brooks also informed the Kadohadachos of the various claims to their lands that some whites had made in Natchitoches, to "which the Indians entirely and unconditionally" objected and desired Brooks "to state [their objections] to the government."[51]

Brooks was more attuned to his own interests than those of the Kadohadachos and immediately began to manipulate the tribe into selling their lands. In March, 1834, Brooks asked Commissioner of Indian Affairs Judge Elbert Herring whether "it would not be best to negotiate for the [Kadohadacho] lands at once before the further progress of the work shall open the eyes of the tribe, as to their importance to the whites." Soon after this Brooks relinquished all responsibility to the Kadohadachos, informing them that he was no longer their agent and that he did "not know what [would] be done" by the United States. Whether Brooks was ordered to do this or did so on his own is unclear; whatever the case, the results were what Brooks desired. The Kadohadachos, denied any protection by the federal government, reluctantly decided that it would be in their best interests to sell their lands for whatever price they could get. They hoped that, by joining their Hasinai kin in Texas, they would receive better treatment from the Mexican government than they had from the United States.[52]

The Kadohadachos had good reason to believe that Mexico would be well-disposed to their entrance, since governmental policy, which had shifted following 1827, was now aimed at establishing the natives' title to the land while curbing the influx of Anglo Americans. Most of these Anglo-American immigrants were southern and had brought with them the attitudes and beliefs of their original homeland; they were Protestants interested in spreading the same slave culture into Texas that had rapidly moved across the South following the War of 1812. This expansion had been carried out at the expense of the Native Americans of the region, including the Cherokees, and now displaced the Kadohadachos. The expanding culture also clashed with the antislavery Catholic beliefs of the Mexicans.[53]

Hostilities broke out between the Anglo Americans and the Mexicans in the 1827 Fredonian Rebellion, in which settlers on the grant of land given to empresario Haden Edwards had attempted to separate from Mexico. With promises of land, Edwards's brother Benjamin enlisted the services of the Cherokee war chief, Richard Fields. The Mexicans, however, persuaded the civil chief, Duwali, to remain loyal, and the Fredonian Rebellion was successfully put down with his assistance. Fields was executed by the Cherokees, and the Mexican government commissioned Duwali as a lieutenant colonel.[54]

Three years later the Mexican Congress passed the Law of April 6, 1830, outlawing further immigration from the United States. In 1831,

Commandant General Terán set in motion a procedure to give the Cherokees and unspecified "agricultural tribes" a grant that included all the lands north of the San Antonio Road between the Trinity and Sabine rivers. Located within this grant were the villages of most of the emigrant natives in Texas, as well as those of the Hasinais and the Nadacos. The Cherokee grant, however, also overlapped two empresarial grants; one to future Commandant Gen. Vicente Filisola, who had taken over the Thorn grant, and the other to New Jerseyite David G. Burnet, who controlled the Edwards grant. Because of the conflicting claims, the Cherokees did not obtain formal approval of their grant from the Mexican government (though in 1833, the governor of Coahuila and Texas announced that the Cherokees and the other tribes could remain in their homes unmolested until the federal government made a decision).[55]

The inroads that Duwali had made with the Mexican government, coupled with continued illegal Anglo-American immigration, caused the Caddos to reevaluate their attitude toward the Cherokees. By 1834, the Caddos began to realize that the Anglo Americans—who were the majority of the nine thousand Euro-Americans who lived in the Department of Nacogdoches—were a much bigger threat than the emigrant tribes of Texas. In addition, Mexico relaxed the Spanish restrictions on native trade, and Nacogdoches became a trading center that competed with the Americans. Although there is no record of an intertribal agreement between the Hasinais and the Cherokees, events suggest that by early 1834, the two groups had made peace in order to collaborate and gain title to their lands.[56]

During his 1834 inspection tour of the province, Col. Juan N. Almonte transmitted the Mexican government's position to the tribes in Texas. Among other things, Almonte was instructed to make certain that all the Indians knew that the Mexican government was "disposed to admit them as an integral part of the Federation" and was willing to grant them full ownership of their lands. On June 1, Almonte met with a group of five hundred members of the various emigrant tribes, along with an embassy from the Nacogdoches Indians. When the Cherokees complained that their lands were being overrun by the Anglo Americans, Almonte assured them that their welfare was a matter of concern to the government, and that his visit was an indication of the sympathy that Mexico felt for them. Partly as a result of Almonte's tour, the Congress of Coahuila and Texas passed a measure in May, 1835, authorizing the governor to settle the Cherokees and other "peaceful and civilized Indians" on vacant lands within the state, where they would be used as a buffer against the hostile Comanches.[57]

Promises of land from the Mexicans and peace with the Cherokees influenced the Kadohadacho decision to succumb to Brooks's pressure, sell their land to the United States, and join their Hasinai kin in Texas. Therefore, in early 1835, the Kadohadacho chiefs and headmen addressed a memorial to President Jackson in which they made "the sorrowful resolution of offering all our lands to you which lie within the boundary of the United States, for sale, at such price as we can agree to in council." On January 28, 1835, Jackson sent the memorial to the secretary of war for his consideration without much comment except to ask "will it not be well to ask an appropriation to cover this expense?"[58]

Clearly, not much attention was paid to the treaty-making process in Washington, and Brooks, appointed as treaty commissioner, was given free reign over the proceedings. On June 3, 1835, Brooks sent the Kadohadacho interpreter Larkin Edwards to inform the tribe that he was ready to negotiate for the purchase of their lands and that he had brought a great many presents for them. Five days later Tarshar arrived, and Brooks showed him the rifles, axes, knives, blankets, and clothes the tribe would receive if they sold their lands. Tarshar admitted that the Kadohadachos "were in great want" of all the items and agreed to bring the rest of his tribe together to treat with Brooks.[59]

On June 25, the entire Kadohadacho tribe—five hundred members which probably included the remnants of the Natchitoches and the Yatasi tribes—gathered at the agency house. Brooks provided them with daily rations and requested them to select representatives for the council to be held the following day. At noon on June 26, Tarshar, his underchief Tsauninot (Father of Children), and twenty-three "chosen councillors" gathered to listen to Brooks's offer. Brooks told the tribe he was "prepared to alleviate" their wants and to place them in a state of independence when compared with their "present destitution." He proclaimed himself a friend sent to obtain the Kadohadacho lands, which he described as "of no more use" to the tribe. He warned them that, "right or wrong," the whites would soon deprive the tribe of the land anyway. Brooks offered to buy the land for goods the tribe could not "otherwise obtain, or long exist without, in this or any other country." In other words, the Kadohadachos were being given the choice to sell their land for what Brooks had to offer or lose it to rapacious whites for nothing.[60]

Tsauninot replied that his tribe was "in great want" and expected Brooks to bring them "relief" by supplying them "with things of much more value . . . than these lands, which yield no game." Stating that the tribe now knew the wishes of the "great father," Tsauninot told Brooks that the councillors would consult with the entire tribe and let him know of their decision the following day.[61]

That night, when the rest of the tribe was told of Brooks's offer, the Kadohadacho people "hung their heads down and were sorrowful." Tarshar then rose and gave an impassioned speech in which he explained the situation for the rest of the tribe, letting them know that, realistically, they had no choice but to sell the land. Pointing out that the Kadohada-chos were starving because of the lack of game, he urged the tribe not to mourn the loss of land, "which yields . . . nothing but misery." Instead, he suggested that the tribe sell the land "and get all we can for it and not wait till the white man steals it away . . . then gives us nothing." Tarshar told the tribe to perform the corn dance if they agreed with him, but not to let the drum beat if they opposed. The entire tribe "all sprang to their feet and performed the dance with universal animation."[62]

The next day the councillors met with Brooks at ten o'clock, and Tsauninot informed him of the tribe's decision. Brooks then asked Tsaun-inot to name a price for the lands and the desired mode of payment, and Tsauninot replied that he expected him to make an offer "as we know not how to fix a price." Brooks offered only to pay them a fixed sum for their "whole country on this side of the [still undetermined] Mexican line, let the quantity of land be small or great." Tsauninot then told Brooks they needed time to deliberate upon a sum.[63]

Late that afternoon Capt. Thomas J. Harrison and a troop of fifty soldiers from the 3d Regiment at Fort Jesup arrived at the council grounds. Along with the captain, two other officers and a surgeon served as wit-nesses to the treaty. That night three white friends of the Kadohadachos who had been invited to help them with the treaty—Joséph Valentín (who had accompanied Dehahuit to Monterrey in 1821), François Bark, and Manuel Flores—arrived at their encampment. Brooks ordered the troops to arrest the trio; Bark was taken into custody, Valentín was sent from the council grounds, and Flores was concealed by the tribe until he could escape. Brooks then had Captain Harrison post a chain of senti-nels around the area to protect against unwanted intrusions: obviously, Brooks did not wish the Kadohadachos to receive counsel from anyone but himself.[64]

Two days later, on June 29, the tribe once again met with Brooks and told him they had been unable to come to a determination on a price and wished to hear his proposal. Brooks responded that, in return for selling all their land and agreeing to remove at their "own expense out of the United States," he was willing to give the Kadohadachos eighty thousand dollars. Thirty thousand dollars' worth of horses and goods were to be paid to tribal members immediately upon signing the treaty. The tribe was to receive ten thousand dollars per annum for the next five years, either in goods or money, depending upon the wishes of the tribe. It seems that the Kadohadachos had already stated to Brooks their wish of joining the Hasinais in East Texas, since Brooks did not offer the Kado-hadachos any lands in the Indian Territory.[65]

At ten in the morning on July 1, 1835, Tarshar told Brooks that the

Kadohadachos agreed to accept his proposal and that the tribe would leave the United States within one year. He stated that, since the tribe might live "some distance from this country," they wanted their annuities to be paid in cash to an agent the tribe would appoint to receive it for them. Brooks agreed to this and retired to his quarters to put the treaty stipulations in writing.[66]

At four o'clock in the afternoon, Brooks gathered the councillors again and had the treaty read to them by the interpreter. During the reading Brooks acted suspiciously; when Lt. J. Bonnell, one of the witnesses, picked up a copy of the treaty to read, Brooks "took hold of the paper, and said that he wished" Bonnell would not read it. Bonnell argued that he was taking notes and wished to see the document, but Brooks "insisted" that he not read it, and the treaty was returned to the agent.[67]

Following the translation of the treaty to the Kadohadachos, Brooks went to each of the twenty-five tribal members and asked them if they understood the interpreter clearly and if they were ready to "sanction it" by affixing their signatures. They all answered in the affirmative, and a pipe was passed around "and congratulations exchanged on having closed the treaty." According to Brooks, all "shook hands and separated in friendship." Brooks and the Kadohadacho headmen then spent the next few days distributing the thirty thousand dollars' worth of goods to the members of the tribe, but since the weather was rainy, the last of the goods was not handed out until July 10. Brooks believed that the Kadohadachos "expressed great satisfaction with everything they received, and with the whole proceeding, from the beginning to the ending. None went away dissatisfied."[68]

The Kadohadachos had sold their lands to the United States for eighty thousand dollars and agreed to remove themselves from the country within one year. Did the tribe make a good deal for their lands, or were they, in effect, swindled by Brooks with the United States receiving the land at bargain prices? In 1963, historian G. W. McGinty looked into this matter and found that the Kadohadachos had actually sold 590,503 acres of land. McGinty calculated that the federal government ultimately received an average of $3.48 per acre of this land upon its resale, for a grand total of $2,068,419. Obviously, the treaty had been a bargain for the United States, since the Kadohadachos had been paid only about sixteen cents for each acre they had sold.[69]

As agent for the tribe, Jehiel Brooks had failed the Kadohadachos miserably, having been more concerned with removing the tribe from their land at a low cost than looking out for the tribe's best interests. Additionally, Brooks himself realized a handsome profit from the treaty. Unknown to the Kadohadachos and the various white witnesses to the proceedings, Brooks had introduced a secret reservation into the treaty that granted land considered to be outside the Kadohadacho territory to two French-speaking mulattos, Touline Grappe and his son François.

The Grappes had formerly been traders and interpreters for the Kadohadachos. Within the Caddo Treaty, four leagues—or about twenty-three thousand acres—of land on Rush Island had been reserved for them. This island contained rich, alluvial bottomland and had been formed between the old western channel of the Red River—the Kadohadachos' eastern boundary—and the newer channel to the east that contained about two-thirds of the river's flow. Henry Shreve had mentioned this island in 1834, noting that it averaged about 2.5 miles in breadth and was 45 miles long. He estimated that, being prime cotton land, it had a potential value of four dollars per acre. Already there were white settlements as large as fifty acres on Rush Island. According to all the whites of the area, as well as the Kadohadachos—who had admitted as much in their boundary determination of 1825—Rush Island was recognized as being outside the Kadohadacho lands.[70]

Brooks, recognizing the potential worth of this island, quietly included it among the lands the Kadohadachos owned and granted it to the Grappes. The witnesses to the treaty all later testified that they had heard nothing mentioned of the Grappe reservation at the negotiations. According to the Grappes, they knew nothing of this until the U.S. Senate ratified the treaty and the president signed it on February 2, 1836. Brooks appeared two weeks later at the Grappes' residence and informed them of their acquisition. The startled Grappes, who were poor, accepted Brooks's offer of six thousand dollars and a slave in return for the land, a fraction of its real worth. Brooks went on to sell the land at a great profit.[71]

Soon after Brooks's actions were made public, both Henry Shreve and members of the Kadohadacho tribe sent memorials to the president informing him of the chicanery within the Caddo Treaty. The matter was not investigated by the House Committee on Indian Affairs until 1841, however; the committee then recommended that the question of fraud should be decided in court. In 1850, the U.S. Supreme Court confirmed Brooks's title to the lands he had acquired from the Grappes on strictly legal grounds. Whether illegal or not, Brooks's actions concerning the Caddo Treaty demonstrated a total disregard for the best interests of the Kadohadachos, for, though the tribe was not directly affected by Brooks's swindle, Brooks had arranged the treaty for personal profit rather than out of a concern for the Kadohadachos.[72]

After three tumultuous decades of relations with the United States in which the tribe had helped the republic secure its southwestern boundary, the Kadohadachos were repaid by being forced to sell their lands and move to Mexico. Nonetheless, many tribal members must have looked upon their banishment with relief. The Kadohadachos could now resettle near their Hasinai kin in Texas, where the Mexican government was more accepting of Indians. Together, the Caddo tribes hoped to recuperate from the shattering occurrences of the past twenty years and start anew; unfortunately, it was not to be.

Chapter 8
The Caddos and the Texas Revolution, 1835–38

[The Kadohadachos] appear to be a poor, miserable people, incapable of the smallest exertion, either as it regards living, or any thing else, except liquor.
—Major B. Riley, U.S. Army,
August 24, 1836[1]

The [Kadohadachos] are in alliance with the Wacoes, and generally join them in their predatory expeditions. This tribe amounts to about 600 souls, and 150 warriors. They are braver and more desperate than the Comanche. . . .
—Report of G. W. Bonnell, Commissioner of Indian Affairs,
Republic of Texas, November 3, 1838[2]

CADDO HOPES FOR REGENERATION in Texas were dashed by the outbreak of the Texas Revolution only months after the signing of the Caddo Treaty of 1835. In contrast with other conflicts between Euro-Americans, this time the Caddo tribes were unable to profit from the war and instead were adversely affected by it. The Kadohadachos suffered a dangerous schism during this period, and all the Caddo tribes were subjected to the belligerence of the Anglo Americans who gained control of the independent Republic of Texas.

The downturn in events following the War of 1812 accelerated the Caddos' amalgamation so much that by 1835 only three tribes remained—the Kadohadachos, Hainais, and the Nadacos. The Kadohadachos' status as the preeminent Caddo tribe—so carefully cultivated by Dehahuit earlier in the century—waned after the treaty of 1835. In compliance with the dictates of the treaty, the majority of the 500 Kadohadachos moved their villages westward to the head of Caddo Lake, where they believed themselves to be on the Mexican side of the unsurveyed international boundary line.[3] The numbers of the three remaining Hasinai tribes—the Hainais, the Nabedaches, and the Nacogdoches—had fallen from about 400 in 1815 to only 225 by 1837. All three tribes, along with a few members of the Ais, gathered at the Hainai village on the Angelina River and were considered as one entity, the Hainais.[4] The Nadacos were the only Caddo tribe that maintained its population levels. Unlike the Kadohadachos, who lived near Shreveport, or the Hainais, who lived near Nacogdoches, the Nadacos resided far from white settlement, on the headwaters of the Sabine River. Isolated from disease and the temptations of the whiskey traders, the Nadaco population remained stable—somewhere around 250—during the period.[5]

Despite the Caddos' sinking fortunes, the tribe's possibility for again profiting from Euro-American conflict arose in the fall of 1835, when circumstances in Mexico caused the Anglo Americans in Texas to rebel. All the tribes of the area realized they were in a good position to obtain land concessions from the whites, and the Cherokees led the negotiations for the Native Americans. In September, Duwali traveled to San Antonio and met with Col. Domingo Ugartechea, military commandant at Bexar, who attempted to enlist the Cherokees and their allies to fight against the rebellious Texans. Duwali returned to his village and held a general council of all the "associated bands"—the emigrant tribes of Texas as well as the Hainais and the Nadacos. Realizing that it would be very difficult for the Mexicans to defeat the more numerous Texans, the tribes concluded that it was in their best interests to cultivate a friendship with the revolutionaries.[6]

For the moment, it appeared that the natives had chosen the most beneficial path, since the rebellious Texans, threatened by an armed Mexican invasion, were in a constant state of alarm. The revolutionaries set up a provisional body to govern Texas in October, 1835, and it immediately took steps to ensure the friendship of the large body of natives allied with the Cherokees. Two agents met with the tribes, and they reported that, if the Texans would "secure [the Indians] in their possessions [and] treat them in a frank, manly, independent manner, [Texas would] secure their friendship and hereafter, if necessary, their cooperation."[7]

Upon the advice of the Indian agents, the Consulate, the new governing body of Texas, agreed to grant the natives land. On November 13, 1835, every member of the Consulate signed a declaration stating that an agreement had been reached with the "Cherokee and their associate bands, twelve in number," including the Hainais and the Nadacos. This agreement temporarily gave the Indians a tract of land lying north of the San Antonio road, from the Sabine River to the Neches. The Texans promised to appoint commissioners to establish the definite boundary of the territory, and three months later, on February 23, 1836, a commission headed by Sam Houston finalized a treaty with the Cherokees and their associate bands. This agreement greatly resembled the treaties made with the natives by the United States; it defined the boundaries of the Indians' land and gave the Republic of Texas the power to regulate trade and commerce. Although the Cherokees and their allies had not received the land westward to the Trinity they desired, they successfully forced the Texans—previously hostile to all native land claims—to accede to their demands. It appeared that a peaceful path had been set out upon by the Indians and the Texans.[8]

On March 2, 1836, only a week after the agreement had been made, a convention of delegates from Texas met at Washington-on-the-Brazos and formally declared independence from Mexico. They then formulated a constitution and provided a provisional government for Texas until the constitution could be adopted. The convention proved to be against granting the tribes land and chose David G. Burnet—the empresario whose land grant conflicted with that of the Cherokees—as president. The treaty with the Indians was not even brought before the provisional government for ratification and, thus, nullified all the previously undertaken peacekeeping efforts.[9]

The decision not to guarantee the natives their lands, coupled with the fact that a large Mexican Army—led by Gen. Antonio López de Santa Anna—was approaching San Antonio caused the Cherokees and their allies to become unfriendly toward the Texans. While the Cherokees remained in their villages "with very hostile feelings, and in a state of preparation for war," the Hainais and the Nadacos assembled at the forks of the Trinity River (the site of present-day Dallas) to judge the progress of Santa Anna's army. There they met with members of the Comanche, Wichita, and Kichai tribes, who had been plundering Anglo-American farms in Texas for the past decade.[10]

Throughout the negotiations between the revolutionaries and the tribes of East Texas, the main body of the Kadohadachos had remained quietly in their villages near the border of Louisiana. The Texans, though, had kept a watchful eye on the tribe because of their traditional ties with the Wichitas, the Texans' enemy. Robert A. Irion, commander of the Texan forces at Nacogdoches, believed that the Kadohadachos were "not formidable on account of numbers, but from their influence with the prairie tribes." As early as October, 1835, the Texans unsuccessfully attempted to enlist the Cherokees and their allies to "act against" the Kadohadachos, Kichais, and Wichitas.[11]

The Texans soon focused on the Kadohadachos as their main threat, and the tribe's strength was exaggerated by the republicans, who considered them to be the responsibility of the United States. In 1831, Mexico and the United States had signed a treaty in which each country pledged to keep the tribes within its territory from crossing the border. Thus, by emphasizing and overstating the Kadohadachos' depredations, the Texans hoped to force the United States to abide by the treaty of 1831 and send American troops to Texas in order to curb the greater native threat, and the Texans' embellished reports of the Kadohadachos have made it difficult to obtain a clear picture of the tribe's actions during this confused period.[12]

There is no doubt, however, that the Kadohadachos were in contact with agents of the Mexican government because the Mexicans also realized the tribe's influential position. Manuel Flores was commissioned to enlist the Kadohadacho warriors to fight against the revolutionaries. Flores lived near the Louisiana-Texas border and was one of the Kadohadachos' friends who had been driven from the treaty grounds by Brooks the year before. Flores met with the tribe in February, 1836, and promised them money and "free plunder" if they would attack the Texans, whom he shrewdly characterized as being Americans. In addition to these promises, Flores frightened the Kadohadachos by claiming that the U.S. government "intended to exterminate them." Flores's cajoling influenced the uncertain Tarshar to lead most of the Kadohadacho warriors into Texas along with the Mexican agent.[13]

The Kadohadachos' entrance into Texas on their way to the forks of the Trinity greatly alarmed the settlers. On March 7, it was reported that the warriors of the tribe—along with the Nadacos, Hainais, Kichais, and Wichitas—were roaming the area north of the white settlements in East Texas and stealing horses. The news of Santa Anna's destruction of the Alamo on March 6 spread quickly through Texas, causing the natives on the Trinity to begin their move south toward the white settlements and Nacogdoches. The Indians' advance panicked the Texans, and they immediately made appeals—that focused on the Kadohadachos—to the United States for assistance in halting the hostile tribes. On March 20, after receiving the news of the disaster at San Antonio, John T. Mason of Nacogdoches addressed an urgent dispatch to the commander of the American troops at Fort Jesup. He begged the officer to send a messenger to the Indians in Texas from the United States, "particularly the Caddoes, to make them keep quiet." By April 9, the native force, overestimated at seventeen hundred warriors, had crossed the Trinity on their way to meet with the Cherokees north of Nacogdoches. As reported by the Texans, the force was "conducted" by the Kadohadachos. The following night the warriors, "piloted" by the Kadohadachos, encamped on the Sabine River.[14]

On April 14, in response to the dangerous situation in Texas, Gen. Edmund P. Gaines, in charge of the U.S. troops at Fort Jesup, ordered thirteen companies to move to the border and encamp on the American side of the Sabine River. Gaines also sent messengers to notify Duwali and Tarshar they would be punished by the American troops if they attacked the white settlers in Texas, many of whom were abandoning their homes and fleeing for the Louisiana border.[15]

Gaines had also been notified of Flores's tampering with the tribe and ordered Lt. J. Bonnell to visit the Kadohadacho villages to gauge the true disposition of the tribe. Upon his arrival, Bonnell found that the Kadohadachos had not planted any corn and that only a few warriors remained, the rest having gone to the prairies "in consequence of what Manuel Flores had told them." Bonnell told the few men he found that the "Americans were their friends, and desired [them] to return to their villages, and live and hunt in peace as usual." The warriors recounted Flores's visit and succeeded in convincing Bonnell that the Kadohadachos' intentions were good. One leading man, Cortes, told Bonnell that he had warned Tarshar as he left for Texas not "to trouble or interfere with the whites in any manner whatever; that they depended on the whites, and was it not for them they would have nothing to eat." Cortes said that he would send runners to the prairies to inform the others in his tribe of Bonnell's wish that they return to their villages. He also asked Bonnell to tell General Gaines that the Kadohadachos "were all very friendly towards the whites."[16]

Despite the protestations of friendship, there is evidence that the Kadohadachos intended to do more than just hunt on the prairies; the fact remains that they did travel with a Mexican agent into embattled Texas. If they meant only to hunt—which they usually did in winter rather than in spring—they certainly chose a dangerous time to do so. Despite the exaggerated claims of the Texans, there can be no doubt that the Kadohadachos did at least join the hostile assembly of tribes at the forks of the Trinity, which included their kin, the Nadacos and the Hainais, as well as their longtime allies the Wichitas and the Kichais. It is highly unlikely that the Kadohadachos would remain aloof from these tribes in order to be faithful to the whites.

News of Bonnell's visit, the advance of the American troops to the Sabine, and Gaines's threats caused the Kadohadachos and the other tribes to hesitate. All possibilities for a combined native attack on the Texans vanished completely with the defeat and surrender of Santa Anna's army at San Jacinto on April 21. Newspaper editor William Parker reported from Nacogdoches on April 29 that these events had caused the Indians to disperse and allayed the panic of the white settlers.[17]

By May 13, the Kadohadachos had returned to their villages, where they addressed a letter (through their interpreter, Larkin Edwards) to General Gaines explaining their actions. They stressed their innocence and claimed that both Flores and the Cherokees had unsuccessfully attempted to embroil them in the conflict between the Mexicans and Texans. Nevertheless, Gaines evidently doubted them, for in a letter to Sec. of War Lewis Cass he stated that the Kadohadachos, along with the Cherokees and others, were "disposed to keep up appearances of a pacific disposition . . . . until a more favorable change occurs in the affairs of those pretended friends."[18]

Throughout the summer of 1836, most of the Kadohadacho men remained in their villages, resigned to await their first annuity payment due September 1. A small group of warriors, however, returned to Texas and joined the Wichitas and Kichais in raiding the white settlements for cattle and horses. Fifty natives armed with guns, bows and arrows, and spears attacked three Texans on June 1 as they were driving their cattle to the town of Nashville on the Brazos. The warriors drove off most of the herd and then attacked a nearby settlement, killing two men. Witnesses reported that half the attackers were Kadohadachos; one claimed that he recognized an "old Indian named Douchey, of the Caddoe tribe, whom he knew well." The rest were Kichais, Tawakonis, and Wacos. This raid, coupled with a rumor that another large Mexican force was headed toward Texas, caused General Gaines in July to order his troops across the border to occupy Nacogdoches.[19]

Reports of Kadohadacho depredations in Texas continued to be transmitted to General Gaines throughout the summer of 1836. On July 19, a Shawnee named Spy Buck testified that he had heard that a number of tribes—including the Kichais, Wichitas, Kadohadachos, and Comanches—had recently killed nine white men on the Sulphur River. Spy Buck also claimed that a group of natives was again gathering at the forks of the Trinity River.[20]

Spy Buck's report was confirmed by a Texan agent who, posing as a Mexican Army officer, visited the Cherokee village in August and met with Duwali. The Cherokee leader informed the agent that he had sent a delegation to Matamoros to meet with the Mexican commander in chief of the military forces of the north, Gen. Vicente Filisola. Duwali believed that the Mexican Army was on its way north and that soon the time would be right for the natives "to make a diversion" on behalf of the Mexicans. The chief bragged that he had "sworn an eternal war against the Americans" and was eager to assist the Mexicans in their campaign. Duwali also claimed that members of other tribes—including the Kadohadachos, Hainais, and Nadacos—had been ready for some time and were now encamped on the Trinity "in a great state of exasperation."[21]

The Cherokee headman seems to have been telling the truth, for a group of Texans visited the Hainai village upon receiving the agent's report and found it evacuated. Obviously, the tribe felt threatened among the panicky white settlers as well as being frightened by the American troops at Nacogdoches. They decided to abandon their ancient village once and for all in favor of living with their kin, the Nadacos. Both groups joined the assemblage at the Trinity River in order to await the arrival of the expected Mexican Army; but they waited in vain, for General Filisola was unable to mount his planned invasion into Texas in either 1836 or 1837.[22]

Other small groups of Caddos abandoned the area entirely. Fifteen families, led by the *canaha*, Monwon, traveled all the way to Mexico in the summer of 1836. They remained there until the following summer, when a smallpox epidemic caused them to return to Texas, where they settled with the Hainais and Nadacos. Another group went in the opposite direction, settling along the Kiamichi River in that eastern part of the Indian Territory reserved for the recently removed Choctaw Indians. This band, known as the White Beads, would remain somewhat aloof from the rest of the Caddos until the 1860s.[23]

In response to the charges against the Kadohadachos, General Gaines again sent an officer to their villages to investigate. Maj. B. Riley arrived among the Kadohadachos in mid-August and found that most were residing quietly in their villages. One band, however, was reported to be "hunting" on the prairies of Texas. Riley found a "great abundance" of whiskey in the villages, which caused him to conclude that the Kadohadachos were "a poor, miserable people, incapable of the smallest exertion, either as it regards living, or any thing else, except liquor." Indeed, Tarshar was drunk when Riley arrived at his village, and the major had to wait until the following morning to address him. At that time Riley informed the hungover Tarshar of the reports of Kadohadacho raids on the Texan settlements and other claims that the tribe intended to join the Mexicans. He said that General Gaines "forbids [this] most positively" and warned that "if any person comes . . . to persuade you to go to war, do not listen to them, but let them know that you intend to be peacable [sic]." The major also advised Tarshar to avoid liquor.[24]

Tarshar sadly admitted that alcohol was a problem and "that the whiskey traders make us miserable by coming among us . . . they make us very poor." He insisted, however, that the tribe had "never fought against the whites, nor ever had any disposition to do so." He soothed Riley by claiming that "all of our children have been raised in this country with the Americans, and we consider ourselves their brothers and best friends, and we like them very much." Tarshar concluded by promising that he would follow the major's advice and report anyone who incited them to go to war. Riley left the Kadohadachos convinced that they were "very peaceably disposed."[25]

Tarshar and most of the Kadohadachos remained quietly in their villages because they were desperately awaiting their first annuity payment of ten thousand dollars and did not want to jeopardize the transaction. Unfortunately, the tribe had given the power of attorney to Jehiel Brooks at the close of the treaty council in 1835, and they depended on him to deliver their money. On September 10, 1836, nine days after the payment was due, Brooks received the Kadohadacho annuity from the Treasury Department in Washington.[26]

In October, Brooks met with the Kadohadacho headmen in Shreveport in order to pay the tribe. The treaty had called for the annuity to be paid in cash. Brooks, however, attempted to pay the tribe in goods rather than money. He showed them ten boxes—each marked as being worth one thousand dollars—which he claimed had been sent directly from President Jackson. However, Brooks would not allow the boxes to be opened until the Kadohadachos had signed a receipt for them, which Tarshar, knowing Brooks's character, refused to do. Brooks then left and hired John C. McLeod as his agent, promising him five hundred dollars if he could procure a signed receipt from the Kadohadachos. The standoff continued for a few days following Brooks's departure until the Kadohadacho *canahas*, being fearful of losing their entire annuity for the year if they did not accept, finally agreed to sign the receipt to receive the boxes of goods.[27]

Upon opening the boxes the Kadohadacho leaders "were very much disappointed and complained that they had not received one-half of what was due them." The boxes contained seven kegs of lead, three boxes of powder, blankets, clothes, trinkets, and about fifty "common" rifles. Larkin Edwards witnessed the transaction, and he believed the contents were worth only between fifteen hundred and two thousand dollars. Three years later, when the matter was officially investigated, it was acknowledged "that Brooks [had] realized an enormous profit."[28]

In response to Brooks's swindle, the Kadohadachos met in council on November 27, 1836, and gave John G. Green the power of attorney to accept their annuity payment for 1837. In an attempt to recover their stolen annuity the tribe addressed a letter to the secretary of war informing him of Brooks's wrongdoing, but the federal government did not respond to the entreaties of the tribe. This inactivity not only calls into question the seriousness of the Jacksonian claims of paternal protection of Indians, it also demonstrates the ineptitude of the administration's handling of the Texas crisis. Although the Jackson administration had been receiving continual reports of Kadohadacho depredations from the Texans, it had failed to supervise the payment of the tribe's annuity. No action was taken by the government even after being informed of Brooks's theft, and the dangerous situation on the border was allowed to worsen.[29]

Rather than spend a miserable winter starving near Shreveport, some of the Kadohadacho warriors entered Texas and joined the bands of marauders who preyed on the white settlers. In November, 1836, a group of Kadohadachos ambushed a troop of Texas Rangers on the Guadalupe River. Two months later, a mixed force of one hundred Kickapoo and Kadohadacho warriors invaded the settlements on the Brazos River near Nashville and killed several families. In response, Maj. Gen. George Bernard Erath, with fourteen Texas Rangers, surprised the raiders eighteen miles east of Austin on Elm Creek. The Texans killed ten warriors before the natives could take shelter in a thicket and return fire. Erath and his followers retreated without incident after the loss of two men.[30]

Texan emissaries William H. Wharton and Memucan Hunt dutifully communicated the reports of Kadohadacho depredations to John H. Forsyth, secretary of state for the new administration of Pres. Martin Van Buren. Wharton and Hunt urged Forsyth to reoccupy Nacogdoches (abandoned by Gaines's force in November, 1836) in order to keep the Kadohadachos "in check." Forsyth referred the matter to Sec. of War Joel H. Poinsett, who informed the Texans on April 14 that the American soldiers would not cross the border to reoccupy Nacogdoches, while also assuring them that the troops would be instructed to "use increased vigilance to restrain all hostile manifestations on the part of the Indians." In July, 1837, the commander at Fort Jesup, Col. James Many, sent an officer to the Kadohadacho villages to investigate the charges against the tribe again. The headmen denied committing any attacks on the whites and "appeared to be very anxious to be on friendly terms with them." It was confirmed, though, that "some of the straggling parties which committed depredations" in the interior of Texas were composed of Kadohadacho warriors.[31]

In the meantime the Nadacos and the Hainais temporarily settled their differences with the Texans. Sam Houston, the first elected president of Texas, realized the dangers and the high cost of continuing the hostilities with the tribes of Texas and attempted to carry out a policy of peace. Houston understood the problems of the tribes and was well-disposed to them since he had married a Cherokee woman and lived with a part of the tribe from 1829 to 1833. In his inaugural address of October 22, 1836, Houston stated that "treaties of peace and amity and the maintenance of good faith with the Indians, present themselves to my mind as the most rational ground on which to obtain their friendship."[32]

Following the failure of Houston's first commission to negotiate a peaceful settlement, the Texas president turned to his old friend Duwali for assistance. In order to win the Cherokees' favor, Houston had resubmitted the Cherokee treaty of February 23, 1836, to the Texas Senate for approval. Duwali, believing that his tribe now stood to profit by friendship with the Texans, agreed to act as Houston's emissary, and in March,

1837, he set out on an extended visit to meet with the prairie tribes. The Cherokee chief found a group of Kadohadachos camped near the Hainai-Nadaco village along the upper Trinity River and got them all to agree to Houston's peace proposition.[33]

Encouraged by Duwali's entreaties, the Hainais and Nadacos pursued peace with the Texans throughout the summer of 1837. In August, a deputation from the two tribes met with a group of East Texan citizens at the residence of Luís Sánchez and asked whether the whites were willing to "conclude a firm and lasting peace" with them. When Col. James Smith announced to the emissaries that the Texans would agree to peace, the Hainais and Nadacos gave a "spontaneous burst or shout of satisfaction which they were unable to restrain."[34]

On August 21, the tribes met in council with Texan commissioners to conclude a peace treaty. The Standing Committee on Indian Affairs recommended that this treaty be ratified by the Texas Senate two months later. Unfortunately, there is no record of whether the Senate followed this advice, and the treaty has subsequently been lost. During this period, however, the Republic of Texas negotiated a series of treaties with various Texas tribes, and it is probable that the Nadaco and Hainai agreement was similar to these. The provisions of these treaties included pledges of perpetual peace and amity by both parties, a promise from the Texans to supply each tribe with an authorized trader, and a promise to punish any aggressions committed upon the Indians by Texas citizens. The Texans jealously guarded their rights to the soil, however, and the treaties did not reserve any land for the tribes.[35] Certainly, the Hainais and the Nadacos accepted the terms and agreed to peace only because it seemed that, by the summer of 1837, the Texans had secured their grip on the area. There was no sign of assistance from General Filisola in Mexico, and the peace with the Texans—so the tribes could settle down and plant their crops in security—seemed to be the only viable alternative that remained. Thus, the Republic of Texas and the two Caddo tribes maintained friendly relations for the remainder of 1837 and into the following summer.

Meanwhile, the main body of the Kadohadachos under Tarshar was awaiting their annuity payment for 1837. Unaware that the Kadohadachos had revoked his power of attorney, Jehiel Brooks applied for the money, undoubtedly in hope of repeating the profitable events of the previous year. John Green, however, was awarded the coveted prize of agent for the Kadohadachos, and on August 11, 1837, he received the ten thousand dollars in Washington. Brooks protested to C. A. Harris, the new commissioner of Indian affairs, claiming that the power of attorney granted to him had placed "its revocation beyond the control of the chiefs."[36]

Commissioner Harris turned the matter over to Secretary of War Poinsett, who, although he was receiving reports of Kadohadacho depredations in Texas, failed to make the connection between the tribe's annuity problems and their hostile activities. Instead of taking actions to clear up the matter, Poinsett asked the attorney general's office for an opinion, not on the wrongdoing of Brooks, but on the legality of the Kadohadacho revocation of Brooks's power of attorney. In other words, had the tribe treated Brooks illegally? Fortunately, the attorney general ruled that the power of attorney "was revocable at the pleasure of its maker," the Kadohadachos.[37]

This small victory for the tribe was a Pyrrhic one, for Green turned out to be an even greedier thief than Brooks. Green returned to Shreveport in September, 1837, contacted Larkin Edwards, and announced that he had brought goods with him with which to pay the Kadohadacho annuity. Green was reluctant to make the payment in Shreveport, so he arranged for Edwards's son to deliver the tribe's goods by boat at a nearby lake. As the year before, the Kadohadachos were extremely disappointed by what they found, for the absent Green had sent only a few kegs of powder and one hundred pounds of lead, "not exceeding fifteen hundred dollars" in worth.[38]

Having their annuity stolen from them two years in a row caused a number of Kadohadachos to abandon the United States once and for all. On November 10, 1837, a company of 18 Texas Rangers headed by Lt. A. B. Benthuysen was attacked by 150 warriors on the headwaters of the Trinity River. Most of the participating Indians were Wichitas, but there were "a few" Kichai and Kadohadacho warriors as well, and 10 Rangers were killed and 3 badly wounded. The survivors limped into a Kadohadacho village located just west of the forks of the Trinity. Benthuysen found the "warriors drawn up to receive us in a hostile manner, they were all armed with Rifles & the squaws had Bows & Arrows." The lieutenant expected a struggle, but "after a good deal of parleying," the Rangers were allowed to stay the night and dress their wounds.[39]

The Kadohadachos who remained in Louisiana decided at the insistence of the neighboring whites to appoint G. H. Scott as their new agent to obtain the 1838 annuity payment. Scott actually lived on the Texas side of the border and had strong ties to the republic. In fact, it seems that Scott, as his subsequent actions reveal, was much more concerned with the interests of Texas than with those of the Kadohadachos. As their agent, he hoped to control the tribe by paying them with food and clothing instead of arms and ammunition, thus preventing them from committing hostile acts in Texas.[40]

Although Tarshar consented to the appointment of Scott as the Kadohadacho agent, he and many others of the tribe had nearly given up hope of ever receiving the annuity. They were torn between waiting yet another miserable year near Shreveport or joining those who had severed ties with the United States to settle in Texas near the Nadacos and the Hainais. Tarshar lacked the bold decisiveness of previous *caddices*, however, and hesitated to take action without the approval of a white benefactor.

Plans were being laid south of the Rio Grande that would soon cause Tarshar and two-thirds of the Kadohadachos to abandon the United States and enter Texas as enemies of the republic. General Filisola and Brig. Gen. Valentin Canalizo, the commanders of the Mexican military forces in the north, had not given up hope of reacquiring Texas. They had remained in contact with Duwali and the Cherokees and had formulated a plan that would employ the tribes of Texas, along with a group of discontented Mexicans located near Nacogdoches, to harass the Texans until a larger Mexican force could enter the province and reclaim it.

By 1838, the Mexicans were ready to put their plan into action. They now felt sure that they could count on the full support of the Cherokees since the Texas Senate—despite the wishes of President Houston—voted in December, 1837, to nullify the treaty of February 23, 1836, upon which Duwali had rested his hopes. Two months later, on February 27, 1838, General Canalizo met with Capt. Vicente Córdova in Matamoros to give him instructions. A Mexican refugee from Nacogdoches, Córdova was considered to be the commander of the loyal Mexican troops in Texas. Canalizo told Córdova that he did not feel the Texans should be allowed to "augment their population, strength, and resources, by remaining in peace." Therefore, he ordered Captain Córdova to travel to Texas and enlist the services of the Native Americans by telling them that "as soon as they have agreed in taking up arms, they will be rewarded according to their merits." Córdova, with the help of Manuel Flores, was ordered to encourage the natives to burn the settlers' homes and crops, steal their livestock, and ruin their commerce.[41]

General Canalizo later assured the Indians that these operations would "ensure the quiet possession of your lands and prevent any adventurer from again disturbing the peaceful repose of your families, or from trampling under foot the soil in which are deposited the remains of your ancestors." Canalizo promised that the Mexican government would send a commissioner to give each tribe "possession of the land they are entitled to" following the success of the campaign.[42]

Upon receiving his instructions, Flores immediately informed the tribes of Córdova's mission and arranged a council to be held upon the captain's arrival. The news of Córdova's mission caused such excitement that the Cherokees and the Kadohadachos sent twenty warriors to Matamoros to escort Córdova across the Rio Grande. Captain Córdova entered

Texas on May 29, 1838, along with the native escort and seventy-two Mexicans, thirty-four soldiers from La Bahía, and Julian Pedro Miracle, who kept a journal of the trip.[43]

As Córdova made his way northward, Duwali arranged for a meeting of all the tribes in East Texas to determine a plan of action. Although the hostile Kadohadachos in Texas did not attend the first council on June 14, they made it known beforehand that they would follow the decision of the Cherokees and their allies. At the council, the Cherokee, Shawnee, Delaware, Kickapoo, and Coushatta headmen informed the Texas emissary, Jeff Wright, that "war was inevitable" if they did not receive the land title granted to them in the treaty of February 1836. They felt the Texans were "making fools of them" and threatened to form a hostile alliance with the Wacos, Kichais, and Tawakonis, if there were no results forthcoming.[44]

By June 20, when Manuel Flores joined the Córdova party just west of the Guadalupe River, the Texans still had not responded to the Indian threats. A group of Kickapoos "kindly" received the Mexicans between the Brazos and the Navasota Rivers and accompanied them almost to the Trinity River, where they met Duwali on July 8. Twelve days later, Captain Córdova held a council with the Cherokees, Delawares, and Shawnees at Duwali's village. The only Kadohadachos present were the ones that had accompanied the party from Matamoros. Córdova asserted that he had five hundred loyal Mexicans near Nacogdoches under his command, and he asked the natives to join his troops in attacking the Texans. Although the Indians had not received a response from President Houston, they objected to making any hostile movements until the arrival of General Canalizo and his troops; however, the group did agree that war against the Texans would begin as soon as "circumstances would permit."[45]

Nine days later Miracle crossed the Neches River and met with "the captain" of the Kadohadachos, who (though unnamed) appears to be Tarshar. Miracle informed the *caddi* of the planned campaign against the Texans, to which Tarshar responded hesitantly; he told Miracle he was reluctant to return to the United States to receive the third annuity payment due in September. Another warrior, Nehomeceno, informed the Mexican that he "preferred to remain with [the Mexicans] and fight" rather than return to Louisiana. Tarshar, bereft of any hopes of ever obtaining any money in Louisiana, finally accepted the invitation. Pressed against the wall by the United States, Tarshar decided to take a large risk by supporting the Mexicans despite doubting Mexico's ability to defeat the Texans. Unfortunately for all the Caddo tribes, his gamble failed.[46]

Córdova and Miracle continued on their trip eastward, and in early August they encamped on the Angelina River near Nacogdoches. There

Córdova gathered together a disappointingly small force of only three hundred Mexican and Indian men. Although a few Kadohadacho warriors were among Córdova's men, most of Tarshar's band was unable to join this contingent before it was discovered by the Texans on August 7. Maj. Gen. Thomas Jefferson Rusk, commander of the Texas militia, immediately called for volunteers, and President Houston also asked Colonel Many to send U.S. troops from Fort Jesup since the Kickapoos, Kadohadachos, and other American Indians had joined "the rebel Mexicans" and were ready to attack and plunder Nacogdoches.[47]

Colonel Many sent an officer to Nacogdoches, who reported on August 18 that "there had been good grounds for fearing such an attack, but the danger was over" since Córdova's force had slipped away from the Texans rather than fight; at first, they moved north toward the Cherokee village on the Sabine River and then westward to the upper Trinity River. The Mexican-Indian force remained intact for another two months, desperately awaiting reinforcements that, it turned out, would never arrive.[48]

The Córdova Rebellion, though unsuccessful, convinced many Texans that President Houston's peace policy was not working and that the Republic of Texas should take a more aggressive stance regarding Indians. A presidential election was upcoming, and many of Houston's political enemies charged that he had been ineffectual in the face of Córdova and the Indians. On September 3, 1838, less than a month after the Córdova Rebellion, Mirabeau Buonaparte Lamar, a proven foe of the tribes, was elected president of Texas. In his first message to the Texas Congress, Lamar boldly stated that he considered Houston's policy of pacification a complete failure and announced that the time had come for "the prosecution of an exterminating war on [Texas' Indian] warriors; which will admit of no compromise and have no termination except in their total extinction or total expulsion." Although Lamar was not inaugurated until December 10, 1838, his election had immediate repercussions. The aggressiveness of Texas troops toward the natives in October and November, coupled with the fact that the commanders often notified President-elect Lamar—not President Houston—of their actions, demonstrates that the hostile energies of Texas had been unleashed by Lamar's election.[49]

This, combined with continuing Kadohadacho depredations in Texas and circumstances in Louisiana concerning the Kadohadacho annuity, resulted in a showdown between the Texans and the tribe before the end of the year. Events leading toward this climax had begun in June, 1838, when ex-Agent Green, in an act of dubious legality, had given the Kadohadacho power of attorney to a Shreveport merchant named Thomas Williamson. Williamson was awarded the ten thousand–dollar annuity payment for 1838 by Commissioner Harris despite the protestations of newly appointed Agent Scott. Williamson then hired his partner, Charles A. Sewall, to conduct business with the Kadohadachos.[50]

Sewall notified the tribe to assemble in Shreveport, and on October 11, they revoked Green's power of attorney and formally approved Sewall as their agent. In Sewall, the tribe had finally obtained an honest agent who would actually serve their needs. By this time, however, Tarshar and two-thirds of the tribe had left Louisiana for the prairies of Texas, and, thus, the mark of the *canaha* Tsauninot, heretofore second chief of the Kadohadachos, was found atop the appointment of Sewall.[51]

Tarshar and his band, severely disappointed at the failure of the Córdova Rebellion, were actively hostile after arriving in Texas, and throughout the fall of 1838, Kadohadacho warriors continually raided the white settlements. G. W. Bonnell, Texas commissioner of Indian affairs, reported that the Kadohadachos were roaming the headwaters of the Brazos, Trinity, and Colorado Rivers and joining the Wacos "in their predatory expeditions." Bonnell characterized them as being "braver and more desperate than the Comanches."[52]

While most of the Kadohadachos had settled in a village with the Hainais and the Nadacos on the western fork of the Trinity River, a few warriors remained with Córdova. On October 14, General Rusk learned that Córdova's troops had gathered at the Kickapoo village on the Trinity downstream from the Caddo encampment, and he mounted an expedition. Rusk was attacked before he could reach the village, however, and the Texas troops lost eleven men before repulsing the attackers, who also left eleven dead on the field. Among the Indian dead were Kadohadacho, Coushatta, Biloxi, and Cherokee warriors.[53]

A week later, on October 21, Brig. Gen. John H. Dyer led eighty Texans within two miles of the Kadohadacho village on the Trinity. The Texans fought a "skirmish" with the tribe, during which six Kadohadacho warriors were killed. General Dyer reported both that the frontier was exposed and that he expected to have to call out his entire force of Rangers to "protect the frontier against" the Kadohadachos and other tribes.[54]

While the Texans were panicking over a feared Kadohadacho onslaught, back in Shreveport Sewall was distributing the first part of the annuity to the 160 remaining members of Tsauninot's band. Over a period of five months, Sewall distributed over thirteen thousand dollars' worth of goods, mainly in the form of food, clothing, and alcohol, to the tribe. On October 25, significantly, he gave the tribe a "scant supply for hunting" that consisted of seventeen rifles, eighteen pistols, eight kegs of powder, and two kegs of lead.[55]

A few days later, a report reached Shreveport that two families had been murdered by Indians just across the border in Texas; and again, on November 7, another report reached Shreveport indicating that a hostile Kadohadacho-Hainai force roamed East Texas. The news that the Kadohadachos had just received arms and ammunition from their agent in Louisiana was communicated across the frontier as well. The tribe, led by Tsauninot, had just begun to travel west for their annual winter hunt "but discovered people on both sides of the border suspected them of hostile intentions"; as a result, they returned to Shreveport to consult with their newfound friend, Charles Sewall. The agent directed Tsauninot and his band to an island in the Red River twelve miles from Shreveport, where they could find game and remain apart from the whites for the winter.[56]

In the meantime General Dyer had assembled a force of four hundred men in northeast Texas to stop Indian raids. Upon learning of the murders of the two families near the border—which he attributed to the newly armed Kadohadachos—Dyer ordered Capt. Edward H. Tarrant and his company of forty militia to "destroy," if possible, the Kadohadachos in Texas; but if that was not possible, Tarrant "was to follow them across the line & exterminate them." On November 23, General Rusk, realizing the seriousness of a body of Texas troops crossing the international border, took command and ordered thirty men of the Port Caddo company of Rangers to assist him. This force of seventy was joined by eighty local Texans led by one-time Kadohadacho agent, G. H. Scott.[57]

Neighboring whites informed the Kadohadachos of the advancing Texas troops, and the tribe immediately retreated to the protection of a canebrake. A few Texan scouts approached the Kadohadacho stronghold on November 23 and were fired upon by the warriors. Tsauninot maintained this hostile stance until the rest of Rusk's force arrived and he realized he was outnumbered. Wisely, Tsauninot opted for peace and called out that "he did not want to fight, but desired a talk."[58]

Rusk and his adjutant, Col. Hugh McLeod, advanced and met Tsauninot and one of his warriors. Rusk told the *canaha* that he did not wish to kill his people, but he insisted that the Kadohadachos either give up their arms and ammunition to their agent in Shreveport and never enter Texas again or be forced to fight "upon the spot." Tsauninot responded that he also did not wish to fight but that his people would starve if they gave up their arms and ammunition and could not hunt. Rusk told the chief that the Republic of Texas would provide sustenance for the Kadohadachos as long as their arms were detained from them. Tsauninot was forced to agree to these terms but stated he could not immediately accompany Rusk to Shreveport, since he had to retrieve the Kadohadacho women and children who were guarding their horses on the other side of a lake. The two parties then exchanged hostages to be returned after the

Kadohadachos arrived in Shreveport to formalize the agreement before Agent Sewall.[59]

Colonel McLeod accompanied Tsauninot as his hostage and was treated "kindly" by the tribe. The *canaha* offered to go to Nacogdoches and remain there until the end of the hostilities between the Texans and the Indians if it would ease matters. Tsauninot insisted that his band was no longer connected with Tarshar's, but that his warriors were often—as in the present instance—suspected of Tarshar's "rascalities."[60]

On November 24, Rusk and the seventy Texas Rangers entered Shreveport, while Scott's men assembled at his ranch just across the border. Five days later, the Kadohadachos met with Rusk and Sewall in Shreveport and signed an agreement in which they agreed to give up their arms—except for ten guns with which to hunt—to Agent Sewall and to remain within the United States, where they would be supported by the Texas government. The Texans also pledged that no whites would be allowed to "molest or interrupt" the tribe or their property. Sufficiently chastised, Tsauninot and his band retreated to a small peninsula between Cross Lake and Caddo Lake, where they quietly remained for the rest of the winter.[61]

His mission successfully accomplished, Rusk and his troops returned to Texas and joined Dyer's forces on their march to the villages of the three Caddo tribes on the forks of the Trinity River. Upon hearing of the approach of four hundred armed Texans, the Caddos—hastily, in fact—abandoned their encampment and traveled west to the upper reaches of the Brazos. They picked up camp so hastily that they left behind buffalo skins, blankets, and even a few guns. The Texans destroyed the remnants of the village but broke off pursuit because it was the dead of winter and their provisions had run out. From the Brazos River, the Caddo tribes eventually retreated across the Red River into Indian Territory, abandoning Texas altogether. Thus, Texan hostility caused both Kadohadacho bands—along with the Hainais and the Nadacos—to spend the winter of 1838–39 in the United States, despite the provisions of the treaty of 1835.[62]

Under the direction of President Lamar, Texans continued their brutal campaign to rid their republic of Indians. In March, 1839, Texas troops caught and defeated Captain Córdova and his force, which had dwindled to only seventy Mexicans and Indians. Flores was killed by the Texans a few months later, and several letters were found on his body that again commissioned him to incite the natives against the Texans. One of these letters was addressed to the captains of the Kadohadachos and the Cherokees.[63]

In response, President Lamar sent nine hundred Texas troops to the Cherokee village in July, 1839. The Indians fired upon the Texans, who then attacked and massacred one hundred Cherokees, including Duwali. The Texas Army destroyed the Cherokee lodges and cornfields and captured and scattered their cattle. Like the Caddo tribes, the remaining Cherokees—as well as the other emigrant bands—fled across the Red River and sought refuge in the Indian Territory.[64]

Although President Lamar's actions eliminated most of the Cherokees and their fellow emigrants from Texas, the Caddo tribes—being natives of Texas—were eventually allowed to return. However, the Caddos had learned a few important lessons during the period of the Texas Revolution: only through unity could they survive, and, even with unity, the tribe could never afford to go to war against the Euro-Americans. From this point on and despite continued pressures, the Caddos would always pursue a policy of peace with the whites.

Chapter 9

The Caddos Return
to Texas, 1839–54

Captains, if you love your children, advise them not bad, but good; and show to them the white path . . . we are made alike, all look alike and are one people, which you must recollect. The Great Spirit our father, and our mother, the earth, sees and hears all we say in council. . . . I hold the white path in my hands, (a string of wampum beads) given by our white brothers. look at it: see, it is all fair. To you Waco and Tawakoni captains and warriors I give it. stop going to war with the white people. they, the white people, gave it unto me: I give it now to you: use it as I have done and your women and children will be happy, and sleep free of danger.
—Nadaco *caddi* Iesh to the Treaty Council,
May 14, 1844[1]

THE 1838 "INVASION" OF THE UNITED STATES by the Texas troops actually had fortunate results for the Caddos. The incident caused the Van Buren administration to investigate the matter, take note of the Kadohadachos' plight, and afford the tribe a modicum of paternal protection sorely lacking in the period following the treaty of 1835. Ultimately, this led to the reunification of the Kadohadachos as well as increased unity among the three Caddo tribes. Together, the Caddos made peace with the Republic of Texas and were allowed to settle on the upper reaches of the Brazos River. For a while, the Caddos thrived in their new home and strove tirelessly to effect peace between the Texans and other tribes. Despite the Caddos' efforts, the Texans, following their entrance into the United States, again assumed a hostile stance toward the tribe. Ironically, the tribe was forced to look to the United States for protection and ultimately formed a friendship with the same government that had forced the Kadohadachos to abandon their homes in 1835.

At the beginning of 1839, the Caddo tribes were gathered in three groups, all located outside the Republic of Texas. The small White Bead group still resided among the Choctaw Indians in the Indian Territory. Tsauninot and his band of Kadohadachos remained in Louisiana near

Caddo Lake, where they found enough game to survive the winter. The rest of the Kadohadachos under Tarshar, as well as the Nadacos and Hainais, had retreated into the Indian Territory west of the White Beads. Iesh, one of the most impressive *caddices* in Caddo history, led the Nadacos. Born in 1806, he was called José María by the whites, and although he was small in stature, Iesh had an indomitable spirit that would guide him in keeping the shattered Caddo tribes together during the desperate decades to come.[2]

Not only did Iesh lead the Nadacos, he exerted a large degree of influence with the Hainais as well. So many Hainai headmen had died during the Texas Revolution that the tribe had no *caddi* and was being led by a prominent *canaha* named Bedi, who often deferred to Iesh. By the time the position of Hainai *caddi* was filled by the young Toweash a few years later, Hainai dependence on Iesh and the Nadacos had been firmly established, and Toweash was considered to be Iesh's "second chief." The Kadohadachos would also experience leadership problems in the future, and Iesh's influence over them increased as well; thus, the stage was set for the ultimate unification of the Caddos.[3]

Soon after retreating into the Indian Territory, small Caddo groups recrossed the Red River into Texas for their winter hunt. One hunting party captured an escaped white woman, kidnapped by the Comanches only thirty miles north of Austin, whom they returned to her kidnappers—she finally, successfully escaped once and for all in 1840. The woman later reported that this band "retired up the Brazos," where they rejoined the rest of the tribe—which had also crossed into Texas—and planted corn.[4]

While the Caddo tribes—except for Tsauninot's band and the White Beads—had returned to Texas, events were taking place in the United States that brought the Kadohadachos' predicament to the attention of the Van Buren administration. Missouri Sen. Thomas Hart Benton and Louisiana Rep. R. J. Garland demanded an inquiry into General Rusk's "invasion" of Louisiana, and in response, Secretary Poinsett ordered an investigation of the Kadohadachos' situation. In March, 1839, Colonel Many met with Tsauninot, and found his homeless band of 162 people "destitute in every respect." The *canaha* explained the tribe's mistreatment at the hands of former agents Brooks and Green but noted that his tribe was "tolerably well satisfied with Sewall . . . [for] he had supplied them well with much provisions."[5]

Colonel Many's report forced the federal government to take an active interest in the Kadohadachos' welfare. While nothing was done to recover the stolen annuities of the previous two years, William Armstrong, agent for the Choctaw Indians (who had recently been removed to the Indian Territory), was entrusted with the Kadohadacho annuity

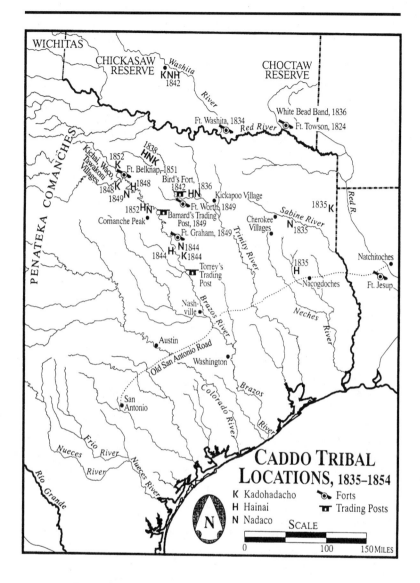

WICHITAS

CHICKASAW
RESERVE **KNH**
1842

Washita
River

CHOCTAW
RESERVE

White Bead Band, 1836

Ft. Washita, 1834

Red River

Ft. Towson, 1824

Natchitoches

1838
HNK
1852
K Ft. Belknap, 1851
1848 **K H** 1848
1848 **N** 1849
Kichai, Waco,
Tawakoni
Villages

PENATEKA COMANCHES

Bird's Fort,
1842

1836

HN Kickapoo Village

1852 **HN** Barnard's Trading
Comanche Peak Post, 1849
Ft. Worth, 1849

Cherokee
Villages **N** 1835

1835 **K**

Sabine River

Red R.

N 1844
1844 **H K** 1844

Ft. Graham, 1849

Torrey's
Trading
Post

Trinity River

1835
H

Nacogdoches

Natchitoches

Ft. Jesup

Nash-
ville

Brazos River

Neches River

Austin

Old San Antonio Road

Washington

San
Antonio

Colorado River

Brazos

River

Nueces *River*

Frio River

Rio Grande

Nueces River

**CADDO TRIBAL
LOCATIONS, 1835–1854**

K Kadohadacho   Forts

H Hainai   Trading Posts

N Nadaco   SCALE

0   100   150 MILES

payment for 1839. He was also instructed to find the Kadohadachos a
permanent home in the Indian Territory. In January, 1840, Armstrong
sent H. G. Rind to meet with Tsauninot and the headmen to determine
their wishes pertaining to the annuity payment. The headmen told Rind
that they had "the utmost confidence in [Sewall], who they say has be-
friended them in all of their difficulties," and they officially retained him
as their agent. Therefore, Rind assigned Sewall the responsibility of
distributing the 1839 annuity to the Kadohadachos under Tsauninot.
In addition, an official agreement was made with the Kadohadacho

headmen "to select . . . and procure a home" for the tribe, with either the Choctaws or any other tribe residing in the Indian Territory.[6]

In August, 1840, Tarshar's son, Bintah, visited Agent Armstrong at Fort Towson, located at the junction of the Kiamichi and the Red Rivers in the Indian Territory. Bintah had been sent by his father to inquire about the final annuity payment due the tribe in 1840, which he felt his band deserved since they had yet to receive any of the previous payments. Bintah also indicated interest in settling among the Choctaws in the Indian Territory, as the Texans would "not let [the Caddos] remain where they are." Armstrong responded encouragingly, and he gave Bintah a medal for his father, telling him to return to Fort Towson in sixty days.[7]

Tarshar, however, waited seven months to contact Armstrong through a member of the Chickasaw tribe, which had also recently been settled in the Indian Territory. The Chickasaw informed the agent that Tarshar's band would arrive at Fort Towson later in the spring to receive the final annuity payment, adding that the *caddi* hoped that he would not have to share the money with Tsauninot's band. Catching wind of Tarshar's desires, Tsauninot moved his band out of Louisiana and into the Indian Territory to be near Fort Towson.[8]

Both bands informed Armstrong that they wished for their annuity to be paid out in cash rather than in goods. In addition, Armstrong recommended that payment be made directly to the heads of each family, rather than through Agent Sewall. Armstrong asked the Choctaw chief if he would allow the Kadohadachos to receive their annuity on his reservation. He gave his approval, feeling that it might be the means "in which the Caddo settle down in his territory as part of [the Choctaw] nation." However, the Choctaw chief insisted that the Kadohadachos could not settle permanently on his lands as an independent tribe, a point which proved to be the Kadohadachos' major obstacle to finding a home in the Indian Territory.[9]

By September, 1841, both Kadohadacho bands were on the Choctaw Reservation waiting to receive their annuity. Both Tarshar and Tsauninot died that fall, and their deaths helped to clear the way for the Kadohadachos' reunification. A leading *canaha*, Red Bear, assumed the position of Kadohadacho leader in the stead of the young and inexperienced Bintah. On November 8, 1841, Armstrong received the ten thousand dollars from the Treasury Department, and he delivered the cash individually to members of both bands later that winter. The fact that all the bands were equal parties in the final annuity payment can be inferred from Red Bear's letter of July, 1842, which stated "with my people are the Anadarkos [Nadacos] and Ionies [Hainais] and we are all as one people." Since there was no mention of the schism within the Kadohadacho tribe, it seems that the split was healed by the fair payment of the final annuity.[10]

Following the receipt of the final annuity payment, the entire Caddo tribe—Kadohadachos, Nadacos, and Hainais—decided to move westward onto the Chickasaw Reservation. In the spring of 1842, they planted crops on the right bank of the Washita River (probably in present Carter County, Oklahoma) where they hoped to settle permanently, even though they had not received the official approval of the Chickasaws. Unforeseen circumstances arose, however, that led the Caddo tribes back across the Red River where they were, ironically, welcomed by the Republic of Texas.[11]

The Caddos' return to Texas was surprising since conflict with the Texan settlers had continued even after the tribe had retreated into the Indian Territory. In July, 1842, the Caddos heard rumors that a party of Texans was on its way across the Red River to seek vengeance from them for stealing horses. Red Bear sought out the headmen of the Creeks—another southeastern tribe resettled in the Indian Territory—for help, claiming that the Caddo tribes were "determined to lay down the hatchet" and seek peace with the Texans. He complained, however, that the Kichais, Wichitas, and Wacos were "constantly bringing horses and scalps" from Texas into the Indian Territory. Red Bear also reported that he had learned "from good authority" that a large number of Texans were about to cross the Red River and that the result of their invasion would "be a general massacre." The only way to avoid this, he felt, would be for the Caddos to evacuate their villages and crops, but Red Bear feared that the Texans would view this move as a sign of hostility. Thus, perhaps to avoid conflict, Red Bear asked Robert M. Jones, an influential Choctaw, to act as an intermediary between the Caddos and the Republic of Texas.[12]

Fortunately for the tribe, the time proved right for peace. Sam Houston had been inaugurated president of Texas for the second time in September, 1841, and had announced the resumption of his peace policy in his message to the Texas Congress. He stated that the Indians, "finding a disposition on our part to treat them fairly and justly, and dreading a loss of trade . . . would be powerfully affected, both by feelings of confidence and motives of interest, to preserve peace and maintain good faith. The hope of obtaining peace by means of war has hitherto proved utterly fallacious." President Houston began implementing this policy in July, 1842, the same month that Red Bear asked the Creeks and Robert Jones for assistance. The president appointed three commissioners to "treat with any and all Indians on the frontiers of Texas" in an attempt to end the warfare between the tribes and the white settlers.[13]

The Texas commissioners met Jones in the Indian Territory in late July, 1842, and arranged a meeting with twenty Caddo warriors who happened to be in the area. The two groups agreed to hold a formal peace "talk" in August at the Caddo villages on the Washita, at which Col. Ethan Stroud gave the warriors tobacco to distribute to the Caddo headmen as a token of peace. Jones sent a letter to Red Bear advising him to "make a white road that you and all others who choose, may travel in peace and safety."[14]

On August 24, 1842, the Caddo *canahas* met with the Texas commissioners and entered into an agreement initiating a three-year period of close relations between the Caddos and the Republic of Texas. Adopting the role they had carried out so often before, the Caddos agreed to be emissaries of peace and visit with the hostile tribes in order to invite them to assemble at the Waco village on the Brazos to meet the Texas commissioners.[15]

After various delays, the treaty council was held in March, 1843, on Tehuacana Creek, about six miles southeast of the present city of Waco. Present were representatives of the Kadohadacho, Hainai, Nadaco, Delaware, Shawnee, Tawakoni, Kichai, Waco, and Wichita tribes, as well as the Republic of Texas, represented by three commissioners and one secretary. Since the Texans had solicited the assistance of the United States in making peace with the tribes, the Cherokee agent, Pierce M. Butler, appeared on behalf of Pres. John Tyler. After the "usual preliminary of smoking [was] finished," a letter from President Houston was read and interpreted for the tribes. Texan commissioner G. W. Terrell made the opening address, and he was followed by Butler, who urged the tribes to make peace.[16]

The headmen of the individual tribes responded the following day. After the chiefs of the Delawares and the Shawnees had agreed to peace, Bintah, who had assumed the position of Kadohadacho *caddi*, rose to speak. He welcomed the Texans as friends and agreed to counsel peace to his people upon his return. Bintah was very pleased, for the Caddo "women and children will now be without fear, the road is cleared for them to travel without danger, I believe that what you have told me is truth, and [I believe] that from this time henceforth we are all friends."[17]

On March 31, 1843, an agreement was signed by all parties. It was "solemnly agreed that the war . . . should cease," and the tribes were invited both to trade with the Texans at Torrey's Trading House on the Brazos River near the Waco village and to plant corn at any place above the post. This agreement was signed by Bintah, Chowa, and Haddabah as chiefs of the Kadohadachos and Hainais, and Iesh signed for the Nadacos. All agreed to meet for another conference at Bird's Fort on the Trinity in the autumn to establish a permanent boundary between the Texans and the Indians.[18]

Since the Caddo tribes had still not received the approval of the United States to settle in the Indian Territory, they—except for the small group of White Beads—immediately moved back to Texas following the signing of the treaty. The Nadacos set up their village on a small stream about eight miles west of the western fork of the Trinity River, where they "planted considerable corn." The Kadohadachos and the Hainais settled on the Brazos River only a small distance away from the Nadacos.[19]

On September 29, 1843, the promised grand council was held at Bird's Fort, and an agreement calling for the end of all warfare between Texas and the Caddo, Wichita, and Delaware tribes was reached. Agents were to be assigned to the tribes in order to hear their complaints and see "that justice is done between them and the whites." Most important, a line of trading houses was to be set up for the tribes on the frontier, and this line was to serve as the boundary between whites and natives, both of whom were forbidden to cross the line without special permission from the president. Once the tribes had "shown that they will keep this treaty, and no more make war upon the whites, nor steal horses from them," the president would authorize the traders to provide them with guns, powder, and lead. This treaty was signed by Bintah and Haddabah for the Kadohadachos, Iesh for the Nadacos, and Toweash for the Hainais. The treaty was approved by the Texas Senate on January 31, 1844, and signed by President Houston three days later.[20]

Following the signing of the treaty at Bird's Fort, Iesh and the Nadacos moved their village to the Brazos, about fifty miles above the council ground on Tehuacana Creek. The Hainais relocated nearby and were considered to be "united" with the Nadacos, even though they now had their own *caddi*, Toweash. The Kadohadachos, along with a small group of Delawares—who would be the Caddos' closest ally in the years to come—also joined the Nadacos, thus forming one large contiguous village (located in the present counties of Bosque and Hill). Most white observers agreed that the Caddos had made a fine choice for their village site; one commented that a "more suitable and pleasant place could not have been selected" by the tribe. The village lay "in the center of a plain two milse long," bordered by hills "covered with horses, they being fine for grazing, present[ing] a lively green as far as the eyes could reach." Flowing diagonally through the plain was a beautiful, clear creek," on the banks of which stood, "in picturesque disorder," the Caddos' traditional grass houses. Adjoining each abode were the Caddo fields; one Texas Indian agent felt that the Caddos had "about 150 acres of the finest corn" he had ever seen, in addition to "innumerable" peas, beans, and pumpkins.[21]

Successful and content in their new homes, all three Caddo tribes, as well as the Delawares, tirelessly strove to maintain the peace. However, the Wichita tribes continued to plunder the white settlements for horses and cattle, and Bintah and Iesh took the lead in trying to convince these tribes to stop their raiding. In February, 1844, Bintah joined Texas Indian Agent Daniel G. Watson as he headed up the Brazos to seek out the hostile Penateka Comanches, who had yet to agree to peace. At the Kichai village—located just above the confluence of the Clear Fork of the Brazos and the Brazos—the party found some Wacos and Kichais driving stolen horses. Bintah forced them to give up their horses and threatened that he would report their actions to President Houston. A few days later at the Nadaco village, Iesh pressured a Waco chief, Lame Arm, to admit to Watson that he and a group of Tonkawas had recently stolen thirteen horses from the white settlements around San Antonio.[22]

The *caddices'* actions impressed Watson so much that he left certificates at the Caddo villages stating that even if the Texans traced stolen horses to their homes, they were not to be considered the perpetrators. Instead, blame was to be placed on the Wacos, Kichais, and Tawakonis, whose villages were on the road that passed through the Caddo towns. The certificate also stated that the Caddos "were doing their best to stop the other [Wichitas] from coming down" to the Texas frontier.[23]

The Caddos continued to pressure the Wichita tribes to follow the "white road" throughout the next few years. The Texans held another council with the Indians at Tehuacana Creek in May, 1844, and included among the tribes were hostile Waco and Tawakoni bands that had not participated in the Bird's Fort Treaty of the previous year. Red Bear took the lead in convincing them to make peace, stating, "I do not like to see guns firing and blood spilled, for I am a friend of peace. . . . I am glad to meet my white brothers here, I am glad to hear their talk. . . . I want we should all live together as brothers, eat out of the same dish, drink from the same cup, smoke the same pipe. . . . Our young men here must not go to war, but kill game and make money, not steal and murder." His words were seconded by Iesh, Haddabah, and Bedi, and soon after Bedi's speech, the Tawakonis and Wacos agreed to abide by the peace and the council was ended. In return for their mediation, the Caddos received hoes, kettles, axes, hatchets, knives, cloth, and other goods from the Texans.[24]

The peace with the Wichita tribes proved to be short-lived, for in late July, both Iesh and Red Bear learned that renegades were planning a raid on Torrey's Trading House. Iesh sent a runner to the post to inform the whites of the proposed attack, while Red Bear and Bintah began mobilizing their forces to go to war against the Wichita tribes. They invited white settlers to join them in attacking the raiders. Upon hearing this, Texas agents, along with Iesh, hurried to the Kadohadacho village to prevent them from battling the Wichitas. Iesh's counsel proved to be decisive, and Red Bear and Bintah called off their attack, as did the Wichitas once they learned that their raid had been betrayed by the Caddos. In return for his good offices, Superintendent Thomas G. Western instructed

Agent Samuel Slater to embrace Iesh "for me as my brother, and say that Gen Houston will approve of his conduct that he was right in preventing bloodshed. . . . [Iesh] is a great man and a good friend."[25]

Soon afterward, the Caddos assisted the Texans in their peacemaking efforts with the Comanches. Texan agents had traveled up the Clear Fork of the Brazos and held talks with the Penateka band of Comanches led by Chief Mopechucope. The Penatekas had agreed to come down to the Kichai village, where a council was held that included the Caddos, Delawares, and the nonhostile Wichita tribes. All the chiefs made very "friendly speeches . . . showing great signs of peace and friendship" to the Comanches and induced the Penatekas to accompany them to Tehuacana Creek and enter into a formal treaty with the Republic of Texas.[26]

Pres. Sam Houston, realizing the great importance of this treaty, opened the council on October 7, 1844, by welcoming the tribes and hoping that the "blood from the path of the Comanche and the white people" could be removed. Houston used the Caddos as an example of the present good relations between the Indians and the Texans and told the Penatekas he knew where the Caddos "make their corn, and my young men can go there, and eat with them and all be happy." Houston wanted the Comanches to follow the Caddo example and settle down to plant crops as well. Following two days of speechmaking and negotiations, a treaty was signed by all the parties present, including the Penateka Comanches, and ratified by the Texas Senate on January 24, 1845. Anson Jones, Texas' final president before it became a state, continued Houston's peace policy and signed the treaty twelve days later.[27]

Throughout the rest of the year, both the Caddos and the Texans demonstrated their willingness to remain friends and abide by the peace treaties. One example of this occurred in early November, 1844, when a Waco raiding party kidnapped the son and daughter of Mrs. Nancy Simpson near Austin. Superintendent Western immediately informed the Caddo tribes of the theft, for he felt they would "take an interest in the matter and through their instrumentality possibly, the double object may be attained of recovering the children and ascertaining who the aggressors are." The Caddos did take actions to recover the children and informed the powerful Comanches of the kidnapping. Wishing to keep the peace as well, the Comanches forced the Wacos to return the boy; however, the girl had been killed soon after she was taken.[28]

The Texans were soon given the opportunity to show their gratitude to the Caddo tribes, and on January 2, 1845, Red Bear and Bedi led a party of Kadohadachos and Hainais into Washington-on-the-Brazos with eight packs of peltries and asked for permission to trade. The two men explained that Torrey charged exorbitant prices for goods at his trading post. Although Superintendent Western refused to allow the two men to barter, since they were forbidden by treaty to come below the line of trading posts, he did give them presents and provisions and made a promise to look into the matter personally.[29]

Western fulfilled his promise by immediately ordering Indian Agents Benjamin Sloat and L. H. Williams to investigate the matter, informing them that it was their duty to "see that all Indians are dealt with fairly, by the traders, and that justice be done them." Western wrote Torrey and told him that "dissatisfaction among the Indians must be prevented, and our Treaties with them must be rigidly complied with." Western's assertiveness on behalf of the Caddos paid off when it was reported later that the problem of high prices had been "rectified by the Govt agents and it was done and the Indians were all satisfied."[30]

A week after Red Bear and Bedi's visit to the capital, a Mexican named Fernandez wrote President Jones, charging that the Caddos had actually been scouting the town to see how many men the Texans had at their disposal. Fernandez claimed that the Caddos and other tribes were planning an attack upon all the whites in the vicinity of Torrey's Trading House. Although Superintendent Western claimed not to be the "least alarmed," he instructed Agents Sloat and Williams to talk to Red Bear and gain information pertaining to the matter.[31]

Red Bear, along with a Spanish-speaking Kadohadacho named Vicente, met with Sloat and Williams at Tehuacana Creek on February 6 to answer the charges. Both denounced Fernandez as a liar, saying that he had claimed to be an officer in the Mexican Army and wanted to make war on the Texans. Vicente told Fernandez that "we were all now friends with the whites and I did not wish to hear him talk that way." Red Bear said that he sent Fernandez from the Caddo camp "very mad because I would not let him have a horse." Upon receiving this information, Superintendent Western responded that "the affair of Red Bear and the Mexican turned out just as I expected, the Bear is a good old Indian and the Mexican a scoundrel."[32]

Despite the continued good relations between the Caddos and Texans, renegade Wacos persisted in plundering the white settlements. This worried the Caddo tribes, who feared that Waco depredations would cause the Texans to retaliate against all the native tribes. Iesh and Bintah met with Texas agents at Tehuacana Creek in January, 1845, and expressed their fears. The Nadaco *caddi* claimed that his young men had left his village because they had heard that, if the Caddos did not join the whites in attacking the Wacos, "the whites would think we were friends to the Waco, and kill us." On the other hand, the Wacos told the Caddos that, if they did not move their villages farther away from the whites, "they will steal our horses, so you see we are between two fires." Both Iesh and Bintah insisted that they were glad to be "in the White Path and hope we shall always keep in the same path." Soon after this meeting, Waco attacks temporarily stopped and peace was maintained.[33]

In June, 1845, however, the Wacos killed two white men on the Colorado River below Austin. In response, a group of white citizens organized an army to attack the Waco village on the Brazos above the Caddos. Again, Iesh reported to the Texan agents that stories were being spread among his men that the whites intended to attack the Caddos "and Burn their villages and kill them all without distinction." The Nadaco *caddi* requested that the Texans desist in their efforts to attack the Wacos and advised them to wait to punish the renegades at a general council planned for September, 1845. Iesh believed that, if the Texans waited for the council to seek retribution against the Wacos, "all [the natives] will understand it and act accordingly."[34]

Superintendent Western accepted Iesh's advice and instructed Agent Williams to tell the Nadaco *caddi* "that he may rest in peace and their women and children shall sleep in quiet." Western insisted that the Texans would not attack the Wacos without the consent of Iesh and the chiefs of all of the other friendly tribes. Even then, Western claimed the "white man will not shed the Red man's blood if he can avoid it," even that of the Wacos, "who are very bad men." The superintendent told Williams to embrace Iesh, "[for] he is my brother," and that he would see him and the rest of the Caddos at the council at Tehuacana Creek.[35]

This council, which began on September 19, 1845, was the final general meeting held between the Republic of Texas and the Indians. Only the renegade Wichita bands, as well as the important Penateka Comanche chiefs, failed to attend. All the tribes promised to maintain the peace and force the Wichitas to stop committing depredations on the white settlers. Toweash, the Hainai *caddi*, summed up the attitude of the Caddo tribes by stating that President Houston had given the Caddos "powder and lead, and told us to go home and shoot deer, and raise corn for our women and children, so that in the cold rainy weather they would not cry for bread and meat. We have done so and found that it is good. All that he has told us was true, and now I can go home to my people and tell them that all is still good, that they can eat and sleep in safety and feel no more afraid." Following the council, the Texans distributed goods and presents to the Kadohadachos, Nadacos, and Hainais, and they left for their villages "peaceably and quiet."[36]

Throughout the rest of 1845, the Caddo tribes and the Republic of Texas maintained the peaceful relations they had enjoyed for the past three years. The Caddos felt secure in their homes, which were located along the Brazos River about forty miles below Comanche Peak. They had been living there for two years and had made many improvements, including nearly one hundred lodges constructed in the traditional manner, "appearing as hay stacks built of poles and grass." The villages were surrounded by the tribes' well-tended fields, and the grassy hills around their settlement were filled with grazing horses. The Texas government enforced their security by providing them with protection against white settlers and by supplying the natives with trade. Unfortunately, the Caddos' period of friendship with Texas was very brief, and the tribe would soon be looked upon again with hostility.[37]

In late 1845, the citizens of the Republic of Texas gave up their independence as an autonomous nation and joined the United States. The federal government quickly took steps to assume its constitutional duty of supervising relations with the native tribes in the new state, and the United States commissioned Cherokee Agent Butler and M. G. Lewis to negotiate a treaty with the Texas tribes. Following various delays, a council got under way at Tehuacana Creek on May 12, and an agreement was reached three days later between the United States and the Comanche, Hainai, Nadaco, Kadohadacho, Lipan Apache, Tonkawa, Kichai, Tawakoni, Wichita, and Waco tribes. The Indians "acknowledged themselves to be under the protection of the United States," and perpetual peace was pledged between the two parties. It was also agreed that blacksmiths, teachers, and "preachers of the gospel" would be sent to reside among the tribes at the discretion of the president. Iesh, Bintah, and Toweash affixed their marks to the treaty, which was approved by the U.S. Senate on February 15, 1847.[38]

The commissioners prevailed upon a number of the chiefs to visit Washington in an attempt to "impress" them with the strength and resources of the United States. Among the natives to make the trip was Iesh, who met with Pres. James K. Polk on July 25 and was presented with a testimonial of friendship. Although the chiefs were quartered in the outskirts to give them more room and freedom from the crowds, a few became sick, and the entire party returned to Texas soon after Iesh's interview. Although the stay in Washington was short, the Nadaco *caddi* was suitably impressed. Iesh later remarked that he had seen "what the white people were and knew it was folly to fight them." For the rest of his life, Iesh maintained a policy of peace and cooperation with the whites, for he realized that the Caddos had no other alternative.[39]

Although the United States was ready to assume responsibility for the Indians, the unique circumstances of Texas' entrance into the Union hampered the federal government's efforts. Unlike the other states, Texas retained complete control of its public lands upon joining the Union. This presented a complex legal problem, for the land occupied by the Texas tribes was not the domain of the United States; thus, the federal government's laws applying to Indians were rendered inapplicable. For this reason, a provision in the treaty of 1846, which extended the federal trade and intercourse laws over the Texas tribes was removed by the Senate. To make matters more difficult, the laws of Texas did not acknowledge that the tribes had any right to the land.[40]

Commissioner of Indian Affairs William Medill spelled out the problem in March, 1847, to Maj. Robert S. Neighbors upon his appointment as special agent to manage Indian affairs in Texas. Medill stated, "It is difficult if not impossible to determine at present how far the department has the power and jurisdiction with respect to the Indian country in Texas." Since the trade and intercourse laws, as well as other laws for the regulation of Indian affairs, could not be applied to Texas, the federal government was almost powerless to deal effectively with the tribes, illegal traders, or encroaching Texans.[41]

To add to the problem, Texas, upon turning over responsibility for the Indians to the federal government, became hostile to the tribes' interests. In the latter years of the Texas republic, the government had been forced to adopt a native peace policy and had pledged paternal protection over the tribes. Now, however, the Texans washed their hands of the problem and gave almost no assistance to the helpless agents of the federal government. As time wore on, the Texas government's policy toward Indians harkened back to that of President Lamar.

The complex legal problems, however, did not immediately come to the fore. Instead, Major Neighbors quickly won the friendship of the tribes by demonstrating his willingness to assist them in whatever problems might arise. The major introduced himself to the Caddos on May 30, 1847, and Neighbors found "everything perfectly quiet in their village, and the Indians well satisfied and friendly." The only complaint that the Caddos had was with the Wichita tribes, who continued to steal horses from both the Texans and the Caddos. This had led to a skirmish between the Caddos and the Wacos in which two Wacos were killed, one of whom was a chief who had visited Washington the previous summer.[42]

Major Neighbors traveled immediately up the Brazos to the Kichai villages to end the hostilities between the tribes and urge the Wichitas to desist in their horse raiding. Neighbors had asked Iesh, now considered to be the leader of the Caddos, to accompany him with a small force of warriors, but the Nadaco *caddi* had been thrown from his horse and was unable to travel. As his replacement, Iesh sent his "second chief," Toweash, the Hainai *caddi*, along with six warriors. Six Delawares, led by John Conner, also traveled with Neighbors, and the party arrived at the Wichita villages on June 10. Having won the confidence of the Caddos and the Delawares, Neighbors adopted a bold stance with the Wichitas, believing "that the friendly Indians would sustain me in any measure I might adopt towards them." In the face of the major's assertiveness, the

Wichita bands agreed to end their depredations and to return all stolen horses and mules. The Wacos and the Caddos also "settled the matter to the satisfaction of both parties."[43]

Neighbors was particularly thankful for Toweash and Conner's assistance. The Texas agent informed Commissioner Medill that "their untiring exertions to effect a friendly arrangement with [the Wichita] bands, gave evidence of the friendly disposition of the people, and their attachment to the United States." The special relationship initiated between Neighbors and the Caddos in 1847 continued in good standing for the following twelve years.[44]

Neighbors visited the Caddo villages again on August 28, when he met with the headmen and "found them all perfectly peaceable and friendly." Their corn crop had been destroyed by the excessive dryness of the summer, however, and this was the first of a trend in which many Caddo corn crops failed due to the dry climate of their new homeland on the plains. Iesh also complained to Neighbors that his people found it difficult to obtain food and that they were forced to scatter in pursuit of game. Unfortunately, this did not alleviate the problem because the increase in white settlements had caused the buffalo and other game to "almost entirely disappear" from the prairies of East Texas. Relatively large numbers of buffalo still roamed the high plains of West Texas, but the fierce Comanches jealously guarded these hunting grounds. Problems of subsistence, rarely an issue in their traditional eastern homelands, continually haunted the Caddos in the drier lands of the west.[45]

Neighbors then traveled up the Brazos to the Wichita villages, where he found large numbers of Kadohadachos and Hainais. Neighbors assembled the tribes at the Kichai village and informed them that presents promised by President Polk had arrived at Torrey's Trading House. The major called for a council to be held there in late September, to which the tribes eagerly agreed.[46]

Neighbors counted 2,200 natives in assembly when the council began on September 27, 1847, most of them from the Caddo, Wichita, and Comanche tribes. In view of the federal government's helplessness concerning the disposition of public lands, Neighbors "avoided as much as possible any discussion of land matters, or questions of boundary." However, Texas governor J. Pinckney Henderson temporarily chose to assist the federal agent, and he and the tribes reached an agreement that a "temporary line"—twenty miles below Torrey's, and thirty miles from the nearest white settlements—would serve as the boundary between the races.[47]

This was done in an effort to allay Indian fears of attack by the white settlers. Throughout the summer of 1847, Texas newspapers published numerous rumors of native hostilities that led to tensions on both sides concerning the outbreak of war. The "temporary line" satisfied the tribes, and each principal chief pledged himself to assist Major Neighbors in "carrying into full effect the several stipulations of the treaty" of 1846. The "friendly dispositions" of the natives convinced Neighbors that they were "sincere in their many professions of friendship for the government and citizens of the United States." The agent informed Commissioner Medill that he felt "fully assured that, unless the Indians are improperly interfered with, we have nothing to fear for the future."[48]

Although the Caddo tribes had established a solid friendship with Major Neighbors, it soon became apparent how limited the federal Indian agent's powers were in two vital areas: preventing illegal traders from introducing alcohol into Indian country and protecting the tribes from encroaching white settlers. The former issue would cause the Caddos only temporary problems, since they had resisted alcohol after their relocation in northwestern Texas in 1842. Three years later, however, the "civilized" tribes of the Indian Territory began crossing the Red River, bringing with them large quantities of liquor, and in August, 1847, Agent Neighbors visited the Nadaco village and found the tribe "in some degree disorganized" due to a recent shipment of whiskey. In early September, while Neighbors was at the Kichai village, a party of traders arrived from the Indian Territory with forty gallons of whiskey. The agent was powerless to arrest them, but "by threatening to induce the Indians to seize their goods and put them to death," Neighbors forced the traders to retreat without selling their goods. On September 11, Neighbors met a party of Cherokees on their way to the Caddo villages with thirty gallons of whiskey, which he seized and destroyed. He immediately informed Commissioner Medill of his actions and stated that "in the absence of all law regulating intercourse" with the natives, he was "confined . . . to the destruction of the spirits."[49]

The traders from the Indian Territory were back in Texas the following year. They opened a trading post at the Kichai village in June, 1848, and were "supplying as much whiskey" as they could sell. The whiskey traders arrived at the Kadohadacho village two months later with eleven barrels of liquor, which the natives were reported to be "drinking in great excess." Major Neighbors informed Medill that he was helpless to interfere because of "the present indefinite position of our Indian affairs . . . having no authority or force to employ for its destruction." Soon after, however, the Caddo tribes successfully policed themselves and prevented the introduction of whiskey into their villages, despite the helplessness of the federal government.[50]

Unfortunately, the Caddo tribes were not able to overcome the federal government's impotence in protecting them from white encroachment. Almost as soon as the council of September, 1847, had ended, white settlers pushed beyond the "temporary line." A man named Spencer settled on the council grounds near Torrey's Trading House and "threatened to shoot the first Indian that came on the land claimed by him." However, Major Neighbors, with the assistance of Governor Henderson and a troop of Texas Rangers, had Spencer removed below the line in December, 1847. Following this altercation, Neighbors traveled through West Texas for about a month, and when he returned in January, 1848, he found the situation had radically changed for the worse. Spencer, along with a man named Moore, had returned to the council ground, and the Texas Rangers had abandoned the enforcement of the "temporary line" agreement. The Ranger captain informed Neighbors that he had been ordered to move the ranger station fifteen miles above the council grounds and not "interfere or prevent any settlers from going above" Torrey's. As a result, white settlement had pushed ten miles above the trading post by March, 1848.[51]

The whites' westward advance reinforced the decision—which Neighbors had suggested the previous fall—of most of the Caddo and Wichita tribes to settle together near the Kichai village on the Brazos, about 150 miles above Torrey's (in present Palo Pinto County). Among the Caddo tribes, only the Nadacos under Iesh stubbornly refused to relocate, and they returned from their winter hunt to the old Caddo villages now only about thirty miles above the highest white settlements. Agent Neighbors met with the Nadaco *caddi* on February 27 and found him "perplexed" and uncertain of what to do. Iesh confessed that he was hesitant to settle and plant corn, since the whites might drive his tribe off before harvest time. Neighbors, in an attempt to restore Iesh's confidence in the United States, advised him to remain where he was, for the federal government "would do him justice" even if the whites moved beyond his village. Major Neighbors was not as confident in his report to Commissioner Medill of March 2, 1848, in which he stated that "a crisis has now arrived" and that the whites' insistence on settling on Indian lands "regardless of the consequences . . . must necessarily and inevitably lead to serious difficulty."[52]

Major Neighbors's forecast of trouble soon materialized, as violence broke out on the frontier and the animosity between the Texans and the natives surfaced. In early April, 1848, Capt. Samuel Highsmith's Ranger company, acting upon the rumored murder of a settler, met a party of Wichitas on the Llano River. The natives fled on sight, but the Rangers overtook the party, drove them into the river, and slaughtered twenty-five warriors. The Wichitas retaliated on April 9 by killing and scalping three surveyors of the Texas Emigration and Land Company near the headwaters of Aquilla Creek. The surveyors were engaged in running the line on the southwest boundary of a large tract granted to W. S. Peters by the Republic of Texas, commonly called the Peters Colony. This line stretched about 130 miles west of the newly founded city of Dallas on the Trinity River well into territory claimed by the Wichitas.[53]

The day after the murder of the surveyors, Capt. M. T. Johnston's troop of Texas Rangers traveled to the Aquilla to supervise the burial of the three men. One of the land company's wagons arrived on the scene, and the driver reported that he had encountered six natives, who had refused to answer his inquiries. The following morning, April 11, a small party commanded by Lieutenant Smith started out in search of the natives; instead, they ran across a sixteen-year-old Kadohadacho boy, who had become separated from his father, with whom he had been hunting. The boy was frightened by the approach of the mounted Rangers and fled on foot, despite their entreaties for him to halt. One of the Rangers grabbed the boy's rifle to stop him, and the boy, feeling threatened, drew his knife to defend himself. A volley was fired by the other Rangers, and the boy was killed. The Rangers left him where he lay, and he was found the next day by a Kadohadacho search party.[54]

During the crisis that followed, Iesh clearly demonstrated that he had become the leader of the entire Caddo tribe, including the Kadohadachos. The murdered boy's brothers immediately took up arms, resolving to obtain vengeance for the murder. Despite the fact that Haddabah—who had become the new Kadohadacho *caddi* upon Bintah's death over the winter—was the boy's uncle, Iesh took charge of the matter and was able to pacify the warriors "with great difficulty." On April 18, the Nadaco *caddi* met with local trader Charles Barnard and "promised to keep his people quiet" until the matter could be investigated. Iesh agreed to abide by the stipulations of the treaty made with the United States, which stated that any citizen charged with the murder of an Indian would be tried and punished by the laws of the state. However, the Nadaco *caddi* insisted that the tribe "was determined to have satisfaction for this outrage." Now it was up to the commander of the Texas Rangers, Col. Peter H. Bell, to see that justice was done.[55]

In response to the Wichita murders of the surveyors and the Kadohadachos' call for revenge, the whites on the frontier mobilized for war. Between two and three hundred Texas citizens organized an attack on the tribes to "drive them out of the country." The Texas Rangers prevailed upon the settlers to "desist" in their planned attack, but in the face of this intense white hostility, Colonel Bell refused to arrest the soldiers responsible for the Kadohadacho boy's murder.[56]

In mid-June, two months after the incident, Iesh and the boy's father protested the lack of progress in the matter to Major Neighbors. Although they agreed to wait, they told Neighbors that unless the murderers were brought to justice, "they will personally seek to take satisfaction out of the company that killed the boy." Neighbors informed Commissioner Medill he fully believed that, "unless the matter is properly noticed . . . it will lead to serious difficulties." Neighbors asked Medill to use his influence to force Colonel Bell to investigate the matter, since he seemed so unwilling to do so on his own.[57]

Prodded by his superiors, Colonel Bell finally took action and met with the Kadohadacho *caddi*, Haddabah, at Torrey's on July 29. The two men agreed to meet again at Torrey's on September 10 to settle the matter, and Colonel Bell vowed to bring the men responsible for killing the boy to the meeting. Despite this promise, when Colonel Bell and a number of Ranger officers arrived to meet the principal chiefs of the entire Caddo tribe, Lieutenant Smith's men were not with them, and the Caddos, who had come to "see punishment inflicted" upon the men, were very upset. Major Neighbors, fearing "serious difficulties" if the issue was not definitely settled at this point, took action to resolve the matter. He used all the influence he "could possibly bring to bear to induce" the Caddos to accept an agreement calling for the tribe to receive five hundred dollars in cash "and give up the idea of revenge." Colonel Bell also agreed to bring the matter before the grand jury at its next session that fall. It was obvious, however, that no Texas grand jury would bring charges against a Texas Ranger for killing an Indian.[58]

For the time being, the arrangement satisfied the Caddos, and Major Neighbors found "everything quiet and peaceable" in the Kadohadacho and Hainai villages when he visited them in October, 1848. Although a large part of the tribes had dispersed for the winter hunt, the agent found "nothing calculated to disturb our peaceful and friendly relations with them." The Nadacos, however, were frightened by the hostility of the white settlers and the Texas Rangers. Instead of returning to their old village in the spring of 1849, the Nadacos decided to join with the Kadohadachos and the Hainais and moved farther up the Brazos. The Nadacos quickly settled into their new home by constructing traditional grass houses and with the other Caddo tribes made "very creditable efforts" at raising corn, beans, pumpkins and melons.[59]

Two years later, federal agents took a census of the Caddos that clearly demonstrated how much the tribes had suffered in the sixteen years since the beginning of the Texas Revolution. The Nadacos were the only Caddo tribe that had been able to maintain its population during this troubled period. Their village containing 202 people was "situated in an extensive rich valley" on the right bank of the Brazos, about 120 miles above the white settlements. The Hainai village stood on the opposite bank of the river from the Nadacos. Toweash's tribe had suffered great losses, for the Hainai population had dropped from just over 200 people in 1837 to only 113 in 1851. The Kadohadacho tribe had also experienced a great loss in population. Their village, located 20 miles upstream from the Nadacos, contained only 161 Kadohadachos, down from 500 in 1835. Some of this loss can be attributed to defection; the troubles in Texas had caused many Kadohadachos and Hainais, along with a few Wacos and Kichais, to abandon Texas and join the Wichitas, who now resided in the western portion of the Indian Territory. Other Caddos joined the White Beads at their village now located on Caddo Creek, a tributary of the Washita River near Fort Arbuckle (in present Carter County, Oklahoma). Even including these groups, the Kadohadacho population had been cut nearly in half since the Texas Revolution. Altogether, the Caddos who lived on the Brazos totaled 476 members, 161 of whom were warriors.[60]

Although there were no outbreaks of violence between the whites and the Indians in the winter of 1848–49, Major Neighbors realized that the quiet situation was temporary and the Caddos' position would continue to deteriorate unless bold steps were taken to resolve the "Indian question" in Texas. On March 7, 1849, Neighbors put forth his solution to Maj. Gen. William J. Worth, U.S. commander of the military forces in Texas. Neighbors called for a statewide reservation system to be implemented, in which the natives would be placed under federal jurisdiction and separated from the whites. He proposed that the federal government should acquire land from Texas "for the permanent location and settlement of the Indians; said land to be divided among the several bands and tribes according to their numbers." The federal trade and intercourse laws would be extended over the Texas tribes, and agents would be provided. To protect the tribes on the reservation, Neighbors called for the federal government to establish in Indian country military posts where the commanders would be in "full co-operation with the Indian agent in carrying into effect all laws or treaty stipulations." Although Neighbors was soon removed from his post as Texas agent by the newly installed Whig administration of Pres. Zachary Taylor, the establishment of an Indian reservation in Texas soon became the federal government's goal.[61]

Unfortunately, the actual implementation of the policy did not come immediately, and the Caddos' suffering continued. The new agent, John Rollins, was a political appointee who remained in Washington throughout the summer of 1849; this left the tribes of Texas without a representative of the federal government which, in view of the state's hostile attitude, was their only ally. Without the steadying influence of Major Neighbors, the frontier erupted in flames, and the Comanches and the Lipan Apaches unceasingly attacked the southern part of the state throughout the summer. At least 171 Texans were killed, 25 were taken captive, and over $100,000 in property was stolen.[62]

The Caddos, however, resisted the Comanches' invitations to join them in their raids and followed Iesh's policy of friendship with the whites. They stayed at their villages all summer and fall and "made a very large crop." In fact, the Caddos saved the lives of two white men who were in their village when a group of Comanches arrived. The Comanches had just been attacked by a party of Texans, five of them had been killed, and they sought revenge on the two white men; but the Caddos "manifested much firmness and friendship" and refused to cede them. The Caddos received nothing from the whites in return for earning the Comanches' enmity. Instead, eager surveyors arrived at the Nadaco village a few months later to mark off the land for a future white settlement.[63]

The federal government, realizing that it had no power to enforce the boundary, continued to push for the establishment of a reservation and the imposition of the trade and intercourse laws. Despite the continued Indian depredations, the Texans refused to accede to the wishes of the federal government. The February, 1850, session of the state legislature rejected a specific proposal to authorize the United States to extend the trade and intercourse laws to the tribes of Texas. The situation became so desperate that Pres. Millard Fillmore tried personally to persuade the Texans to "assign a small portion of her vast domain for the provisional occupancy of the small remnants of tribes within her borders." Commissioner of Indian Affairs Luke Lea suggested the appointment of a commission to confer with Texas authorities "for the purpose of effecting the conventional arrangements indispensable to a satisfactory adjustment" of Indian affairs, such as the extension of the trade and intercourse laws. Despite the fact that William M. Williams, chair of the Texas House Committee on Indian Affairs, responded favorably to these entreaties and called upon his state to adopt the proposals of the federal government, the Texas legislature once again refused to comply.[64]

In June, 1851, two representatives of the federal government made separate visits to the Caddo and Wichita villages on the Brazos. Col. Samuel Cooper, with Maj. Henry H. Sibley and a company of the 2d Cavalry, left Fort Graham on June 5 to spend a week meeting with the various tribes. Almost as soon as Cooper left, Special Indian Agent Jesse Stem arrived at the villages accompanied by Col. William J. Hardee and a troop of dragoons. The previous September, Congress had provided for two sub-agents to assist Agent Rollins, and Agent Stem had been assigned to supervise the agricultural tribes of the Brazos, while John Rogers was placed in charge of the Comanche and Lipan Apache tribes.[65]

Both Cooper and Stem held talks with the Caddo headmen, and their reports were very similar. Both claimed that the Caddos were "perfectly peaceable" and "professed the most cordial feelings towards our government and people." However, the tribe's headmen strongly desired that "a permanent boundary should be fixed, so that they might have a country where they could be secure from encroachments of the white settlements." Only then could the Caddos build up their villages and raise their crops without fear of being "forced to abandon their homes, the fruits of their labor, and the graves of their kindred." Iesh—who Stem felt was "the most influential chief on the Brazos"—complained to the agent that the boundary line was constantly being crossed by whites "who marked trees, surveyed lands in [the natives'] hunting grounds, and near their villages . . . [and] this is not just."[66]

The Caddos also complained that, because of the scarceness of game, they found it difficult to obtain enough to eat and at times were "in a starving condition." They "expressed a desire" to be provided with better farming implements, which had been promised in the treaty of 1846, so that they might cultivate their crops "to better advantage and to greater extent." The headmen also asked to be furnished with a few cows and hogs to overcome the want of game. Agent Stem arranged a conference to be held in the fall and promised to bring them hoes, ploughs, and harnesses. He also wanted to teach the tribes how to raise potatoes, which he felt would fare better in the dry country. Colonel Cooper recommended that the government should supply the tribes with these items, which "would greatly contribute to their comfort, and might through their influence, effect a salutary change in the temper and feelings" of some of the hostile tribes.[67]

Despite the reports of Stem and Cooper concerning the tenuous situation of the agricultural tribes of the Brazos, no action was taken by the federal government to protect them. In fact, matters were actually made worse by the establishment in the summer of 1851 of Fort Belknap on the Clear Fork of the Brazos. The post, located above the Caddo and Wichita villages, served as an invitation for the whites to stream into and beyond the native settlements.[68]

Following their annual winter hunt, the Nadacos and the Hainais returned to their villages in early 1852 only to find the area surveyed and surrounded by white settlers. They were forced to move down the Brazos to an unoccupied tract of land near Comanche Peak, in present Hood County. This land was of a lesser quality, and the corn crop of 1852 was "unusually small." Combined with their inability to construct adequate shelters, the Nadacos and Hainais "experienced an unusual amount of sickness and mortality" throughout the year. Agent Stem reported that their precarious situation had caused the tribesmen to "have no courage for vigorous and hopeful effort." The Kadohadachos, on the other hand, moved their village upstream near Fort Belknap, in present Young County. Realizing the desperate situation of the tribe, Major Sibley purchased the land on which the Kadohadachos resided and gave them written permission to live on his property for five years. However, because the land was "previously uncultivated," the Kadohadachos were only able "to make but little" corn for the year.[69]

The Kadohadachos' problems were exacerbated by the untimely death of their *caddi*, Haddabah, in the summer of 1853. George W. Hill, Stem's replacement, reported in August that there was no clear successor to Haddabah as *caddi*, and, thus, the tribe was "much scattered and divided in sentiment." In their misery, they again took up whiskey, which they obtained from the soldiers at Fort Belknap. Hill told the old men of the tribe to gather the people to select a chief, and he promised to "remove as far as possible [the] evils" of liquor upon his return the following month.[70]

Before returning to the Kadohadacho village, Hill held a council on September 15 with most of the Hainai and the Nadaco warriors one hundred miles down the Brazos at the trading post recently established by George Barnard. Iesh did most of the talking for both of the tribes and "urged with force the necessity" of the government procuring a home for him and his people, around which "his white brother could pass" to the west. He told Hill that "the buffalo was gone and but a few deer were left and the white people had most of them"; thus, he again asked to be provided with cattle and hogs. Agent Hill was forced to reply that he could not do anything for them until he received orders from the "white father."[71]

On September 26, Hill returned to the Kadohadacho village and met with the *canahas*, who "after much effort" had still been unable to choose a new leader. They requested that Hill "give them one," whom they promised "to hold up and make strong." Expecting this, Hill had gathered information about the various *canahas* and chose Tinah, "a sensible and good man," to be the new Kadohadacho chief. In a symbolic gesture, Hill "delivered . . . the papers and principal effects of Haddabah" to Tinah. The *canaha* then promised to make his tribe refrain from drinking whiskey and requested that Hill give them a permanent home. Although the agent was unable to fulfill this request, he did travel with a group of Kadohadachos to Barnard's Trading Post and purchased "articles of necessity to enable them to make" their fall hunt.[72]

In late 1853, just in time to save the desperate Caddo tribes from further despair, the Texas government at last realized that something had to be done to solve the state's Indian problem. In his message to the Texas legislature on November 9, 1853, Governor Bell—the former commander of the Texas Rangers—recommended that the United States be given the authority to settle the natives on a reservation to be located within the boundaries of the state. The Texas legislature followed the governor's advice and on February 6, 1854, passed an act giving the federal government jurisdiction over twelve leagues of the state's vacant land "for the use and benefit of the several tribes of Indians residing within the limits of Texas."[73] The reservation proposal of Agent Neighbors was at last being put into effect, five full years after it had first been suggested. The Caddos hoped they could finally settle down on the reservation and end the wandering they had been forced to endure since 1835.

Conclusion

UNFORTUNATELY FOR THE CADDOS, it would be another two decades before they were able to settle permanently on lands they could call their own. At first, however, it seemed that the reservation they chose on the Brazos River, fifteen miles downstream from Fort Belknap, would be the answer to their problems. Consisting of eight leagues, or 37,152 acres, the Brazos Reserve (in present Young County) contained fertile land, abundant water, and good pastures, and the Caddos eagerly began settling there in late 1854. The Kadohadachos, along with a small group of Delawares, settled near the east line of the reserve, while the Nadacos and Hainais settled in a village about 1.5 miles to the west of the Kadohadachos. As a result of Iesh's leadership over the two tribes, the term Nadaco began to be used for both, and the designation of Hainai was temporarily dropped.[1]

The first census of March, 1855, counted 204 Nadacos and 160 Kadohadachos on the Brazos Reserve, a loss of 110 people since the previous count in 1851. Much of this loss can be attributed to members of the tribe who had taken refuge in the Indian Territory. Over the next few years, these refugees trickled back across the Red River, and by 1859, there were 218 Nadacos and 244 Kadohadachos on the reserve. About 200 Caddos remained in the Indian Territory at the White Bead village.[2]

The Nadacos and the Kadohadachos—along with the Wacos, Tawakonis, and Tonkawas, who also settled on the Brazos Reserve—eagerly began planting crops and raising houses. The federal agents provided them with oxen, ploughs, and farming utensils, and by 1857, the Caddos raised four thousand bushels of wheat, a return more successful than that of the "white citizens" of the area. As a part of the federal government's effort to "civilize" the natives, tribesmen were furnished with hogs, cattle, and chickens, and taught the art of husbandry, and the Caddos eagerly sent their children to a school where they were taught to read and write English. The federal agents were well satisfied with the "progress" of the tribe, and felt that the condition of the Indians would soon "bear comparison" with the white frontier citizens.[3]

Although the Caddos and the other tribes of the Brazos Reserve made great strides within the reservation system, uncontrollabe external forces hampered the overall success of the reserve. The hostile Comanches to the northwest emerged as the primary enemy, attacking both the natives on the Brazos Reserve and the white frontier settlements. Despite the Caddos' many demonstrations of friendship—they assisted both the Texas Rangers and the U.S. cavalry in fighting the Comanches—the unceasing attacks on the hapless Texans caused them to suspect the tribes of the Brazos Reserve and oppose its very existence. On May 23, 1859, a group of three hundred Texans attacked the reserve tribes, and it was necessary for U.S. troops to disband the white "posse." For the protection of the natives, the federal government decided to move the tribes of the Brazos Reserve—as well as the friendly Penateka Comanches on the Upper Reserve—north of the Red River. In August, 1859, under escort of federal troops, the tribes moved to land in the Indian Territory leased from the Choctaw and Chickasaw Indians. They were joined there by the refugee Caddos and the White Beads, as well as by the entire Wichita tribe.[4]

Bad luck followed the Caddos to their new home, located on the Washita River, in present Caddo County, Oklahoma. The Civil War broke out two years after their removal from Texas, and the Indian Territory was occupied by the Confederates. Although the tribes of the so-called Wichita Reservation signed a treaty with the Confederacy, the Caddos were uneasy with the Texas troops assigned to guard the region. Iesh died in the summer of 1862, and leadership fell into the hands of the unsure Tinah. In October, 1862, the Wichita Agency was destroyed by a group of natives armed by the Union forces, and as a result, the Caddos—along with the Wichitas and Penateka Comanches—abandoned the area and took refuge in Union-controlled Kansas.[5]

It was not until 1867—after five years of great suffering—that the Caddos and their allies were able to return to the Wichita Reservation. Since their lands were leased and not their own, however, the tribes of the reservation feared being dispossessed and forced to move again. Therefore, in 1872, a delegation of reservation tribesmen concluded a treaty in Washington that set the boundaries of the reservation as being all lands lying between the Canadian and Washita Rivers between 98° and 98°40'. Although this agreement was never ratified by Congress, the Wichita Reservation was recognized as consisting of 743,610 acres. Much to the chagrin of the Caddos and the other tribes, the reservation was combined with that of their former enemies, the Kiowas and Comanches in 1878.[6]

Once again, the Caddos began planting crops and building houses on the reservation. The tribe was also provided with stock, and a school was built for its children. In 1874, the Kadohadachos and the Nadacos met in council and agreed to unite under the new Kadohadacho *caddi*, Nahahsanah (or Guadeloupe), as the unified Caddo Indian tribe. However, just as the tribe was getting used to its new homes and arrangements, Congress passed the Dawes Act, calling for the abandonment of the reservation system and the allotment of the land to individual tribal members. After long delays, allotments amounting to 152,714 acres were distributed to 965 natives—534 of them Caddos—of the Wichita Reservation, with the surplus being sold by the federal government to whites.[7]

The Caddo tribe—despite the attempts of the U.S. government to destroy it—remained intact, and a measure of home rule was provided through the terms of the Oklahoma Indian Welfare Act of 1938 and its acceptance by the enrolled Caddo voters. The tribe ratified a constitution, which remained in effect until 1976, when it was replaced by a completely new document. Today, the Caddo tribal complex is located on thirty-seven acres of ground controlled by the tribe, located seven miles north of Gracemont, in Caddo County, Oklahoma.[8]

Notes

Abbreviations

ADM Bolton, Herbert Eugene, ed. *Athanase de Mézières and the Louisiana-Texas Frontier, 1768–1780*. 2 vols. Cleveland: Arthur H. Clark, Co., 1914.

AJHP Houston, Andrew Jackson. Papers. Archives, Texas State Library. Austin, Texas.

BA Bexar Archives. Eugene C. Barker Library. University of Texas, Austin.

CAL Letters Received by the Office of Indian Affairs. Caddo Agency 1824–1842. National Archives Microfilm Publications M–234, Roll 31.

CO *Chronicles of Oklahoma*.

CRHC Hume, C. Ross. Collection. Western History Collections. University of Oklahoma, Norman.

DCRT Garrison, George Pierce, ed. *The Diplomatic Correspondence of the Republic of Texas*. 3 vols. Washington: Government Printing Office, 1908–1911.

DDOIHC Duke, Doris. Oral Indian History Collection. Western History Collections. University of Oklahoma, Norman.

DSP Starr, James Harper. Papers (includes Papers of Kelsey H. Douglass). Eugene C. Barker Library. University of Texas, Austin.

HED United States Congress. House of Representatives. *Executive Documents*.

HR	United States Congress. House of Representatives. *Reports.*
LBC	Rowland, Dunbar, ed. *Official Letter Books of W. C. C Claiborne.* 6 vols. Jackson: Printed for the Mississippi State Department of Archives and History, 1917.
LHQ	*Louisiana Historical Quarterly.*
MBLP	Gulick, Charles A., Jr., Katherine Elliott, and Harriet Smither, eds. *The Papers of Mirabeau Buonaparte Lamar.* 6 vols. Austin: Von Boeckmann-Jones, 1921–1927.
NSFFL	Letterbook of the Natchitoches-Sulphur Fork Factory, 1809–1821. National Archives Microfilm Publications T1029, Roll 1.
PSTCHS	*Preliminary Studies of the Texas Catholic Historical Society.*
SED	United States Congress. Senate. *Executive Documents.*
SMV	Kinnaird, Lawrence, ed. *Spain in the Mississippi Valley.* 3 vols. Washington: Government Printing Office, 1946–1949.
SR	*Senate Reports*
SWHQ	*Southwestern Historical Quarterly* (from July 1897 to April 1912, this appeared as the *Texas State Historical Association Quarterly*).
TAL	Letters Received by the Office of Indian Affairs from the Texas Agency. Photostat Copy. Eugene C. Barker Library. University of Texas, Austin.
TIP	Winfrey, Dorman, ed. *The Indian Papers of Texas and the Southwest, 1825–1916.* 5 vols. Austin: Texas State Library, 1959–1961.
TMCZ	Leutnegger, Benedict, ed. and trans. *The Texas Missions of the College of Zacatecas in 1749–1750.* Documentary Series no. 5. San Antonio: Old Spanish Missions Historical Research Library at San Jose Mission, 1979.
TRP	Jenkins, John, ed. *The Papers of the Texas Revolution, 1835–1836.* 8 vols. Austin: Presidial Press, 1973.

TTR   *Telegraph and Texas Register* (Houston, Texas).

WTSHAYB *West Texas State Historical Association Year Book.*

Introduction

1. The Gentleman of Elvas, "The Narrative of the Expedition of Hernando de Soto," *Spanish Explorers in the Southern United States, 1528–1543*, 233.

2. Both Amaye and Naguatex are thought to have been located around the Great Bend of the Red River, near the present-day common boundary of Oklahoma, Texas, and Arkansas. For the latest discussion of the route of Moscoso, see Timothy K. Perttula, *The Caddo Nation: Archaeological and Ethnohistoric Perspectives*, 19–27; also, John Reed Swanton, ed., *Final Report of the United States De Soto Commission*; and Charles T. Hudson, Chester DePratter, and Marvin T. Smith, "Hernando de Soto's Expedition through the Southern United States," in *First Encounters: Spanish Explorations in the Caribbean and the United States, 1492–1570*, eds. Jerald T. Milanich and Susan Milbrath, 77–98.

3. The Gentleman of Elvas, "Expedition of de Soto," 238–46.

4. The Caddos call themselves *Hasinai*, meaning "our people." The term Caddo derives from the French (and subsequently the Anglo-American), abbreviation of Kadohadacho, the name of the Caddo confederacy located on the Red River around the Great Bend. At the time of early relations with the United States, the Kadohadachos were the most powerful of the Caddo confederacies; thus, as the various Caddo tribes gradually banded together during the nineteenth century, they became collectively known as the Caddos. Since one of the confederacies is also known as the Hasinai, I have chosen to use the term Caddo to designate all the tribes of the three confederacies—Kadohadacho, Hasinai, and the Natchitoches. James Mooney, *The Ghost Dance Religion and the Sioux Outbreak of 1890*, 1092–93; Vynola Beaver Newkumet and Howard L. Meredith, *Hasinai: A Traditional History of the Caddo Confederacy*, 117.

5. Rex Strickland, "Moscoso's Journey through Texas," 120; Newkumet and Meredith, *Hasinai*, 107, 121, 124; Perttula, *Caddo Nation*, 24–25.

6. These include William Joyce Griffith, *The Hasinai Indians of East Texas As Seen by Europeans, 1687–1772*, 43–165; Herbert Eugene Bolton, *The Hasinais: Southern Caddoans as seen by the Earliest Europeans*; John Reed Swanton, *Source Material of the History and Ethnology of the Caddo Indians*; Donald G. Wycoff, "Caddoan Cultural Area: An Archeological Perspective," *Caddoan Indians* 1:25–280; Robert W. Neuman, "Historical Locations of Certain Caddoan Tribes," *Caddoan Indians* 2:9–158; Charles H. Lange, "A Report on Data Pertaining to the Caddo Treaty of July 1, 1835: The Historical and Anthropological Background and Aftermath," *Caddoan Indians* 2:59–320; Jack T. Hughes, "Prehistory of the Caddoan Speaking Tribes," *Caddoan Indians* 3:9–411; Helen Hornbeck Tanner, "The Territory of the Caddo Tribe of Oklahoma," *Caddoan Indians* 4:9–144; Newkumet and Meredith, *Hasinai*; and Perttula, *Caddo Nation*.

7. William B. Glover, "A History of the Caddo Indians," 872–946.

Chapter 1. The Caddos

1. Newkumet and Meredith, *Hasinai*, 4–6.

2. The term "Caddoan" is used to indicate the language spoken by the Caddos as well

as that spoken by the Arikaras, Pawnees, Wichitas, and Kichais. The term "Caddos" applies only to the tribes of the three Caddo confederacies that are the subject of this study. See "Comparative Caddoan," 113–51, and "The Classification of the Caddoan Languages," both by Allan R. Taylor; Wallace L. Chafe, "Siouan, Iroquoian, and Caddoan," *Native Languages of the Americas*, ed. Thomas A. Sebeck 1:527–72; Alexander Lesser and Gene Weltfish, *Composition of the Caddoan Linguistic Stock*; and Douglas R. Parks, ed., *Caddoan Texts*.

　　3. Jack T. Hughes, "Prehistory of the Caddoan-Speaking Tribes," 95, 302; Donald G. Wycoff, "The Caddoan Cultural Area: An Archaeological Perspective," *Caddoan Indians* 1:10.

　　4. Good first-hand accounts of the nonagricultural historical pursuits of the Caddos are Fray Francisco Casañas de Jesús María to the Viceroy of Mexico, August 15, 1691, in "Descriptions of the Tejas or Asinai Indians," ed. and trans. Mattie Austin Hatcher, *SWHQ*, 210–11; Fray Isidro Felís de Espinosa on the Asinai and their Allies, also in "Descriptions," ed. and trans. M. A. Hatcher, *SWHQ*, 152, 155, 157, which is the English translation of Isidro Felíx Espinosa's *Chrónica apostólica, y seráphica de todos los colegios de propaganda fide de esta Nueva-Espana, de Missioneros Franciscanos observantas: Erigidos con authoridad pontifica, y regia, para la reformaciones de los fieles, y conversion de los gentiles*, 419–38; Pierre and Jean-Baptiste Talon, "Voyage to the Mississippi through the Gulf of Mexico," in *La Salle, the Mississippi, and the Gulf*, ed. Robert S. Weddle, 229–33, 255; Henri Joutel, "Historical Journal," in *The Journeys of René-Robert Cavelier, Sieur de La Salle*, ed. Isaac Joslin Cox 2:172; Wycoff, "Caddoan Cultural Area," 14.

　　5. Robert W. Neuman, *An Introduction to Louisiana Archaeology*, 218; Wycoff, "Caddoan Cultural Area," 36–37. For a description of Caddo agriculture, see Talon, "Voyage to the Mississippi," 229; Casañas to the Viceroy, August 15, 1691, 211, and Espinosa on the Asinai, 152, both in "Descriptions," ed. and trans. M. A. Hatcher, *SWHQ*.

　　6. Wycoff, "Caddoan Cultural Areas," 52. The two most important sites of these prehistoric mounds are at the Davis Site Park near Alto, Texas, and at the Spiro Mound Site Park near Spiro, Oklahoma. Many important studies have been published on both of these, including H. P. Newell and A. D. Krieger, "The George C. Davis Site, Cherokee County, Texas," 1–271; Dee Ann Story, ed., *Archeological Investigations at the George C. Davis Site, Cherokee County, Texas, Summers 1979 and 1980*; and James A. Brown and Robert E. Bell, *The First Annual Report of Caddoan Archaeology, Spiro Focus Research*.

　　7. Neuman, *Louisiana Archaeology*, 319; Espinosa on the Asinai, in "Descriptions," ed. and trans. M. A. Hatcher, *SWHQ*, 156; Hughes, "Prehistory," 329.

　　8. Perttula, *Caddo Nation*, 6–9, 85.

　　9. Donald E. Chipman, *Spanish Texas, 1519–1821*, 28–30; John Ewers, "The Influence of Epidemics on the Indian Populations and Cultures of Texas," 108.

　　10. The past two decades have brought a welcome influx of works that have revolutionized the way we perceive Native American population decline. These studies have estimated the 1492 population of America north of Mexico to be anywhere from 7 million to as high as 18 million, up from estimates in the 1920s of only 1 million. These new figures imply that the native population had declined by 90 percent by the end of the nineteenth century. These studies also demonstrate that epidemic disease often preceded direct contact between the aboriginal populations and the European intruders. See Alfred W. Crosby, "Virgin Soil Epidemics as a Factor in the Aboriginal Depopulation in America," 289–99; Henry F. Dobyns, *Their Number Become Thinned: Native American Population Dynamics in Eastern North America*; Russell Thornton, *American Indian Holocaust and Survival: A Population History Since 1492*; and Ann F. Ramenofsky, *Vectors of Death: The Archaeology of European Contact*.

　　11. Timothy K. Perttula, "European Contact and Its Effects on Aboriginal Caddoan Populations between A.D. 1500 and A.D. 1680," in *Columbian Consequences*, ed. D. H. Thomas 3:512–15.

12. The exact population of the Caddo confederacies at the time of the first prolonged European contact, as with any other time, is very difficult to establish. In 1928, Mooney estimated the Caddo population in 1690 to have been 8,500. In 1942, Swanton lowered that figure to 8,000. More recently, Thornton has suggested a method of estimation that multiplies the population of an aboriginal group at its nadir in the historic period by either twenty or twenty-five. The Caddos reached this nadir in the 1890s, when their population stood at about 500. Using this method, we can estimate the Caddo population to have ranged between 10,000 and 12,500. I think that 10,000 is an acceptable approximate figure, but the reader should understand that determining exact populations is virtually impossible. James Mooney, *The Aboriginal Population of America North of Mexico*, 12–13; Swanton, *Source Material*, 13; Thornton, *American Holocaust*, 30.

13. Stephen Williams, "The Aboriginal Location of the Kadohadacho and Related Tribes," in *Explorations in Cultural Anthropology*, ed. Ward Goodenough, 545.

14. Swanton, *Source Material*, 12–13.

15. Herbert Eugene Bolton, "The Native Tribes about the East Texas Missions," 249–76.

16. Jean Cavelier, "Relation," *The Journeys of René-Robert Cavelier*, ed. Isaac J. Cox 1:298; Henri de la Tonty, "Memoir," in *Historical Collections of Louisiana*, ed. B. F. French 1:72–73.

17. The best secondary overviews of the historical culture of the Caddos are Swanton, *Source Material*; Griffith, *Hasinai Indians*; and Bolton, *Hasinais*. The best first-hand accounts include Joutel, "Historical Journal," 132–81; Father Anastasius Douay, "Narrative of La Salle's Attempt to Ascend the Mississippi in 1687," in *The Journeys of René-Robert Cavelier*, ed. Isaac J. Cox 1:222–67; and Espinosa on the Asinai, 150–80; and Casañas to the Viceroy, August 15, 1691, 206–18, 283–304, both in "Descriptions," ed. and trans. M. A. Hatcher, *SWHQ*.

18. Griffith, *Hasinai Indians*, 59–63; Bolton, *Hasinais*, 82–84; Casañas to the Viceroy, August 15, 1691, 213; and Espinosa on the Asinai, 160, both in "Descriptions," ed. and trans. M. A. Hatcher, *SWHQ*.

19. Espinosa on the Asinai, 158, 160–61; Casañas to the Viceroy, August 15, 1691, 288, 190; and Fray Francisco Hidalgo to Fray Isidro Cassos, November 20, 1710, 51–52, all in "Descriptions," ed. and trans. M. A. Hatcher, *SWHQ*.

20. Casañas to the Viceroy, August 15, 1691, 296; and Espinosa on the Asinai, 165–66, both ibid.

21. Casañas to the Viceroy, August 15, 1691, 284; Espinosa on the Asinai, 165–66, both in "Descriptions," ed. and trans. M. A. Hatcher, *SWHQ*. Secondary works on Caddo religion and beliefs include George A. Dorsey, *Tradition of the Caddo*; A. de Zavala, "Religious Beliefs of the Tejas or Hasinai Indians," 39–43; Mary Austin Hatcher, "Myths of the Tejas Indians," 107–18; C. E. Castañeda, "Myths and Customs of the Tejas Indians," 167–74; Newkumet and Meredith, *Hasinai*, 4-12; and Bolton, *Hasinais*, 138–57.

22. "These allied tribes do not have one person to govern them as with us a kingdom is accustomed to have a ruler whom we call a king." Casañas to the Viceroy, August 15, 1691, in "Descriptions," ed. and trans. M. A. Hatcher, *SWHQ*, 286; Joutel, "Historical Journal," 136; Fray Damian Massanet, "Letter to Don Carlos de Sigüenza," in *Spanish Exploration in the Southwest, 1542–1706*, ed. Herbert Eugene Bolton, 378. See also Donald G. Wycoff and Timothy G. Baugh, "Early Historic Hasinai Elites: A Model for the Material Culture of Governing Elites," 225–88; and Bolton, *Hasinais*, 74–81.

23. Casañas to the Viceroy, August 15, 1691, in "Descriptions," ed. and trans. M. A. Hatcher, *SWHQ*, 217.

24. Ibid.; Espinosa on the Asinai, in "Descriptions," ed. and trans. M. A. Hatcher, *SWHQ*, 156.

25. Newkumet and Meredith, *Hasinai*, 29–30.

26. Ibid., 30, 34; Fray Juan Agustín de Morfi, *Excerpts from the Memorias for the History of the Province of Texas*, ed. and trans. Frederick C. Chabot, 30–31, 34, 43; Espinosa on the Asinai, in "Descriptions," ed. and trans. M. A. Hatcher, *SWHQ*, 156–57; Bolton, *Hasinais*, 92–93.

27. Newkumet and Meredith, *Hasinai*, 9, 32–33; Espinosa on the Asinai, 156–57; and Casañas to the Viceroy, August 15, 1691, 211, both in "Descriptions," ed. and trans. M. A. Hatcher, *SWHQ*; Bolton, *Hasinais*, 93–97.

28. Espinosa on the Asinai, in "Descriptions," ed. and trans. M. A. Hatcher, *SWHQ*, 154; Douay, "Narrative," 232.

29. Douay, "Narrative," 232; Joutel, "Historical Journal," 138; Fray Francisco Hidalgo to the Viceroy, November 4, 1716, in "Descriptions," ed. and trans. M. A. Hatcher, *SWHQ*, 56. For discussions on Caddo housing, see also Clarence H. Webb, "House Types among the Caddo Indians," 49–75; and E. N. Wilmsen, "A Suggested Development Sequence for House Forms in the Caddoan Area," 35–49.

30. Joutel claims that each house contained about fifteen or twenty people ("Historical Journal," 137); Douay states that each house contained two families ("Narrative," 232). For descriptions of Caddo marriage, see Espinosa on the Asinai, 64; and Casañas to the Viceroy, August 15, 1691, 217, 283–84, both in "Descriptions," ed. and trans. M. A. Hatcher, *SWHQ*; Newkumet and Meredith, *Hasinai*, 46–48; and Bolton, *Hasinais*, 70, 87–88.

31. Fray Gaspár José de Solís, "Diary of a Visit of Inspection of the Texas Missions Made by Fray Gaspár José de Solís in the Year 1767–1768," 70; Espinosa on the Asinai, in "Descriptions," ed. and trans. M. A. Hatcher, *SWHQ*, 64; Newkumet and Meredith, *Hasinai*, 48.

32. Newkumet and Meredith, *Hasinai*, 15–16; Memorial of the College of Zacatecas to the King, January 15, 1750, *TMCZ*, 46; Espinosa on the Asinai, in "Descriptions," ed. and trans. M. A. Hatcher, *SWHQ*, 157; Solís, "Diary," 70.

33. Espinosa on the Asinai, 157; and Casañas to the Viceroy, August 15, 1691, 211, both in "Descriptions," ed. and trans. M. A. Hatcher, *SWHQ*; Solís, "Diary," 61; Bolton, *Hasinais*, 100–103.

34. Espinosa on the Asinai, 152–53, 176–77; and Casañas to the Viceroy, August 15, 1691, 210–11, both in "Descriptions," ed. and trans. M. A. Hatcher, *SWHQ*; Bolton, *Hasinais*, 108–109.

35. Espinosa on the Asinai, 176; and Casañas to the Viceroy, August 15, 1691, 213, both in "Descriptions," ed. and trans. M. A. Hatcher, *SWHQ*; Newkumet and Meredith, *Hasinai*, 41–45.

36. Espinosa on the Asinai, 175–77; Casañas to the Viceroy, August 15, 1691, 213–14, 285; and Hidalgo to the Viceroy, November 4, 1716, 55, all in "Descriptions," ed. and trans. M. A. Hatcher, *SWHQ*; Joutel, "Historical Journal," 140.

37. For first-hand accounts of Caddo torture, see Joutel, "Historical Journal," 162–65; and Talon, "Voyage," 238-39.

38. Gilbert C. Din and Abraham P. Nasatir, *The Imperial Osages: Spanish-Indian Diplomacy in the Mississippi Valley*; Newkumet and Meredith, *Hasinai*, 73.

39. Swanton, *Source Material*, 7.

40. Lawrence E. Aten, *Indians of the Upper Texas Coast*; W. W. Newcomb, Jr., *The Indians of Texas*, 133–53; Thomas Frank Schilz, "People of the Cross Timbers: A History of the Tonkawa Indians." Recent scholarship suggests that the Tonkawas were relative latecomers to the area, not emigrating from the High Plains until the mid-seventeenth century. See W. W. Newcomb and T. N. Campbell, "Southern Plains Ethnohistory: A Reexamination of the Escanjaques, Ahijados, and Cuitoas," in *Anthropological Perspectives of Plains Natives and Their Past*, eds. Donald G. Wycoff and Jack L. Hofman.

41. Newcomb, *Indians*, 247–77; Earl Henry Elam, "The History of the Wichita Indian Confederacy to 1868," 1–70.

42. Newcomb, *Indians*, 103–31; Thomas Frank Schilz, *The Lipan Apaches in Texas*.

43. Elizabeth A. H. John, *Storms Brewed in Other Men's Worlds: The Confrontation of Indians, Spanish, and French in the Southwest, 1540–1795*, 59–63; Donald E. Worcester, "The Spread of Spanish Horses in the Southwest," 225–32.

44. Herbert Eugene Bolton, "The Jumano Indians in Texas, 1650–1771," 68; J. Charles Kelley, "Juan Sabeata and Diffusion in Aboriginal Terms," 981–95; John, *Storms Brewed*, 169–70; Douay, "Narrative," 232.

45. Russel M. Magnaghi, "Changing Material Culture and the Hasinai of East Texas," 413–17.

46. Tonty, "Memoir," 73.

47. See Lewis Hanke, *The Spanish Struggle for Justice in the Conquest of America*; and Herbert Eugene Bolton, "The Mission as a Frontier Institution in the Spanish-American Colonies," 42–61.

48. Philip W. Powell, *Soldiers, Indians, and Silver: The Northward Advance of New Spain, 1550–1600*; Herbert Eugene Bolton, "Defensive Spanish Expansion and the Significance of the Spanish Borderlands," in *The Trans-Mississippi West*, eds. James F. Willard and Colin B. Goodykoontz, 1–42.

49. John, *Storms Brewed*, 54–57.

50. Herbert Eugene Bolton, "The Spanish Occupation of Texas, 1519–1690," 4–6.

51. Quoted in Carlos E. Castañeda, *Our Catholic Heritage in Texas, 1519–1936*, 1:205.

52. "I notice that this name Tejas includes all the friendly tribes. The name is common to all of them. . . . And, since this name is a general term, it must be used for no other reason than to indicate the long-standing friendship which they entertain towards each other. And, therefore, among all these tribes 'Tejias' means friends." Casañas to the Viceroy, August 15, 1691, in "Descriptions," ed. and trans. M. A. Hatcher, *SWHQ*, 286.

53. Bolton, "Spanish Occupation," 10–12; Fernando del Bosque, "Diary," 291–309.

54. Archbishop of Guadalajara, "Informe a el Arzobispo de Mexico . . . dando Relasion de las Tierras de Coahuila," quoted in Bolton, "Spanish Occupation," 16.

55. Bolton, "Spanish Occupation," 16.

56. Declaration of Juan Sabeata at El Paso, October 20, 1683, in *Pichardo's Treatise on the Limits of Louisiana and Texas*, ed. Charles Wilson Hackett 1:138–39.

57. Juan Domínguez de Mendoza, "Itinerary," 329, 340; J. W. Williams, "New Conclusions on the Route of Mendoza, 1683–1684," 111–34; Seymour V. Connor, "The Mendoza-López Expedition and Location of San Clemente," 3–29.

58. Fray Nicolás López to the Viceroy, 1686, in *Historical Documents Relating to New Mexico, Nueva Vizcaya and Approaches Thereto, to 1773*, ed. Charles Wilson Hackett 3:361; Castañeda, *Our Catholic Heritage*, 1:318.

Chapter 2. The Caddos and the Arrival of the Europeans, 1686–94

1. Jean Cavelier, "Account of La Salle's Voyage to the Mouth of the Mississippi, His Landing in Texas and March to the Mississippi," in *The Journeys of René-Robert Cavalier*, ed. Isaac J. Cox 1:286.

2. Carta e Informe del Padre Damian Manzanet al Virrey Conde de Galve, June 14, 1693, in *Primeras Exploraciones y Poblamiento de Texas, 1686–1694*, ed. Lino Gómez Canedo, 50.

3. John Anthony Caruso, *The Mississippi Valley Frontier: The Age of French Exploration and Settlement.*

4. For the background of La Salle's Texas expedition, see Henry Folmer, *Franco-Spanish Rivalry in North America, 1524–1763*, 137–46; Robert S. Weddle, *Wilderness Manhunt: The Spanish Search for La Salle*, 15–23; and Castañeda, *Our Catholic Heritage*, 1:281–85.

5. La Salle's landfall on the coast of Texas, rather than at the mouth of the Mississippi, has long been cause for historical debate. For the latest and seemingly definitive word, see Peter H. Wood, "La Salle: Discovery of a Lost Explorer," 294–323. See also Minet, "Journal of Our Voyage to the Gulf of Mexico," in *La Salle, the Mississippi, and the Gulf*, ed. Robert S. Weddle, 92–113.

6. Herbert Eugene Bolton, "The Location of La Salle's Colony on the Gulf of Mexico," *Mississippi Valley Historical Review* 2 (1915):26–34.

7. Castañeda, *Our Catholic Heritage*, 1:294; Douay, "Narrative," 231; Cavelier, "Account of La Salle's Voyage," 286.

8. Douay, "Narrative," 231–32.

9. Ibid., 232–34; Cavelier, "Account of La Salle's Voyage," 286, 297; Joutel, "Historical Journal," 147.

10. Douay, "Narrative," 235–36.

11. Joutel, "Historical Journal," 146, 148–49.

12. Ibid., 124–27; Douay, "Narrative," 238–46; Talon, "Voyage to the Mississippi," 229.

13. Joutel, "Historical Journal," 133–34, 136; Cavelier, "Account of La Salle's Voyage," 297.

14. Joutel, "Historical Journal," 147, 159–64.

15. Ibid., 166–67; Douay, "Narrative," 248; Talon, "Voyage to the Mississippi," 239.

16. Douay, "Narrative," 248–53; Joutel, "Historical Journal," 168–84. One of the Frenchmen in the party drowned in the Red River while at the Kadohadacho village. His body was recovered and the priests performed a burial service for him. He was interred on a hill near the village, and every morning while the French party remained with the Kadohadachos, the wife of the *caddi* visited the grave and placed a small basket of corn on it. This was in accordance with traditional Caddo burial rites, and seems to demonstrate how strongly the Kadohadachos felt for their newfound friends. For information concerning the Quapaws, see W. David Baird, *The Quapaw Indians: A History of the Downstream People*.

17. Tonty, "Memoir," 71–73.

18. Ibid., 74.

19. Ibid., 74–75.

20. Ibid., 76–78.

21. An informative, entertaining account of the Spanish reaction can be found in Weddle, *Wilderness Manhunt*.

22. Alonso de León, "Itinerary of the Expedition of 1689," 388–404; and Fray Damian Massanet, "Letter to Don Carlos de Sigüenza," 363, both in *Spanish Exploration in the Southwest, 1542–1706*, ed. H. E. Bolton; Walter J. O'Donnell, "Documents: La Salle's Occupation of Texas," 116–17.

23. De León, "Itinerary of the Expedition of 1689," 404.

24. Massanet, "Letter to Don Carlos de Sigüenza," 363–64.

25. William Edward Dunn, *Spanish and French Rivalry in the Gulf Region of the United States, 1678–1702: The Beginnings of Texas and Pensacola*, 110–14; Robert Carlton Clark, *The Beginnings of Texas, 1684–1718*, 22–23.

26. Dunn, *Spanish and French Rivalry*, 119; Clark, *Beginnings of Texas*, 22–23. The Colegio de la Santa Cruz de Querétaro was founded in 1683 by the Franciscan Order for the purpose of training missionaries to be sent to spread the faith among the "heathen Indians" of New Spain. See Michael B. McCloskey, *The Formative Years of the Missionary*

College of Santa Cruz of Querétaro, 1683–1733.

27. Alonso de León, "Itinerary of the Expedition of 1690," in *Spanish Exploration in the Southwest, 1542–1706*, ed. H. E. Bolton, 415–16; Massanet, "Letter to Don Carlos de Sigüenza," 375–76; Talon, "Voyage to the Mississippi," 240–41.

28. De León, "Itinerary of the Expedition of 1690," in *Spanish Exploration in the Southwest, 1542–1706*, ed. H. E. Bolton, 416–17; Massanet, "Letter to Don Carlos de Sigüenza," 380.

29. Massanet, "Letter to Don Carlos de Sigüenza," 380–82; De León, "Itinerary of the Expedition of 1690," 417. While talking with the Nabedache *caddi* Father Massanet became convinced that the Hasinais had been visited by Mother Maria de Jesus de Agreda, a Spanish woman who claimed to have been transported by angels to the unknown regions north of New Spain in the 1620s. Father Alonso de Benavides had popularized her story in 1631, and Massanet had been inspired by his pamphlet to travel to Texas to seek converts. The caddi told Massanet how his mother had told him that "in times past they [the Hasinais] had been visited frequently by a very beautiful woman, who used to come down from the heights, dressed in blue garments." Massanet was certain that the woman was Mother Maria, and the story caused him to be even more assured that the Hasinai would accept Christianity. See Dunn, *Spanish and French Rivalry*, 107.

30. De León al Virrey, July 12, 1690, in *Primeras Exploraciones*, ed. L. G. Canedo, 123; Massanet, "Letter to Don Carlos de Sigüenza," 382–83, 386.

31. The *caddi*'s brother abandoned the Spanish return party soon after it left the Nabedache village and went back home.

32. Massanet, "Letter to Don Carlos de Sigüenza," 383.

33. Casañas to the Viceroy, August 15, 1691, in "Descriptions," ed. and trans. M. A. Hatcher, SWHQ, 209–10.

34. Fray Miguel Fontcuberta to the Custodian, September 4, 1690, in *Historical Documents Relating to New Mexico* 2:283–84.

35. Casañas to the Viceroy, August 15, 1691, in "Descriptions," ed. and trans. M. A. Hatcher, SWHQ, 288–89.

36. Ibid., 290–93.

37. Ibid., 294, 298.

38. Diary Kept by the Missionaries, in "The Expedition of Don Domingo Terán de los Ríos into Texas," ed. M. A. Hatcher, 57; Casañas to the Viceroy, August 15, 1691, in "Descriptions," ed. and trans. M. A. Hatcher, SWHQ, 294–95, 303.

39. Casañas to the Viceroy, August 15, 1691, in "Descriptions," ed. and trans. M. A. Hatcher, SWHQ, 294–95, 299.

40. Massanet al Virrey, September, 1690, in *Primeras Exploraciones*, ed. L. G. Canedo, 159–65.

41. Instructions Given by the Superior Government to be Observed in the Expedition to the Province of Texas, January 23, 1691, in "Expedition of Don Domingo Terán de los Ríos," ed. M. A. Hatcher, 6.

42. Massanet, "Letter to Don Carlos de Sigüenza," 384. The Instructions to Terán include the following: "Efforts shall be made to satisfy [the Nabedache *caddi*'s] doubts concerning the death of the Indian. My [the viceroy's] regrets over his death, the steps taken for the punishment of the aggressor, and other details that may help to satisfy him shall be explained." Instructions Given by the Superior Government, January 23, 1691, in "Expedition of Don Domingo Terán," ed. M. A. Hatcher, 5. Espinosa claims the Indian died of sickness and was baptized (*Crónica apostólica*, 414).

43. Diary Kept By the Missionaries, in "Expedition of Don Domingo Terán de los Ríos," ed. M. A. Hatcher, 57–58; Casañas to the Viceroy, August 15, 1691, in "Descriptions," ed. and trans. M. A. Hatcher, SWHQ, 289.

44. Diary Kept By the Missionaries, 66–67; and Itinerary and Daily Account of

Do-mingo de Terán, 18–20, both in "Expedition of Don Domingo Terán de los Ríos," ed. M. A. Hatcher.

45. Itinerary and Daily Account of Domingo de Terán, in "Expedition of Don Domingo Terán de los Ríos," ed. M. A. Hatcher, 28; Massanet to the Viceroy, 1692, in *Primeras Exploraciones*, ed. L. G. Canedo, 264.

46. Itinerary and Daily Account of Terán, in "Expedition of Don Domingo Terán de los Ríos," ed. M. A. Hatcher, 28–29.

47. The Caddo tribes often designated the youngest male heir as *caddi* to ensure longevity of reign. See Talon, "Voyage to the Mississippi," 239; and Espinosa on the Asinai, in "Descriptions," ed. and trans. M. A. Hatcher, *SWHQ*, 175.

48. Itinerary and Daily Account of Terán, in "Expedition of Don Domingo Terán de los Ríos," ed. M. A. Hatcher, 33–34; Massanet al Virrey, 1692, in *Primeras Exploraciones*, ed. L. G. Canedo, 263.

49. Dunn, *Spanish and French Rivalry*, 137; Itinerary and Daily Account of Terán, in "Expedition of Don Domingo Terán de los Ríos," ed. M. A. Hatcher, 39.

50. Carta e Informe del Padre Damian Manzanet al Virrey Conde de Galve, June 14, 1693, in *Primeras Exploraciones*, ed. L. G. Canedo, 309–10.

51. Ibid., 311–13.

52. Ibid., 314–15.

53. Ibid.

54. Diario de Gregorio de Salinas Verona, in *Primeras Exploraciones*, ed. L. G. Canedo, 295; Dunn, *Spanish and French Rivalry*, 141–42.

55. Massanet al Virrey, February 17, 1694, in *Primeras Exploraciones*, ed. L. G. Canedo, 318–19.

56. Ibid., 319–20. Four of the Spanish soldiers, led by Jose Urrutia, deserted the party and returned to the Hasinais. They dug up the metal ornaments and gave them to the Hasinais as a peace offering. Their firearms and their willingness to join the Hasinais in battle made the tribe accept the presence of the four Spaniards. Fray Juan Agustín de Morfi, *History of Texas, 1673–1779*, 1:183; Clark, *Beginnings of Texas*, 43.

Chapter 3. The Caddos and the Establishment of the Europeans, 1694–1731

1. Bénard de la Harpe, *The Historical Journal of the Establishment of the French in Louisiana*, 94.

2. Hidalgo to the Viceroy, November 4, 1716, in "Descriptions," ed. and trans. M. A. Hatcher, *SWHQ*, 56.

3. Verner W. Crane, *The Southern Frontier, 1670–1732*, 45–46; Daniel H. Usner, Jr., *Indians, Settlers, and Slaves in a Frontier Exchange Economy: The Lower Mississippi Valley Before 1783*, 16.

4. La Harpe, "Account of the Journey of Bénard de la Harpe: Discovery Made by Him of Several Nations Situated in the West," 252.

5. The population figures are estimates at best. In 1719, La Harpe claimed that among the four Kadohadacho tribes—and part of the Yatasis—there were four hundred persons "who are able to provide two hundred warriors." Four years later, Sieur Derbanne stated there were 400 men among the Kadohadachos alone. La Harpe also claimed that ten years before, there had been 2,500 Kadohadachos and attributed the subsequent population loss to increased warfare. There were certainly more than 400 Kadohadachos left in 1719, since

that is the figure given for the tribe throughout the early part of the nineteenth century, after the tribe had suffered through another one hundred years of sickness and warfare. La Harpe's assumption of 200 Kadohadacho warriors—Derbanne's 400 may be a bit too high—is certainly more accurate. If this is the case, it can be reasoned that the Kadohadacho population stood at 1,000 in 1719. This figure is arrived at from the observations of other Europeans, who calculated that several families—perhaps two or three—lived in one Caddo house, and that the total number of people per dwelling was between fifteen and twenty. Thus, one warrior per five people is a conservative estimate. Multiply the number of warriors by five and a workable population figure—inexact, to be sure—can be reached for the Caddo tribes. La Harpe, "Account of the Journey," 254; Katherine Bridges and Winston DeVille, eds. and trans., "Natchitoches and the Trail to the Rio Grande: Two Early Eighteenth Century Accounts by the Sieur Derbanne," 255.

6. Again, the population figure is inexact. In one account, La Harpe claims there were 150 Natchitoches, Yatasi, and Doustionis left in 1719. Half of the Yatasis, however, had taken refuge with the Kadohadachos. Since there were about 225 Yatasis and Natchitoches in 1770, La Harpe's figures are certainly too low. The Kadohadacho population declined by 75 percent by 1721; by using the same percentage, the Natchitoches totals stood at 500 in the same year. La Harpe, "Account of the Journey," 85.

7. Ibid., 85, 253–54.

8. Hidalgo to the Viceroy, November 4, 1716, in "Descriptions," ed. and trans. M. A. Hatcher, SWHQ, 56; Hidalgo to the Viceroy, April 8, 1718, in Provincias Internas 181:231–32. The population figures for the Hasinai confederacy are probably the most reliable. In 1721, the Spanish reestablished the missions in the Hasinai country and held great celebrations, during which they fed and clothed all the present members of the various tribes. Father Juan Antonio de la Peña kept close records of the number of Hasinais who attended these functions, and since they were receiving many gifts from the Spanish, it must be assumed that most of the tribal members were present. For all four Hasinai groups, Peña counted 1,348 men, women, and children. That makes a total of 1,500, if 150 members were absent. Juan Antonio de la Peña, "Diary of the Aguayo Expedition," 42–50.

9. For French plans before 1698, see Robert S. Weddle, The French Thorn: Rival Explorers in the Spanish Sea, 1682–1762, 124–26.

10. M. de Bienville, "Journal of the Overland Journey from the Taensas to the Village of the Yataches," in Iberville's Gulf Journals, ed. Richebourg Gaillard McWilliams, 146–47.

11. In 1806, the Red River raft was described as being a series of logjams "100 feet in width, and extend[ing] for 200 yards along [the river's] course. This raft rises nearly three feet above the water, and is covered with bushes and weeds: the trees of which it is composed are Cotton Wood, Cypress, Red Cedar, &c. and they lie so close that the men could walk over it in any direction." Thomas Freeman and Peter Custis, An Account of the Red River in Louisiana, Drawn Up from the Returns of Messrs. Freeman and Custis to the War Office of the United States, who explored the Same in the Year 1806, 13.

12. Bienville, "Journal," 151–56.

13. There is some confusion about this trip. I have followed Clark, Beginnings of Texas, 48; John, Storms Brewed, 198; and Weddle, French Thorn, 178, in view of what occurred later. La Harpe states that Saint Denis was ordered to explore the Red River but returned without further information concerning the Spaniards ("Historical Journal," 25). However, André Pénicault claims Bienville and St. Denis traveled together to the Kadohadacho villages and learned that the Spaniards had abandoned the area (Fleur de Lys and Calumet: Being the Pénicault Narrative of French Adventure in Louisiana, 54–55). Pénicault wrote his story late in life and is known to have made many misstatements concerning dates, his presence at important happenings, and claims of heroic deeds. See Elizabeth McCann, "Pénicault and His Chronicle of Early Louisiana," 288–304.

14. Declaration of St. Denis, June 22, 1715, in Pichardo's Treatise, ed. C. W. Hackett

4:306; Castañeda, *Our Catholic Heritage* 2:17–19; Clark, *Beginnings of Texas*, 47–48.

15. Pénicault mistakenly claims the attack on the Chitimachas took place in 1705, while La Harpe correctly states that it occurred in 1707. Pénicault, *Fleur de Lys*, 100–101, 109–13; La Harpe, "Historical Journal," 55; Jay Higginbotham, *Old Mobile: Fort Louis de la Louisianne, 1702–1711*, 292.

16. Marcel Giraud, *A History of French Louisiana, 1, The Reign of Louis XIV, 1698–1715*, 300–301; Clark, *Beginnings of Texas*, 50; Henry Folmer, *Franco-Spanish Rivalry in North America, 1524–1763*, 229–31.

17. Passport from Cadillac to St. Denis, September 12, 1713, in *Pichardo's Treatise*, ed. C. W. Hackett 1:219. The Acolopissas attacked the Natchitoches upon their departure and killed seventeen men. Pénicault, *Fleur de Lys*, 145–46; Cadillac to Ponchartrain, October 26, 1713, in *Mississippi Provincial Archives: French Dominion*, eds. and trans. Dunbar Rowland and Albert Godfrey Sanders 2:203.

18. Declaration of St. Denis, June 22, 1715, in *Pichardo's Treatise*, ed. C. W. Hackett 4:306; Pénicault, *Fleur de Lys*, 147–49.

19. La Harpe, "Historical Journal," 85; Pénicault, *Fleur de Lys*, 194.

20. Robert Carlton Clark, "Louis Juchereau de Saint-Denis and the Reestablishment of the Tejas Missions," 11.

21. Saint Denis's trip to Mexico has been told many times. He arrived at the presidio at San Juan Bautista in the summer of 1714 and was then escorted to Mexico City, where he was interrogated by Spanish officials. He returned to Texas—and then went on to Mobile—two summers later at the head of the Spanish entrada led by Capt. Domingo Ramón. Since I do not want to recount the moves and countermoves of the French and Spanish in Texas, I have chosen to abandon strict chronology here in order to concentrate on the development of the French trade with the Caddos on the Red River. For a concise overview of Saint Denis's trip, see Jack Jackson, Robert S. Weddle, and Winston DeVille, *Mapping Texas and the Gulf Coast: The Contributions of Saint-Denis, Oliván, and Le Maire*, 5–8.

22. Bridges and DeVille, "Natchitoches and the Trail to the Rio Grande," 241; Clark, *Beginnings of Texas*, 80; Marcel Giraud, *Histoire de la Louisiane Française, 2, Annees de Transition, 1715–1717*, 181–82; Fray Francisco Céliz, *Diary of the Alarcón Expedition into Texas, 1718–1719*, 77, 83.

23. Folmer, *Franco-Spanish Rivalry*, 245–46. The Natchitoches and the Doustionis received one hundred livres' worth of presents apiece, while the Hasinais and the Kadohadachos received three hundred livres' worth apiece. Minutes of the Council of Commerce, October 26, 1719, in *Mississippi Provincial Archives*, eds. and trans. D. Rowland and A. G. Sanders 3:267; La Harpe, "Account of the Journey," 85; Pénicault, *Fleur de Lys*, 216–17; Giraud, *Histoire de la Louisiane* 2:367.

24. La Harpe, "Account of the Journey," 246–51.

25. Ibid., 251–52.

26. Ibid., 253–56, 384–85, 524–35; Mildred Mott Wedel, *La Harpe's 1719 Post on Red River and Nearby Caddo Settlements*; Kathleen K. Gilmore, *French-Indian Interaction at an Early Eighteenth Century Post: The Roseborough Lake Site, Bowie County, Texas*.

27. La Harpe, "Account of the Journey," 384–85, 524–35; John, *Storms Brewed*, 214–16; Elam, "History of the Wichita Indian Confederacy," 98–104.

28. Espinosa on the Asinai, in "Descriptions," ed. and trans. M. A. Hatcher, *SWHQ*, 160.

29. A Spanish expedition into Texas in 1709 learned, through other tribes, that Bernardino was still opposed to Catholicism. See Espinosa, "Diary of the Espinosa-Olivares-Aguirre Expedition of 1709," 8–10.

30. Bernardino had left the Hasinai country with twenty-five warriors and the French party. They were attacked by a group of either Lipan Apaches or Karankawa Indians at the Colorado River, but the joint Hasinai-French force repulsed the attack. Saint Denis then

negotiated a truce between the warring tribes, and most of the Hasinai warriors returned to their villages. Declaration of St. Denis, in *Pichardo's Treatise*, ed. C. W. Hackett 4:308–309; Morfi, *History of Texas, 1673–1779*, 1:171; Clark, "Louis Juchereau de Saint-Denis," 13–14.

31. Morfi, *History of Texas, 1673–1779*, 1:185; Clark, "Louis Juchereau de Saint-Denis," 19–20. The Colegio de Nuestra Señora de Guadelupe was the sister college of the Colegio de Santa Cruz and was founded at Zacatecas in 1707. See McCloskey, *Formative Years*, 98–99.

32. Espinosa, "The Ramón Expedition: Espinosa's Diary of 1716," 20; Don Domingo Ramón, "Diary of His Expedition into Texas in 1716," 19–20.

33. Espinosa, "The Ramón Expedition," 21; Ramón, "Diary of His Expedition," 21.

34. Espinosa, "The Ramón Expedition," 22. Mission San Francisco de los Tejas was located near San Pedro Creek; thus, the Nabedaches were often referred to as the San Pedros.

35. Ibid., 22–24.

36. Morfi, *History of Texas, 1673–1779*, 1:186–87.

37. Espinosa, "The Ramón Expedition," 22; Hidalgo to the Viceroy, November 4, 1716, in "Descriptions," ed. and trans. M. A. Hatcher, *SWHQ*, 56–57; Hidalgo to Father Pedro de Mesquía, October 6, 1716, 215–18; and Hidalgo to the Viceroy, April 8, 1718, 231–32, both in *Provincias Internas* 181.

38. Espinosa, *Chrónica apostólica*, 443–45; Hidalgo to the Viceroy, November 4, 1716, in "Descriptions," ed. and trans. M. A. Hatcher, *SWHQ*, 56–61; Charmion Clair Shelby, "St. Denis's Declaration Concerning Texas in 1717," 172.

39. The Alarcón expedition crossed the Rio Grande on April 9, 1718. In the party were seventy people, cattle, sheep, chickens, six droves of supply-laden mules, and five hundred horses. Alarcón was instructed to found a mission and presidio on the San Antonio River, resupply the missionaries in East Texas, and station more soldiers at the presidio among the *Hasinais*. Céliz, *Diary of the Alarcón Expedition*, 43, 73; Clark, *Beginnings of Texas*, 86.

40. Céliz, *Diary of the Alarcón Expedition*, 76–83. Among the Indians baptized was Angelina, a Hasinai who had already been baptized in Mexico and had learned Spanish. Alarcón persuaded Angelina to live with her family near the Mission La Purísima Concepcion in the hope that others would follow her lead and congregate. The Angelina River is named after her.

41. Father Olivares to the Viceroy, June 22, 1718, in *Provincias Internas* 181:251; Espinosa, *Chrónica apostólica*, 450.

42. Morfi, *History of Texas, 1673–1779*, 1:191; Espinosa, *Chrónica apostólica*, 453–55.

43. "Commission de Commandant," in *Découvertes et établissements des Français dans l'ouest et dans de Sud de l'Amérique Septentrionale (1614–1754)*, 6:220–21; John, *Storms Brewed*, 212; Shelby, "Projected French Attacks upon the Northeastern Frontier of New Spain, 1719–1721," 457–72; Pénicault, *Fleur de Lys*, 221; Minutes of the Council of Commerce in Louisiana, December 2, 1721, in *Mississippi Provincial Archives*, eds. and trans. D. Rowland and A. G. Sanders 2:265.

44. Eleanor C. Buckley, "The Aguayo Expedition into Texas and Louisiana, 1719–1722," 27.

45. Peña, "Diary of the Aguayo Expedition," 39.

46. Ibid., 40.

47. Ibid., 41.

48. Ibid., 41–42.

49. Ibid., 44–45.

50. Ibid., 47–48.

51. Ibid., 57–59.

52. Pedro de Rivera, *Diario y Derrotero de lo Caminado, Visto, y Observado en la Visita*

que Hizo a los Presidios de Nueva Espana Septentrional el Brigadier Pedro Rivera, 80, 164–65. An overview of Rivera's inspection tour, which also included New Mexico, Chihuahua, and Coahuila, is provided by Retta Murphy, "The Journey of Pedro Rivera, 1724–1728," 125–41.

53. Rivera, *Diario*, 80, 162–63; Morfi, *History of Texas, 1673–1779*, 2:258–59.

54. Morfi, *History of Texas, 1673–1779*, 1:83; Charles O'Neill, ed., *Charlevoix's Louisiana: Selections from the History and the Journal of Pierre F. X. Charlevoix*, 123–24; M. Perier to Comte de Maurepas, December 10, 1731, in *Mississippi Provincial Archives: French Dominion*, eds. and trans. Dunbar Rowland, Albert Godfrey Sanders, and Patricia Galloway 4:105; Giraud, *History of French Louisiana, 5, The Company of the Indies, 1723–1731*, 387.

55. Morfi, *History of Texas, 1673–1779*, 2:249–50; Espinosa, *Chrónica apostólica*, 460.

Chapter 4. The Caddos
between Two Empires, 1731– 67

1. Don Jacinto de Barrios y Jáuregui to the Viceroy, November 8, 1751, in *Pichardo's Treatise*, ed. C. W. Hackett 4:16.

2. Marilyn McAdams Sibley, "Across Texas in 1767: The Travels of Captain Pages," 609.

3. John Sibley, "Historical Sketches of the Several Indian Tribes in Louisiana, south of the Arkansas, and between the Mississippi and the River Grande," in *American State Papers, Class II, Indian Affairs*, 721; Report of Tomás Felipe Winthuisen, August 19, 1744, BA.

4. Herbert Eugene Bolton, *Texas in the Middle Eighteenth Century: Studies in Spanish Colonial History and Administration*, 41; Deposition of Don Joseph González, 1750, BA; Investigation of Joachin de Orobio Bazterra, January 12, 1746, BA.

5. Documents discussing the Caddo trade include the Report of Tomás Felipe de Winthuysen, August 19, 1744, BA; Investigation of Joachin de Orobio Bazterra, January 12, 1746, BA; Proceedings of the Junta de Guerra y Hacienda relative to the French intrusion in Spanish dominions, February 1, 1754, BA; and Don Pedro Sierra, January 27, 1761, BA. See also Hiram Ford Gregory, "Eighteenth Century Caddoan Archeology: A Study in Methods and Interpretation"; Usner, *Indians, Settlers, and Slaves*, 176–79, 260–66.

6. The most detailed list of gifts and trade goods to be supplied to the Caddos comes from the period just after the transferal of Louisiana to Spain. It was drawn up by Athanase de Mézières, a French soldier who had been in Louisiana since 1733 and had been stationed at Natchitoches since as early as 1743. In 1769, he was assigned the position of lieutenant governor of Natchitoches by the Spanish governor of Louisiana, Alejandro O'Reilly. The following list of presents was approved by O'Reilly on January 22, 1770, and probably bears a close resemblance to the annual presents the Kadohadachos (as well as the other Caddo tribes) received from the French during the period covered by this chapter.

To the nation of Grandes Cados, for their annual present:

A hat trimmed with galloons	Twenty pounds of powder
An ornamented shirt	Forty pounds of balls
Two fusils	One pound of vermillion
Two blankets of two and one-	Two pounds of glass beads
half points	One pound of thread
Three ells of cloth	One ax

Two ordinary shirts	Two adzes
A copper kettle	Twenty-four large knives
Forty small knives	Two jugs of brandy
Forty-eight awls	Six mirrors
Forty-eight worm-screws	Two pounds of wire
Two hundred flints	One flag
Twenty-four steels	Half a piece of cord
Forty-eight hawksbells	Twenty-five pounds of salt
Two hundred needles	Two hatchets
Ninety ells of tape	One ell of ribbon for the
Ten rolls of tobacco	medal

(O'Reilly to de Mézières, January 22, 1770, ADM 1:132–33.)

Twelve days later, de Mézières made a contract with a Natchitoches merchant to trade European goods to the Caddos in return for deer skins, bear's fat, and buffalo hides. Again, this list is representative of the trade between the French and the Caddo tribes in the period covered by this chapter.

List of Goods necessary for the annual Supply of the Village of the Grand Cadaux:
Forty staple fusils of good caliber
Sixty ells of Limbourg, red and blue
Thirty woolen blankets, twenty of two and one-half points and ten of three points
Four hundred pounds of French gun powder
Nine hundred pounds of bullets, caliber thirty to thirty-two
Thirty pickaxes
Thirty hatchets
Thirty tomahawks
Fifty shirts, half gingham and half white
One gross of hunters' knives with three nails
One gross of pocket knives with horn or dog's head handles
Six dozen of large boxwood combs
Six dozen pairs of large scissors
Sixty pounds of small glass beads, sky blue, white, and black
One thousand flints
Six dozen large steels
Six dozen awls
Six pounds of pure vermillion
Six dozen mirrors of pliant copper
Six pieces of scarlet tavelle
Twelve pounds of copper wire suitable for bracelets and worm-screws

(Contract of Juan Pisneros with Athanase de Mézières, February 3, 1770, ADM 1:143–46.)

7. Solís, "Diary of a Visit of Inspection," 61; Louis de Blanc to Governor Estevan Miró, January 20, 1790, SMV 2:295–97.

8. Contract of Juan Pisneros with Athanase de Mézières, February 3, 1770, ADM 1:143–46.

9. Report of Fray Ignacio Antonio Ciprián to the General Commissary, October 27, 1749, TMCZ, 24; Solís, "Diary of a Visit of Inspection," 70.

10. Once again, the population totals for the Caddo confederacies are estimations at best. The only data for the Kadohadachos comes from a French trader, who stated in 1773

that the Petit Caddos had sixty warriors while the Kadohadachos had ninety, which implies about seven hundred fifty tribal members. See J. Gaignard, Journal of an Expedition up the Red River, 1773–1774, ADM 2:83. While there are reports on the population of the Hasinais, it is difficult to ascertain their exact numbers. In 1749, Fray Ignacio Antonio Ciprián, a Franciscan missionary in Texas, claimed that the Nacogdoches tribe had 22 rancherias and 120 warriors, which translates to about 600 men, women, and children. This total seems too high, for if the other three tribes of the Hasinai had relatively the same population, there would be about 2,400 Hasinais. Report of Fray Ignacio Antonio Ciprián to the General Commissary, October 27, 1749, TMCZ, 26.

Don Manuel Antonio de Soto Bermúdez, an officer from Los Adaes, made a tour through the Hasinai country three years after Fray Ciprián's report. The Nacogodoches *caddi* told Bermúdez that his tribe had "eleven large rancherias and in them fifty-two Indians bearing arms, and that in addition to these there were many young men almost capable of handling muskets." There is no mention of a catastrophic epidemic that hit the Hasinais between 1749 and 1752, so it seems that Ciprián had possibly counted the teenage boys as being warriors. If the report of Bermúdez is correct, there would be about 260 people in the Nacogdoches tribe. The Nasoni *caddi* told Bermúdez that among the Nasonis and the Nadacos (soon to merge into one tribe), there were twenty-nine rancherias with sixty "adult Indians bearing arms," which translates into a total population of about 300. If the Hainais and the Nabedaches had about the same numbers, it would seem that the total Hasinai population stood at about 1,200 in 1752. There are no other reports of their population until after the disastrous epidemic of 1777–78. Report of Bermúdez, November 16, 1752, in *Pichardo's Treatise*, ed. C. W. Hackett 4:56, 58.

The totals for the Natchitoches and the Yatasis are derived from a 1770 list of presents ordered for the two tribes, as well as for the Kadohadachos and the Petit Caddos. Among the gifts were forty pounds of balls for the Kadohadachos (who have already been shown to have had ninety warriors), twenty pounds of balls for the Petit Caddos (who had sixty warriors), twelve pounds of balls for the Yatasis, and eight pounds of balls for the Natchitoches (List of the effects which should be given to the three Indian nations of the Post of Natchitoches, copied from the Instruction drawn by the Most Excellent Senor Conde de Orreilli, ADM 1:132–34). Another document from 1770 states that the Kadohadachos should receive forty rifles, the Petit Caddos thirty, and the Yatasis fifteen. The two documents imply that the Yatasis had about half the population of the Petit Caddos, and the Natchitoches total was about three-fourths that of the Yatasis (Contract of Juan Piseros with de Mézières, February 3, 1770, ADM 1:143–45).

11. See especially the Report of Bermúdez, November 16, 1752, in *Pichardo's Treatise*, ed. C. W. Hackett 4:55–58.

12. Williams, "Aboriginal Location," 549.

13. Memorial of the College of Zacatecas to the King, January 15, 1750, TMCZ, 47; Solís, "Diary of a Visit of Inspection," 70.

14. For discussions of Caddo religion that do not mention the *xinesi*, see the Report of Fray Ignacio Antonio Ciprián to the General Commissary, October 27, 1749, TMCZ, 23–28; and Memorial of the College of Zacatecas to the King, January 15, 1750, TMCZ, 42–53.

15. George Sabo III, "Reordering Their World: A Caddoan Ethnohistory," in *Visions and Revisions: Ethnohistoric Perspectives on Southern Cultures*, 25–41.

16. Memorial of the College of Zacatecas to the King, TMCZ, 44, 49.

17. Report of Tomás Felipe Winthuisen, August 19, 1744, BA; Nicolás de LaFora, *The Frontiers of New Spain: Nicolás de LaFora's Description, 1766–1768*, 166; Solís, "Diary of a Visit of Inspection," 67.

18. Memorial of the College of Zacatecas to the King, January 15, 1750, TMCZ, 49; Report of Fray Ignacio Ciprián, TMCZ, 27.

19. Elam, "History of the Wichita Indian Confederacy," 105–109; John, *Storms Brewed*, 305–306.

20. Ernest Wallace and E. Adamson Hoebel, *The Comanches: Lords of the South Plains*; John, *Storms Brewed*, 249–56, 307–14; William Edward Dunn, "Apache Relations in Texas, 1718–1750," 198–274.

21. Schilz, "People of the Cross Timbers," 75–79; Bolton, *Texas in the Middle Eighteenth Century*, 149–51.

22. Schilz, "People of the Cross Timbers," 81–85; Bolton, *Texas in the Middle Eighteenth Century*, 232–33.

23. Deposition of Lieutenant Don Joseph Gonzáles, 1750, BA; Certification of the Reverend Father Friar Pedro Rámirez, August 20, 1750, BA.

24. Don Jacinto de Barrios y Jáuregui to the Viceroy, November 8, 1751, in *Pichardo's Treatise*, ed. C. W. Hackett 4:16; Report of Don Manuel Antonio de Soto Bermúdez, in *Pichardo's Treatise*, ed. C. W. Hackett 4:54–59.

25. Ibid., 57–59.

26. Fray José de Calahorra to Gov. Barrios y Jáuregui, February 23, 1753, ibid., 61.

27. Proceedings of the Junta de Guerra y Hacienda relative to the French intrusion in Spanish dominions, February 1, 1754, BA. Another reason that Gov. Barrios y Jáuregui allowed the illicit trade between the French of Louisiana and the Spanish and Indians of East Texas to continue was because he was heavily involved in it himself (see Weddle, *French Thorn*, 291–301). For an overview of trade on the Louisiana-Texas frontier, see David J. Weber, *The Spanish Frontier in North America*, 172–74, 186–88.

28. Certification of Gov. Barrios y Jáuregui, October 29, 1755, BA.; Deposition of Don Pedro Sierra, January 27, 1761, BA.

29. John, *Storms Brewed*, 307–14; William Edward Dunn, "The Apache Mission on the San Saba River: Its Founding and Failure," 379–414; Robert S. Weddle, *The San Sabá Mission: Spanish Pivot in Texas*.

30. Eyewitnesses reported that the unnamed Hainai *caddi* demanded horses from the mission priests, who told him he could get horses from the nearby presidio. The *caddi* then commandeered the horse of Father Alonso Giraldo de Terreros and rode off to the presidio. He soon returned enraged, for the soldiers there had fired upon him and his party. When Father Terreros attempted to escort the *caddi* back to the presidio, the Indians began their attack and the priest was killed. Deposition of Juan Leal, March 22, 1758, 75; Deposition of Father Fray Miguel de Molina, March 22, 1758, 85–86; and Deposition of Andres de Villareal, 68–72, all in *The San Sabá Papers*, eds. Paul Nathan and Lesley Byrd Simpson.

31. John, *Storms Brewed*, 350–51; Henry Easton Allen, "The Parrilla Expedition to the Red River in 1759," 60–61, 66–70.

32. Fray José de Calahorra Sáenz to Gov. Martos y Navarrete, May 27, 1760, in "The Tawakoni-Yscani Village, 1760: A Study in Archeological Site Identification," by Leroy Johnson and Edward B. Jelks, 409–10.

33. Diary of Fray Calahorra, October 24, 1760, ibid., 412–13.

34. John, *Storms Brewed*, 357–58.

35. Decree of Gov. Martos y Navarette, September 15, 1762, BA; John, *Storms Brewed*, 362–63.

36. Decree of Gov. Martos y Navarette, September 15, 1762, BA.

37. Fray Calahorra to Gov. Martos y Navarette, July 30, 1765, BA.

Chapter 5. Decline:
The Caddos and Spain, 1767–1803

1. Report by de Mézières of the Expedition to Cadodachos, October 29, 1770, *ADM* 1:208.

2. De Mézières to Teodoro de Croix, November 15, 1778, *ADM* 2:231–32.

3. Louis de Blanc to Esteban Miró, March 27, 1790, *SMV* 3:316.

4. De Mézières to Bernardo de Gálvez, May, 1779, *ADM* 2:252–53; De Mézières to Luis de Unzaga y Amézaga, May 20, 1770, *ADM* 1:199.

5. Report by de Mézières of the Expedition to Cadodachos, October 29, 1770, *ADM* 1:208; J. Gaignard, Journal of an Expedition up the Red River, 1773–1774, *ADM* 2:83. See Chapter 4n.10, for a discussion of Kadohadacho, Yatasi, and Natchitoches population totals. Both Houhan and Cocay played important roles in events that occurred between 1767 and 1768. However, the Spanish designated Cocay as medal chief of the Yatasis in 1770. See Antonio de Ulloa to Hugo Oconor, 1768, *ADM* 1:129; Ulloa to Marqués de Grimaldi, August 18, 1768, *SMV* 2:65–69; Agreement made with the Indian Nations in Assembly, April 21, 1770, *ADM* 1:157.

6. De Mézières to Luis Unzaga y Amézaga, July 3, 1771, *ADM* 1:249; José de la Peña to Luis Unzaga y Amézaga, September 14, 1772, *ADM* 2:16. See Chapter 4n.10 for Hasinai population totals. The Spanish designated the Nadaco *caddi*, as well as Bigotes, as medal chief in recognition of Nadaco independence from the Hasinai. See de Mézières to Croix, September 30, 1779, *ADM* 2:290.

7. Abraham P. Nasatir, *Borderland in Retreat: From Spanish Louisiana to the Far Southwest*, 6–14.

8. De Mézières to the Barón de Ripperdá, July 4, 1772, *ADM* 1:304; De Mézières to Unzaga y Amézaga, May 20, 1770, *ADM* 1:166–68; Din and Nasatir, *Imperial Osages*, 70.

9. De Mézières to Unzaga y Amézaga, November 29, 1770, *ADM* 1:193–94; Din and Nasatir, *Imperial Osages*, 73–74.

10. John, *Storms Brewed*, 380, 388.

11. David M. Vigness, "Don Hugo Oconor and New Spain's Northeastern Frontier, 1764–1766," 27–40.

12. Ulloa to Oconor, 1768, *ADM* 1:128–29.

13. Ibid.

14. Nasatir, *Borderlands in Retreat*, 15–18.

15. Barón de Ripperdá to the Viceroy, July 6, 1772, *ADM* 1:327; Alejandro O'Reilly to de Mézières, September 23, 1769, *ADM* 1:130–31; Report by de Mézières of the Expedition to Cadodachos, October 29, 1770, *ADM* 1:208.

16. O'Reilly to de Mézières, January 22, 1770, *ADM* 1:132–34; Statement of Payment for Indian Presents, January 9, 1770, *SMV* 1:154–55. Alexis Grappe was appointed trader for the Kadohadachos, Fazende Moriere (de Mézières's brother-in-law) for the Petit Caddos, and Sieur Dupin for the Yatasis. See the Contract of Juan Piseros with de Mézières, Natchitoches, February 3, 1770, 143–46; and Instructions for the Traders of the Cadaux D'Acquioux and Hiatasses Nations, February 4, 1770, 148–50, both in *ADM* 1.

17. Agreement Made with the Indian Nations in Assembly, April 21, 1770, *ADM* 1:157–58. The Spanish would often decorate a leading chief with the royal medal in recognition of his eminent position among his tribe, his friendship with Spain, and his importance in diplomatic relations. Being a medal chief usually reinforced the man's authority. See John C. Ewers, "Symbols of Chiefly Authority in Spanish Louisiana," in *The Spanish in the Mississippi Valley, 1762–1804*, ed. Francis McDermott, 272–86.

18. De Mézières to Unzaga y Amézaga, February 1, 1770, 140–42; and Agreement

Made with the Indian Nations in Assembly, April 21, 1770, 157–58, both in *ADM* 1. Unzaga y Amézaga succeeded O'Reilly as governor of Louisiana in 1770. Unfortunately, the new governor and de Mézières did not always agree on Indian policy, particularly regarding de Mézières's policy of peace with the Norteños.

19. De Mézières to Unzaga y Amézaga, June 10, 1770, *ADM* 1:175.

20. De Mézières to Unzaga y Amézaga, September, 27, 1770, 204–206; and Report by De Mézières of the Expedition to Cadodachos, October 29, 1770, 206–208, both in *ADM* 1. For the Spanish viewpoint, see Depositions Relative to the Expedition to Cadodachos, October 30–31, 1770, *ADM* 1:220–30; Fray San Miguel Santa María y Silva to the Viceroy, July 21, 1774, *ADM* 2:68–74.

21. Report by de Mézières of the Expedition to Cadodachos, October 29, 1770, *ADM* 1:209–11.

22. Ibid., 211–13; Elam, "History of the Wichita Indian Confederacy," 137–39.

23. Ripperdá to Unzaga y Amézaga, December 31, 1771, 264; and De Mézières to Unzaga y Amézaga, July 3, 1771, 249–50, both in *ADM* 1.

24. Ripperdá to Unzaga y Amézaga, December 31, 1771, *ADM* 1:265.

25. Ibid., 266.

26. Treaty with the Taovayas, October 27, 1771, *ADM* 1:256–60.

27. For an overview of the problems caused by Oconor, see Donald Worcester, "Spaniards, Frenchmen, and Indians," 42–43; Joseph F. Park, "Spanish Indian Policy in Northern Mexico, 1765–1810," 224–25.

28. Ripperdá to the Viceroy, July 6, 1772, 328; and De Mézières to Ripperdá, July 4, 1772, 305, both in *ADM* 1; José de la Peña to Unzaga y Amézaga, September 14, 1772, *ADM* 2:18–19.

29. De Mézières to Ripperdá, July 4, 1772, 312–13; Ripperdá to the Viceroy, July 6, 1772, 326–27; and the Viceroy to Ripperdá, September 16, 1772, 349–51, all in *ADM* 1.

30. Ripperdá to Unzaga y Amézaga, December 31, 1771, *ADM* 1:266–68.

31. De Mézières to Unzaga y Amézaga, February 25, 1772, 283–84; and Ripperdá to the Viceroy, July 6, 1772, 329, both in *ADM* 1.

32. De Mézières to Unzaga y Amézaga, August, 20, 1772, *ADM* 1:337–38; De la Peña to Unzaga y Amézaga, September 14, 1772, 23–24; and Ripperdá to Unzaga y Amézaga, February 11, 1773, 27, both in *ADM* 2; De la Peña to Unzaga y Amézaga, January 18, 1773, *SMV* 2:211–12.

33. John Francis Bannon, *The Spanish Borderlands Frontier, 1513–1821*, 179–80. For a first-hand account of Rubí's inspection tour, see LaFora, *The Frontiers of New Spain*; and Morfi, *History of Texas, 1673–1779*, 2:419–21.

34. Bolton, *Texas in the Middle Eighteenth Century*, 387, 391.

35. Ibid., 394–401. Index of *oficios* which Col. Domingo Cabello, governor of Texas, submits to the Commandant General of the Interior Provinces of New Spain, August 13–16, 1779, BA.

36. Bolton, *Texas in the Middle Eighteenth Century*, 418–40.

37. De Croix to Cabello, May 14, 1779, BA.

38. Bolton, *Texas in the Middle Eighteenth Century*, 441–46.

39. De Mézières to Croix, November 15, 1778, 231; and De Mézières to Croix, March 18, 1778, 189, both in *ADM* 2.

40. See footnote 303, *ADM* 2:250; Bernardo de Gálvez to de Mézières, October 28, 1777, *ADM* 2:138. Pedro Vial reported that he visited the Nadaco village on the Sabine River in 1788 and that it consisted of fourteen or fifteen grass houses (*Pichardo's Treatise*, ed. C. W. Hackett 3:444–46).

41. See footnote 303, *ADM* 2:250; Pierre Rousseau and Louis de Blanc to Miró, March 20, 1787, *SMV* 3:198; De Blanc to the Barón de Carondolet, November 20, 1792, *SMV* 4:98; Sibley, "Historical Sketches," 721–24.

42. De Mézières to Croix, November 15, 1778, ADM 2:232–33.

43. De Mézières to Unzaga y Amézaga, May 2, 1777, 131; and De Mézières to Unzaga y Amézaga, September 14, 1777, 141–42, both in ADM 2.

44. De Mézières to Gálvez, May 1779, ADM 2:250–52. The wording in this letter makes it unclear whether the *caddi* is actually Tinhioüen. Elizabeth John interprets this document to imply that Tinhioüen died in the epidemic of 1778 (*Storms Brewed*, 523). However, later documents continue to mention a "Tenihuan," "Thenioan," and "Tini-ouan" as being the chief of the Kadohadachos. See Miró to Francisco Cruzat, March 24, 1786, 171; José de la Peña to Miró, September 22, 1787, 234–35; and De Blanc to Miró, August 5, 1788, 259, all in SMV 3.

45. Gálvez to De Mézières, June 1, 1779, ADM 2:253–54.

46. Din and Nasatir, *Imperial Osages*, 137–40; Domingo Cabello, Daily Record of Occurrences for September 1782, BA.

47. Miró to Cruzat, March 24, 1786, 171–72; and Miró to Gálvez, August 1, 1786, 182–83, both in SMV 3; Din and Nasatir, *Imperial Osages*, 153–55.

48. Miró to Cruzat, March 24, 1786, 172; and Miró to Gálvez, August 1, 1786, 183–84, both in SMV 3.

49. Rousseau and de Blanc to Miró, March 20, 1787, SMV 3:198–99.

50. José de la Peña to Miró, September 22, 1787, SMV 3:234.

51. De Blanc to Miró, March 27, 1790, 316; and de Blanc to Miró, August 5, 1788, 259, both in SMV 3.

52. De Blanc to Miró, September 30, 1789, SMV 3:281.

53. De Blanc to Miró, March 27, 1790, SMV 3:317.

54. Croix to Ripperdá, September 15, 1778; and Croix to Cabello, March 9, 1779, in BA. De Mézières to the Viceroy, February 20, 1778, 178; Croix to Bernardo de Gálvez, September 10, 1778, 218; and Croix to José de Gálvez, September 23, 1778, 220–24, all in ADM 2.

55. Index of *oficios*, August 13–20, 1779, BA.

56. Borme to Bernardo de Gálvez, December 29, 1779, ADM 2:330; Cabello to Croix, August, 17, 1780, BA.

57. Ibid.

58. Strength report and daily record of occurences at San Antonio de Bexar Presidio for September 1782, Domingo Cabello, BA.

59. Cabello to Don Pedro Piernas, January 13, 1783, SMV 3:70; John, *Storms Brewed*, 635–36.

60. Cabello to Piernas, January 13, 1783, 70–71; Cabello to the Governor of Louisiana, September 20, 1783, 80–85, both in SMV 3. The Hasinais were to receive 6 axes, 3 hatchets, 3 mattocks, 3 guns, 18 pounds of gunpowder, 36 pounds of balls, 8 ells of cloth, 7 shirts, 3 pounds of vermilion, 3½ dozens of heavy knives, 7 pounds of beads, 4 dozens of combs, and 8 bundles of tobacco. In comparison, the Bidais were to receive the same amount as the Hasinais, the Tonkawas and Tawakonis twice as much, and the Taovayas four times as much.

61. Cabello, Strength Report of September 1783, BA.

62. Ibid.

63. Cabello to Gil Ybarbo, José María de Armán, and Andres Benito Courbiere, April 5, 1785, BA.

64. John, *Storms Brewed*, 653, 690–700.

65. Cabello to Don Jacobo de Ugarte, September 10, 1786; and Ugarte to Cabello, October 5, 1786, both in BA.

66. De Blanc to Miró, February 28, 1790, 301–303; and Letter of Miró, 1788, 256, both in SMV 3.

67. Rafael Martínez Pacheco to Don Juan Ugalde, July 6, 1789, BA.

68. De Blanc to Miró, January 20, 1790, 295–97; de Blanc to Miró, February 28, 1790, 301–302; and de Blanc to Miró, September 2, 1790, 321, all in *SMV* 3.

69. Peña to Miró, August 17, 1789, 232–33; and de Blanc to Miró, March 30, 1791, 407, both in *SMV* 3; de Blanc to Carondelet, February 18, 1792, *SMV* 4:9–13.

70. Carondolet to Don Ygnacio DeLino, June 29, 1792, 56; and Carondolet to Zénon Trudeau, December 22, 1792, 107, both in *SMV* 4.

71. Sibley, "Historical Sketches," 721; Williams, "Aboriginal Location," 553.

72. J. Villasana Haggard, "The House of Barr and Davenport," 46; Barr and Davenport to José Gaudiana, September 2, 1809, BA.

Chapter 6. Resurgence: The Caddos and the Louisiana-Texas Frontier, 1803–15

1. Address to the Caddo Chief, September 5, 1806, *LBC*, 4.

2. By the beginning of the nineteenth century, the Euro-Americans referred to the Kadohadachos as "Caddos." I will continue to use the term Kadohadacho for the Red River Caddos and Hasinai for the East Texas branch of the tribe. The term "Caddos" will be used to include all of the Caddo confederacies.

3. Background on the southwestern border situation can be found in "The Louisiana-Texas Frontier," *SWHQ* 10 (July 1906): 1–75, and *SWHQ* 17 (October 1913): 140–75; "The Explorations of the Louisiana Frontier, 1803–1806," 151–74, 274–84; and *The Early Exploration of Louisiana*, all by Isaac J. Cox; and in Dan L. Flores's excellent *Jefferson and Southwestern Exploration: The Freeman and Custis Accounts of the Red River of 1806*.

4. "Historical Sketches," 721; *A Report From Natchitoches in 1807*, 95, both by J. Sibley. Sibley was born in Massachusetts in 1757 and served as a surgeon's mate in the Revolutionary War. He arrived in Louisiana in 1802 and settled in Natchitoches the following year. See G. P. Whittington, "Doctor John Sibley of Natchitoches, 1757–1832," 467–72.

5. Sibley, *Report From Natchitoches*, 95; Sibley to Governor William C. C. Claiborne, October 10, 1803, in *The Territory of Orleans, 1803–1812*, ed. Clarence E. Carter, 75–76.

6. Sibley, "Historical Sketches," 721–24.

7. Ibid., 722; Sibley, *Report From Natchitoches*, 96. In 1814, Sibley reported that the Nabedaches had one hundred warriors, while the Hainais had fifty-four. I believe that he included the Nacogdoches warriors in the Nabedache total. Sibley to Secy. of War John Armstrong, August 10, 1814, in "Doctor John Sibley and the Louisiana-Texas Frontier, 1803-1814," ed. Julia Kathryn Garrett, *SWHQ* 49 (April 1946),: 609.

8. "Historical Sketches," 722; and *Report From Natchitoches*, both by J. Sibley, 96.

9. "Historical Sketches," 722–23; and *Report From Natchitoches*, both by J. Sibley, 94–96.

10. "Historical Sketches," 724; and *Report from Natchitoches*, 96–97, both by J. Sibley; Dan L. Flores, "The Red River Branch of the Alabama-Coushatta Indians: An Ethnohistory," 57–59. For an overview of the emigrant tribes, see Fred B. Kniffen, Hiram F. Gregory, and George A. Stokes, *The Historic Indian Tribes of Louisiana, From 1542 to the Present*, 83–105.

11. Sibley, *Report From Natchitoches*, 11–12, 15–16; Sibley to Secy. of War Henry Dearborn, January 10, 1807, 294–95; and Sibley to Dearborn, April 3, 1807, 297–98, both

in "Doctor John Sibley and the Louisiana-Texas Frontier," ed. K. J. Garrett, *SWHQ* 45 (January 1942); Sibley to Secretary of War William Eustis, October 20, 1809, *HR* 1035, 105–106.

12. Sibley, "Historical Sketches," 725.

13. Sibley to Eustis, November 28, 1812, in "Doctor John Sibley and the Louisiana-Texas Frontier," ed. K. J. Garrett, *SWHQ* 49 (January 1946): 418; Manuel María de Salcedo, "A Governor's Report on Texas in 1809," 614.

14. Daniel Clark to Secy. of State James Madison, September 29, 1803, *The Territory of Orleans, 1803–1812*, ed. C. E. Carter, 63.

15. Sibley to William Claiborne, October 10, 1803, ibid., 75–76.

16. Claiborne to Edward Turner, February 25, 1804, *LBC* 1:386.

17. See footnote number 20, in "Doctor John Sibley and the Louisiana-Texas Frontier," ed. K. J. Garrett, *SWHQ* 45 (January 1942): 300.

18. Don Jacobo de Ugarte to Juan Bautista de Elguezábal, November 26, 1803; and Nemesio Salcedo to Elguezábal, July 17, 1804, both in BA.

19. Elguezábal to Salcedo, June 3, 1804; and Salcedo to Elguezábal, July 17, 1804, both in BA.

20. Claiborne to Thomas Jefferson, August 30, 1804, *LBC* 2:287.

21. Turner to Claiborne, October 13, 1804, 385; and Claiborne to Turner, November 3, 1804, 390, both in *LBC* 2; Turner to Claiborne, November 21, 1804, *The Territory of Orleans, 1803–1812*, ed. C. E. Carter, 336. Sibley gave Dehahuit the fated flag the following year.

22. Cox, *Early Exploration of Louisiana*, 164. Upon Sibley's appointment as permanent agent in 1805, Secretary Dearborn instructed him to "encourage a few of the Principal Chiefs of some of the considerable Tribes or Nations to make a visit to the seat of Government; and, if practicable, to induce the Great Chief of the Caddos [the only tribe mentioned by name] to be of the party . . . " (Dearborn to Sibley, October 17, 1805, *The Territory of Orleans, 1803–1812*, ed. C. E. Carter, 515).

23. Dearborn to Sibley, December 13, 1804, *The Territory of Orleans, 1803–1812*, ed. C. E. Carter, 352–53; Valle to Elguezábal, March 22, 1805, BA.

24. Sibley, "Historical Sketches," 721–22.

25. Quoted in Cox, *Early Exploration of Louisiana*, 165; Claiborne to Sibley, June 10, 1805, 125; and Claiborne to Jefferson, July 14, 1805, 185, both in *LBC* 3.

26. Valle to Elguezábal, May 23, 1805; and Valle to Eguezábal, October 3, 1805, both in BA.

27. Valle, Diary containing events occurring during the entire month of June 1805; and Valle to Elguezábal, August 10, 1805, both in BA.

28. Quoted in Flores, *Jefferson and Southwestern Exploration*, 55.

29. Salcedo to Antonio Cordero, October 8, 1805, BA.

30. Sebastian Rodriguez to Cordero, February 13, 1806, BA.

31. For a study of the factory system, see Francis Paul Prucha, *American Indian Policy in the Formative Years: The Indian Trade and Intercourse Acts, 1790–1834*. For details of the trade, see List of articles at the United States Trading House at Natchitoches for the ensuing year, January 4, 1811, NSFFL.

32. Flores, *Jefferson and Southwest Exploration*, 88; Juan Ygnacio Ramón to Francisco Viana, June 2, 1806, BA.

33. Flores, *Jefferson and Southwest Exploration*, 123–25; Ramón to Viana, June 20, 1806, BA; T. Freeman and P. Curtis, *Account of the Red River*, 20–21.

34. T. Freeman and P. Curtis, *Account of the Red River*, 20–21.

35. Ibid.

36. Flores, *Jefferson and Southwestern Exploration*, 162–63; T. Freeman and P. Curtis, *Account of the Red River*, 23–25.

37. T. Freeman and P. Curtis, *Account of the Red River*, 26–27.

38. Ibid., 27–28. The leader of the three Kadohadachos was named Grand Ozages. He traveled with the American party up the Red River and all the way back to Natchitoches, "and was Particularly Servisable [sic] in hunting, as a Guide & keeping the Other Indians together, and is in Major Freemans [sic] Opinion one of the Best Indians he ever saw." Sibley later presented Dehahuit with a regimental coat to give Grand Ozages in recognition of his assistance (*Report From Natchitoches*, 21).

39. Flores, *Jefferson and Southwestern Exploration*, 173; T. Freeman and P. Curtis, *Account of the Red River*, 35–36; *Pichardo's Treatise*, ed. C. W. Hackett 3:422–29.

40. T. Freeman and P. Curtis, *Account of the Red River*, 35–36.

41. Claiborne to His Excellency Governor Herrera, August 26, 1806, 384; and Herrera to Claiborne, August 28, 1806, 392, both in *LBC* 3.

42. The boundaries of the Neutral Ground were never officially described beyond a general statement that the Arroyo Hondo on the east and the Sabine River on the west were to serve as boundaries. J. Villasana Haggard, "The Neutral Ground Agreement Between Louisiana and Texas, 1806–1821," 1001–1128.

43. Address to the Caddo Chief, September 5, 1806, *LBC* 4:3–5.

44. Sibley to Dearborn, January 10, 1807, in "Doctor John Sibley and the Louisiana-Texas Frontier," ed. K. J. Garrett, *SWHQ* 45 (January 1942): 295; Sibley, *Report From Natchitoches*, 13–14.

45. Sibley, *Report From Natchitoches*, 20–21.

46. Ibid., 23–24; Sibley to Dearborn, July 3, 1807, in "Doctor John Sibley and the Louisiana-Texas Frontier," ed. K. J. Garrett, *SWHQ* 45 (January 1942): 381.

47. Sibley, *Report From Natchitoches*, 23, 26–27; Viana to Cordero, July 23, 1807, BA.

48. Sibley, *Report From Natchitoches*, 48–60. At this council there were 90 Kadohadacho, 45 Nabedaches, 34 Nadacos, 24 Nacogdoches, 16 Hainais, 8 Kichais, 18 Tawakonis, and 80 Comanches.

49. Ibid., 63–65.

50. Ibid., 63–64.

51. Sibley to Dearborn, August 8, 1807, in "Doctor John Sibley and the Louisiana-Texas Frontier," ed. K. J. Garrett, *SWHQ* 46 (July 1942): 83–84.

52. Viana to Cordero, September 18, 1807, BA.

53. Record of Goods Supplied by Barr and Davenport, November 11, 1807; and List of Indian Presents, January 11, 1808, both in BA.

54. Salcedo to Bernardo Bonavía, June 14, 1809; Bonavía to Salcedo, June 16, 1809; Salcedo to Pedro López Pirelos, June 18, 1809; and Bernardo Montero to Salcedo, May 13, 1812, all in BA.

55. Salcedo to José María Guadiana, August 19, 1809; and Barr and Davenport to Guadiana, September 2, 1809, both in BA; Flores, *Jefferson and Southwestern Exploration*, 307.

56. Sibley to Eustis, January 30, 1810, in "Doctor John Sibley and the Louisiana-Texas Frontier," ed. K. J. Garrett, *SWHQ* 47 (April 1944): 388–89.

57. Sibley to Eustis, December 31, 1811, in "Doctor John Sibley and the Louisiana-Texas Frontier," ed. K. J. Garrett, *SWHQ* 49 (January 1946): 403.

58. Harry M. Henderson, "The Magee-Gutierrez Expedition," *SWHQ* 55 (July 1951): 43–61; Sibley to Eustis, May 18, 1812, *HR* 1035.

59. Sibley to Eustis, July 14, 1812, in "Doctor John Sibley and the Louisiana-Texas Frontier," ed. K. J. Garrett, *SWHQ* 49 (January 1946): 412; Salcedo to Soto, August 11, 1812, BA.

60. Sibley to Eustis, August 5, 1812, 414; and Sibley to Eustis, February 12, 1813, 421, both in "Doctor John Sibley and the Louisiana-Texas Frontier," ed. K. J. Garrett, *SWHQ* 49 (January 1946).

61. Sibley to [Gen. John] Armstrong, October 6, 1813, in "Doctor John Sibley and

the Louisiana-Texas Frontier," ed. K. J. Garrett, *SWHQ* 49 (April 1946): 602.

62. Ibid., 603.

63. Linnard to General John Mason, September 3, 1813; and Linnard to Mason, October 14, 1813, both in NSFFL.

64. A Talk from W. C. C. Claiborne, Governor of Louisiana, to the Chief of the Caddo, October 18, 1813, *LBC* 6:276–77.

65. Sibley to Armstrong, August 10, 1814, in "Doctor John Sibley and the Louisiana-Texas Frontier," ed. K. J. Garrett, *SWHQ* 49 (April 1946): 609.

66. Claiborne to Jackson, October 28, 1814, *LBC* 6:293–94.

67. Claiborne to James Monroe, December 20, 1814, 328–29; Claiborne to Thomas Gales, September 15, 1815, 364, both in *LBC* 6; Sibley to Monroe, January 10, 1815, in "Doctor John Sibley and the Louisiana-Texas Frontier," ed. K. J. Garrett, *SWHQ* 49 (April 1949): 611; Glover, "History of the Caddo Indians, 907.

Chapter 7. Disruption of the Caddo World and the Treaty of 1835

1. Journal of the proceedings at the agency-house, Caddo nation, Louisiana, in forming and completing a treaty for the cession of land, & c., between the commissioner on the part of the United States and the Caddo nation of Indians, *HR* 1035, 118.

2. Juan Antonio Padilla, "Texas in 1820: Report of the Barbarous Indians of the Province of Texas by Juan Antonio Padilla, Made December 27, 1819," 47–52; Jean Louis Berlandier, *The Indians of Texas in 1830.*

3. Berlandier, *Indians of Texas*, 52; Padilla, "Texas in 1820," 47–49.

4. Padilla, "Texas in 1820," 48; Berlandier, *Indians of Texas*, 108.

5. As usual, the exact population totals for the Caddos are difficult to ascertain. In 1819, Padilla grossly overestimated the Kadohadacho total as being 2,000. In 1820, Jedediah Morse estimated the Kadohadacho population to be 450, while the Natchitoches had 100 and the Yatasis 40. That same year the citizens of Hempstead County, Arkansas, claimed that there were 300 Kadohadacho warriors, which would put their tribal total around 1,500, again an overestimation. In 1825, the U.S. government published a census of Indian tribes that stated there were 450 Kadohadachos, 25 Natchitoches, and 36 Yatasis. In 1828, a Spanish official, Gen. Manuel Mier y Terán, overestimated the Kadohadacho population at 300 families with 400 warriors. Ten years later, after a decade of decline, 500 Kadohadachos were present to negotiate a treaty with the United States. This number probably included the Yatasis and the Natchitoches.

Morse estimated the population of the Hasinai tribes to be 890, but he seemed to believe that the Tejas and Hainai were two different tribes. Padilla claimed that there were 200 Nacagdoches, 500 Nabedaches, and 400 Hainais, another overestimation. The Hempstead citizens believed that the Nabedaches had 60 warriors (which would imply 300 people), and the Hainai had 100 warriors (500 people); they did not mention the Nacogdoches. Terán's figures of 1828 seem close to being correct. He stated that there were 23 Hainai families (165 people) and 15 Nabedache families (75 people). Jean Louis Berlandier, who accompanied Terán in 1828, also stated that there were 50 Nacogdoches families totaling 200 people. In 1837, the Standing Committee on Indian Affairs of the Republic of Texas stated that the Hasinai population—which included the Hainai, Nacogdoches, Nabedaches, and a few Ais—numbered only 225. Later evidence suggests this number to be close to the truth. Sibley's earlier estimate for the Hasinai—450 or so—seems to be more correct than the others.

Morse reports the Nadaco population as being 180 people, while Padilla stated that there were about 200. The Hempstead County citizens believed there were 150 Nadaco warriors, which translates to about 750 people, a figure that is much too high. In 1828, Terán actually visited the Nadaco village and counted 29 families (145 people). In 1851, there were 202 Nadacos. Somewhere between 200 and 250 Nadacos in 1815, then, seems to be about right. Jedediah Morse, *A Report to the Secretary of War of the United States on Indian Affairs*, 373–74; Padilla, "Texas in 1820," 47–53; Grand jury presentment in Hempstead County, April 1820, in *The Territory of Arkansas, 1819–1825*, ed. Clarence E. Carter, 196–97; Statement showing the names and numbers of the different tribes of Indians now remaining within the limits of the several States and Territories, and the quantity of land claimed by them, respectively, January 10, 1825, *American State Papers, Indian Affairs* 2:545–47; Berlandier, *Indians of Texas*, 103–39; Journal of the proceedings at the agency-house, Caddo Nation, *HR* 1035, 116.

6. The Kadohadachos were well aware of the situation, and did not recognize any boundary settlement between Euro-Americans as affecting them anyway. In 1830, Gen. Manuel de Mier y Terán asked Dehahuit "whether his people's lands lay in Mexico or in the United States. Once the chief had got the question straight, he answered that he was neither on Mexican nor American territory, but on his own land which belonged to nobody but him" (Berlandier, *Indians of Texas*, 107).

7. Passport for Andres Valentín and Chief Caddo to travel to Bexar, July 20, 1816; Marcel Soto to Mariano Velo, July 23, 1816; and Ignácio Pérez to Commandant Gen. Joaquín de Arredondo, November 7, 1816, all in BA; Padilla, "Texas in 1820," 47–48. In the summer of 1819, the Spanish at San Antonio heard a rumor that Dehahuit had died. Governor Martínez ordered the trader Marcel Soto to go to the Kadohadacho village and have the leaders come to Bexar and choose their new chief in front of the governor. Martínez felt that "this plan would have the object of being friendly with them in order to make them contented and have them maintain the constant loyalty which until the present they have observed with the Spanish government." Martínez to Arredondo, July 18, 1819, 249; and Martínez to Arredondo, November 14, 1819, 280–81, both in *The Letters of Antonio Martínez, Last Spanish Governor of Texas, 1817–1822*, ed. Virginia H. Taylor.

8. Claiborne to Jamison, May 18, 1816, *LBC* 6:401.

9. John Fowler to Thomas McKenney, May 19, 1817, in "The Red River Valley, North of Natchitoches, 1817–1818: The Letters of John Fowler," ed. Russell M. Magnaghi, 291; T. Freeman and P. Custis, *Account of the Red River*, 21.

10. Sibley to Eustis, July 17, 1811, in "Doctor John Sibley and the Louisiana-Texas Frontier," ed. K. J. Garrett, *SWHQ* 49 (July 1945): 119; W. A. Trimble to John C. Calhoun, August 7, 1818, in *Report to the Secretary of War*, by J. Morse, 258–59.

11. Jamison to the secretary of war, March 31, 1817, in *The Territory of Louisiana-Missouri, 1815–1821*, ed. Clarence E. Carter, 257; Trimble to Calhoun, August 7, 1818, in *Report to the Secretary of War*, by J. Morse, 259; Fowler to McKenney, April 8, 1817, in "The Letters of John Fowler," ed. Russell M. Magnaghi, 289.

12. Jamison to the secretary of war, March 31, 1817, in *Territory of Louisiana-Missouri*, ed. C. E. Carter, 257–58.

13. Jamison to the secretary of war, May 10, 1817, ibid., 302–303; Fowler to McKenney, May 10, 1817, NSFFL.

14. Russell M. Magnaghi, "Sulphur Fork Factory, 1817–1822," 167–75; Fowler to McKenney, August 10, 1818; Fowler to McKenney, July 4, 1818; and Fowler to McKenney, August 29, 1818, all in NSFFL.

15. Martínez to Arredondo, June 2, 1818, in *Letters of Antonio Martínez*, ed. V. H.

Taylor, 139; Fowler to Jamison, April 16, 1819, in *The Territory of Arkansas, 1819–1825*, ed. C. E. Carter, 70–71.

16. Fowler to Jamison, April 16, 1819, 70–71; and Jamison to the secretary of war, May 26, 1819, 69–70, both in *Territory of Arkansas, 1819–1825*, ed. C. E. Carter.

17. McKenney to the secretary of war, July 16, 1819, ibid., 86–87.

18. Gov. William Miller to the secretary of war, June 20, 1820, ibid., 194–95.

19. The secretary of war to George Gray, November 13, 1823, 565–66; and Gray to McKenney, October 1, 1824, 703–704, both in ibid.

20. Gray to the secretary of war, December 30, 1824, ibid., 739–40.

21. Fowler to McKenney, May 9, 1817, in "Letters of John Fowler," ed. R. M. Magnaghi, 291; Fowler to McKenney, July 4, 1818, NSFFL; Jamison to the secretary of war, May 10, 1817, in *Territory of Louisiana-Missouri*, ed. C. E. Carter, 302–303. The Kickapoos, Delawares, and Shawnees were all Algonkian speakers originally located in Pennsylvania and Ohio. Following the American Revolution the tribes were scattered, and a few splinter groups crossed the Mississippi and settled in Spanish Louisiana. The Kickapoos settled in the Osage country, while the Delawares and Shawnees were relocated near Cape Girardeau, Missouri. From these locations they gradually made their way to Texas. See H. Allen Anderson, "The Delaware and Shawnee Indians and the Republic of Texas, 1820–1845," 232–33; Ariel Gibson, *The Kickapoo Indians: Lords of the Middle Border*.

22. Sibley, *Report from Natchitoches*, 16; Trimble to Calhoun, August 7, 1818, in *Report to the Secretary of War*, by J. Morse, 257. The Cherokees, of Iroquoian linguistic stock, lived in the southeastern Appalachian highlands by the sixteenth century. In 1791, the Cherokees signed a treaty with the United States and began adapting the "outward trappings of Western material culture." Some tribesmen, however, preferred to move away from the Anglo Americans, and, like the Delawares and Shawnees, crossed the Mississippi River and settled in Spanish Louisiana along the tributaries of the St. Francis, White, and Arkansas Rivers. See the excellent work of Dianna Everett, *The Texas Cherokees: A People between Two Fires, 1819–1840*, 6–10.

23. Fowler to McKenney, August 10, 1818, NSFFL; Trimble to Calhoun, August 7, 1818, in *Report to the Secretary of War*, by J. Morse, 259; Padilla, "Texas in 1820," 47.

24. Jamison to the secretary of war, May 10, 1817, in *Territory of Louisiana-Missouri*, ed. C. E. Carter, 302–303; Everett, *Texas Cherokees*, 16; Governor Miller to the secretary of war, June 20, 1820, 195; and David Brewls to the secretary of war, April 26, 1821, 285, both in *Territory of Arkansas, 1819–1825*, ed. C. E. Carter.

25. Fray Francisco Maynes to Antonio Martínez, November 10, 1820; and Jose Vivero and Francisco del Corral to Martínez, March 28, 1821, both in BA; Depositions of Pierre Rublo and Joseph Valentín, *HR* 1035, 33–35.

26. Gran Cado to Martínez, March 4, 1822; and Martínez to the *ayuntamiento* of Bexar, November 22, 1821, both in BA.

27. Martínez to the *ayuntamiento* of Bexar, November 22, 1821; Martínez to Gaspar Lopez, January 20, 1822; Dia Juin to Martínez, January 22, 1822; and Gran Cado to Martínez, March 4, 1822, all in BA.

28. Everett, *Texas Cherokees*, 25–28. In a letter to Governor Martínez, dated January 22, 1822, Dehahuit asked if the governor had someone who could write his letters for him. Dia Juin to Martínez, January 22, 1822, BA.

29. Everett, *Texas Cherokees*, 30–34.

30. Ibid., 31–32.

31. Quote from Ernest William Winkler, "The Cherokee Indians in Texas," 126; Everett, *Texas Cherokees*, 40–42. By this time, the Anglo Americans knew the Taovayas as the Wichitas.

32. The tribes and their population: 55 Biloxis, 45 Apalaches, 120 Pascagoulas, 180 Coushattas, 36 Yatasis, 25 Natchitoches, 27 Adaes, and 450 Kadohadachos. Statement

showing the names and numbers of different tribes of Indians now remaining within the several States and Territories, and the quantity of land claimed by them, respectively, January 10, 1825, 545–47; and Gray to the secretary of war, October 1, 1825, 706, both in *American State Papers, Indian Affairs* 2; Gray to the secretary of war, May 26, 1825, 52–53; and McKenney to Gray, November 16, 1825, 152–53, both in *Territory of Arkansas, 1825–1829*, ed. C. E. Carter.

33. Gray to the secretary of war, September 30, 1825, in *Territory of Arkansas, 1825–1829*, ed. C. E. Carter, 117–18.

34. Henry Conway to Edmund P. Gaines, June 25, 1822, in *Territory of Arkansas, 1819–1825*, ed. C. E. Carter, 445; Baird, *Quapaw Indians*, 65.

35. Treaty with the Quapaw, January 19, 1825, 529–30; and Gov. William Izard to the secretary of war, September 3, 1825, 706, both in *American State Papers, Indian Affairs* 2; Baird, *Quapaw Indians*, 68–69.

36. Governor Izard to the secretary of war, September 3, 1825; and Governor Izard to the secretary of war, September 24, 1825, both in *American State Papers, Indian Affairs* 2:706; Gray to the secretary of war, April 30, 1826, in *Territory of Arkansas, 1825–1829*, ed. C. E. Carter, 237–38; Baird, *Quapaw Indians*, 70–74.

37. Governor Pope to the secretary of war, April 17, 1832, 497–98; McKenney to the secretary of war, April 28, 1829, 22; Governor Pope to the secretary of war, June 22, 1829, 44–45; and Governor Pope to the secretary of war, April 17, 1832, 497–98, all in *Territory of Arkansas, 1829–1836*, ed. C. E. Carter; Baird, *Quapaw Indians*, 76–79.

38. Gray to the secretary of war, June 13, 1827, in *Territory of Arkansas, 1825–1829*, ed. C. E. Carter, 479–81; José María Sánchez, "A Trip to Texas in 1828," 279.

39. Thomas Dillard to the secretary of war, August 12, 1828, in *Territory of Arkansas, 1825–1829*, ed. C. E. Carter, 728–29.

40. Jehiel Brooks to Peter Bean, July 7, 1830, in *Territory of Arkansas, 1829–1836*, ed. C. E. Carter, 258–59.

41. Ibid.

42. Brooks to the secretary of war, August 16, 1830, 256; and Brooks to Bean, July 7, 1830, 258–59, both in *Territory of Arkansas, 1829–1836*, ed. C. E. Carter.

43. Jacksonian policy toward the Native Americans is one of the most controversial subjects in U.S. history. For various interpretations, see Ronald N. Satz, *American Indian Policy in the Jacksonian Era*; Michael Paul Rogin, *Fathers and Children: Andrew Jackson and the Subjugation of the American Indian*; and Francis Paul Prucha, "Andrew Jackson's Indian Policy: A Reassessment," 527–39.

44. Brooks to John Eaton, September 17, 1830, CAL.

45. Brooks to Eaton, January 14, 1831; and Brooks to Eaton, February 16, 1831, both in CAL.

46. Brooks to Hugh L. White, July 8, 1831, CAL.

47. Caddo Chief to the president of the United States, May 28, 1831, CAL.

48. Brooks to Judge E. Herring, commissioner of Indian affairs, March 20, 1834, *HR* 1035, 113.

49. Brooks to Herring, April 9, 1833, CAL.

50. Brooks to Herring, April 4, 1833; and Brooks to Henry Leavenworth, April 6, 1833, both in CAL.

51. Brooks to Herring, June 8, 1833, CAL.

52. Brooks to Herring, March 20, 1834, 113; Memorial of the chiefs and head men of the Caddo to the President, undated, 99, both in *HR* 1035.

53. For an excellent view of southern attitudes, see James Oakes, *The Ruling Race: A History of American Slaveholders*. For the attitudes of the Anglo Americans in Texas, see Randolph B. Campbell, *An Empire for Slavery: The Peculiar Institution in Texas, 1821–1865*, 10–49.

54. Edmund Morris Parson, "The Fredonian Rebellion," 10–52; Everett, *Texas Cherokees*, 42–47.

55. Everett, *Texas Cherokees*, 61–66.

56. Juan D. Almonte, "Statistical Report on Texas," 206; Everett, *Texas Cherokees*, 73.

57. Helen Willits Harris, "Almonte's Inspection of Texas in 1834," 197–98, 204–205.

58. Memorial of the chiefs and head men of the Caddo to the President, undated, *HR* 1035, 99-100.

59. Journal of the proceedings at the agency-house, Caddo Nation, ibid., 116.

60. Ibid., 116–17. That the other Red River Caddo tribes were included is evidenced by the fact that a man named Chowabah signed the treaty. In 1843, the Caddos were visited by the artist J. M. Stanley, who recorded that he had painted a Natchitoches chief named "Cho-wee, or Bow." Most likely this is the Chowabah from 1835. Swanton, *Source Material on the History and Ethnology of the Caddo Indians*, 96.

61. Journal of the proceedings at the agency-house, Caddo Nation, *HR* 1035, 116–17.

62. Ibid., 117.

63. Ibid., 117–18.

64. Ibid., 118–19; Deposition of Joseph Valentín, December 10, 1840, *HR* 1035, 28–29.

65. Journal of the proceedings at the agency-house, Caddo Nation, *HR* 1035, 119.

66. Ibid., 120.

67. The Caddo Indian Treaty, 74–77; Journal of the proceedings at the agency-house, Caddo Nation, 120; and Testimony of Captain J. Bonnell, March 31, 1842, all in *HR* 1035, 58–60.

68. Journal of the proceedings at the agency-house, Caddo Nation, ibid., 120.

69. G. W. McGinty, "Valuating the Caddo Land Cession," 59–73.

70. The best look at the Caddo Treaty and the actions of Brooks is in Charles H. Lange's "A Report on Data Pertaining to the Caddo Treaty of July 1, 1835: The Historical and Anthropological Background and Aftermath," *Caddoan Indians* 2:159–322; Henry M. Shreve to Herring, April 30, 1834, CAL.

71. Testimony of Jacques Grappe, *HR* 1035, 65–67.

72. Lange, "A Report," 291–92.

Chapter 8. The Caddos and the Texas Revolution, 1835–38

1. Maj. B. Riley to Gen. Edmund P. Gaines, Aug 24, 1836, *HED* 351, 815–18.

2. Report of G. W. Bonnell, Texas Commissioner of Indian Affairs, November 3, 1838, *SR* 171, 46–47.

3. Caddo Chiefs to the secretary of war, January 9, 1837, CAL.

4. Report of Standing Committee on Indian Affairs, October 12, 1837, in *TIP* 1:23. Again, all the Caddos called themselves Hasinai, meaning "our people." By 1835 or so, the tribes of the Hasinai confederacy had merged into one group, led by the Hainai. For the sake of clarity, I have chosen—in accordance with contemporary usage—to call this group the Hainai.

5. The Nadaco number is an estimate; there were no reliable figures for the Nadacos until 1851, when they numbered 202. Since the population of the tribe probably did not rise in the difficult period from 1835 to 1851, this figure seems accurate. E. B. Ritchie, ed., "Copy of Report of Colonel Samuel Cooper, Assistant Adjutant General of the United States, of Inspection Trip from Fort Graham to the Indian Villages on the Upper Brazos

made in June, 1851," 331.

6. Mosely Baker and F. W. Johnson to the Chairman of the General Council of Texas, October 23, 1835, in *TRP* 2:200. For the important role the Cherokees played in the Texas Revolution, see Everett, *Texas Cherokees*, 70–98.

7. Baker and Johnson to the Chairman, October 23, 1835, *TRP* 2:200. The best overview of Texan-Indian relations is Anna Muckleroy, "The Indian Policy of the Republic of Texas."

8. The other "associate bands" were the Shawnees, Delawares, Kickapoos, Quapaws, Choctaws, Biloxis, Alabamas, and Coushattas, as well as a group called the Caddo of the Neches. This was probably a small group of Kadohadachos that had abandoned Louisiana prior to the rest of the tribe. Houston et al., Treaty, November 13, 1835, *TRP* 4:415; Treaty Between Texas and the Cherokee Indians, February 23, 1835, *TRP* 1:14–17.

9. Muckleroy, "The Indian Policy of the Republic of Texas," 1–4.

10. Depositions of C. H. and William Sims, M. B. Menard, and letter of James and Ralph Chester to the Committee of Vigilance and Safety of Nacogdoches, April 11, 1836, 775–76; and Report of A. Hotchkiss, March 21, 1836, 377, all in *HED* 351.

11. Irion to Memucan Hunt, September 20, 1837, *DCRT* 1:260; Baker and Johnson to the Chairman, October 23, 1835, *TRP* 2:201.

12. For the opinion that the Texans were embellishing their reports regarding the Kadohadachos, see Maj. Gen. Alexander Macomb to Secy. of War Lewis Cass, April 25, 1836, *TRP* 6:77–78. Macomb notes that he had met with a Colonel Darrington, who was of the opinion that the Kadohadachos "cannot be concerned in attacking the Texians, and that they are but few in number and quite insignificant." Macomb also states that the governor of Louisiana believed that "there was a scheme of those interested in the Texian speculations, who had been instrumental in making General Gaines believe that the Mexican authorities were tampering with the Indians within our boundaries, and at the same time exciting, by false representations here, the sympathies of the people in favor of the Texians, with a view of inducing the authorities of the United States to lend their aid in raising in this city [New Orleans] a force composed of interested persons, which force should move to the Texian frontiers, under the call of General Gaines, and afterwards, under false pretensions, actually march into Texas and take part in the war now raging between the Texians and the Government of Mexico. . . ."

13. Lieut. J. Bonnell to Gaines, April 20, 1836, 774–75; Larkin Edwards to Gaines, May 13, 1836, 814–15; and Bonnell to Gaines, June 4, 1836, 809–10, all in *HED* 351.

14. Greenwood to the President of the Convention, March 7, 1836, *TRP* 5:17; Mason to Nelson, March 20, 1836, 773–74; Depositions of C. H. and William Sims, M. B. Menard, and letter of James and Ralph Chester to the Committee of Vigilance and Safety of Nacogdoches, April 11, 1836, 775–76; and Irion to Mason, April 12, 1836, 779, both in *HED* 351.

15. Gaines to Lewis Cass, April 20, 1836, *HED* 351, 771–73.

16. Bonnell to Gaines, April 20, 1836, ibid., 774–75.

17. William Parker to the editor of Natchez *Free Trader*, April 29, 1836, *TRP* 6:120.

18. Edwards to Gaines, May 13, 1836, 814–15; and Gaines to Cass, June 7, 1836, 787–88, both in *HED* 351.

19. Riley to Gaines, August 24, 1836, 815–18; and Sterling Robertson to Gaines, June 16, 1836, with copies of the depositions of James Dunn and Montgomery Shackleford, 792–94, both in *HED* 351; Thomas Maitland Marshall, *A History of the Western Boundary of the Louisiana Purchase, 1819–1841*, 175–79.

20. Bonnell to Gaines, July 19, 1836, *HED* 351, 796–98.

21. Bonnell to Gaines, August 9, 1836, with copies of reports of Menard and Isadore Pantallion, *HED* 351, 799–803.

22. Sam Houston to Gaines, September 12, 1836, AJHP; George Browning to Sam

Houston, September 16, 1836, *TRP* 8:484.

23. Mary Idanish Interview; and J. B. Thoburn Deposition, September 22, 1928, both in CRHC; Sadie Weller Interview, DDOIHC.

24. Riley to Gaines, August 24, 1836, *HED* 351, 815–18.

25. Ibid.

26. W. B. Lewis, Treasury Department, to Commissioner of Indian Affairs T. Hartley Crawford, February 8, 1842, CAL.

27. Caddo Chiefs to the secretary of war, January 9, 1837, ibid.; Deposition of Larkin Edwards, December 16, 1840, 36; and Deposition of Charles Sewall, December 15, 1840, 35–36, both in *HR* 1035.

28. Deposition of Edwards, December 16, 1840, ibid., 36; Caddo Chiefs to the secretary of war, January 9, 1837; and Col. James B. Many to Secy. of War Joel Poinsett, April 19, 1839, all in CAL.

29. Caddo Chiefs to the secretary of war, January 9, 1837, CAL.

30. J. Pinckney Henderson to William H. Wharton and Memucan Hunt, January 21, 1837, *DCRT* 2:177–78; *TTR*, January 13, 1837; Maj. George Bernard Erath, in "Memoirs," ed. Lucy A. Erath, 228.

31. Henderson to Wharton and Hunt, February 19, 1837, 194–95; and Poinsett to Forsyth, April 14, 1837, 206, both in *DCRT* 2; W. H. Secrest to Sam Houston, March 1, 1837, *TIP* 1:21; Abstract of correspondence, *SED* 14, 59–60.

32. See Jack Gregory and Rennard Strickland, *Sam Houston with the Cherokees, 1829–1833*; Muckleroy, "Indian Policy," 8.

33. Muckleroy, "Indian Policy," 16; Commissions of Kelsey Douglass and Henry Millard, November 12, 1836, DSP; Everett, *Texas Cherokees*, 84–85; William Goyens to Houston, May 10, 1837, *TTR*.

34. *TTR*, September 9, 1837.

35. Report of Standing Committee on Indian Affairs, October 12, 1837, *TIP* 1:27. The other treaties made at this time were between the Republic of Texas and the Tonkawa Indians, the Lipan Indians, the Comanche Indians, and one joint treaty with the Wichita and Kichai Indians (*TIP* 1:28–32, 46–48, 50–54).

36. Brooks to Harris, May 5, 1837; Lewis to Crawford, February 8, 1842; and Brooks to Harris, February 6, 1838, all in CAL.

37. B. J. Butler to Poinsett, March 31, 1838, CAL.

38. Deposition of Edwards, December 16, 1840, *HR* 1035, 36–37; G. H. Scott to Poinsett, August 29, 1838; and Many to Poinsett, April 19, 1839, both in CAL.

39. Benthuysen to Mirabeau Buonaparte Lamar, December 8[?], 1838, *MBLP* 1:592–94.

40. Scott to Poinsett, August 29, 1838; and Caddo Chiefs to Martin Van Buren, February 4, 1838, both in CAL.

41. Everett, *Texas Cherokees*, 88. The best treatment of these events, known as the Córdova Rebellion, is found in *After San Jacinto: The Texas-Mexican Frontier, 1836–1841*, ed. Joseph Milton Nance, 113–41.

42. The basic outline of the plan is contained in a group of messages sent in 1838 and 1839. Private instructions for the captains of friendly Indians of Texas, by His Excellency the General-in-chief Vicente Filisola; Valentin Canalizo to Don Vicente Córdova, February 27, 1838; Instructions to the captains and chiefs of the friendly nations, and to which they ought to conform; the plan of the campaign for the security of their homes, by Valentin Canalizo, February 27, 1839; Canalizo to the Chiefs of the tribes, February 27, 1839, all in *SED* 14, 13–14, 31–36.

43. Memorandum book of Pedro Julian Miracle, ibid., 14.

44. Jeff Wright to Houston, June 13, 1838; and Wright to Houston, June 17, 1838, both in AJHP. At a council later in the week, Duwali was more conciliatory to the Texans. Wright to Houston, June 25, 1838, AJHP.

45. Memorandum book of Pedro Julian Miracle, *SED* 14, 15–16.

46. Ibid., 14–16.

47. Nance, *After San Jacinto,* 119–20; Abstract of correspondence, *SED* 14, 60.

48. Abstract of correspondence, *SED* 14, 60–61; Nance, *After San Jacinto,* 120–21.

49. Lamar had served as private secretary to Gov. George M. Troup during the struggle with the federal government over jurisdiction of the Creek lands in the 1820s. By threatening to mobilize the state militia, Governor Troup had succeeded in carrying out the fraudulent Treaty of Indian Springs, by which the state of Georgia obtained 4.7 million acres of land from the Creeks. A. K. Christian, "Mirabeau Buonaparte Lamar," 50–51; Charles P. Roland, *Albert Sidney Johnston: Soldier of Three Republics,* 81–86; Muckleroy, "Indian Policy," 128–29.

50. Charles A. Sewall to the Commissioner of Indian Affairs, January 8, 1839; Scott to Poinsett, August 29, 1838; and Lewis to Crawford, February 8, 1842, all in CAL.

51. Sewall to the Commissioner of Indian Affairs, January 8, 1839; and Appointment of Charles A. Sewall, procuration by Caddo Chiefs, October 11, 1838, both in CAL.

52. Report of Bonnell, November 3, 1838, *SR* 171, 46–47.

53. Ibid.; Colonel Hugh McLeod to Lamar, October 22, 1838, *MBLP* 2:265–67.

54. John H. Dyer to J. S. Mayfield, October 21, 1838, *MBLP* 2:256–57.

55. Statement of Merchandise Received by Caddo Indians from Charles A. Sewall, *HR* 1035, 125–29; Deposition of Sewall, January 8, 1839, CAL.

56. A. Horton to Rusk, November 7, 1838, TJRP. Deposition of Sewall, January 8, 1839; Sewall to Commissioner of Indian Affairs, January 8, 1839, all CAL.

57. Thomas F. Ruffin, "Invasion of Caddo Parish by General Thomas Jefferson Rusk's Republic of Texas Army, 1838," 72–73; McLeod to Lamar, November 21, 1838, *MBLP* 2:298–99; Sewall to Commissioner of Indian Affairs, January 8, 1839, CAL.

58. Ruffin, "Invasion of Caddo Parish," 73; Rusk to Albert Sidney Johnston, February 25, 1839, *SED* 14, 24; Sewall to Many, November 26, 1838, *HED* 71, 5; McLeod to Lamar, November 23, 1838, *MBLP* 2:302–303.

59. Rusk to Johnston, February 25, 1839, *SED* 14, 24–25; McLeod to Lamar, December 1, 1838, *MBLP* 2:308.

60. McLeod to Lamar, December 1, 1838, *MBLP* 2:308.

61. Agreement between the Caddo Indians and Maj. Gen. Thomas J. Rusk, November 29, 1838, *SED* 14, 26–27; Many to Poinsett, April 19, 1839, CAL.

62. McLeod to Lamar, January 9, 1839, *MBLP* 2:406; Glover, "History of the Caddo Indians," 937.

63. Nance, *After San Jacinto,* 125–30, 136–37; Canalizo to the Chiefs of the tribes, February 27, 1839, *SED* 14, 35.

64. Christian, "Mirabeau Buonaparte Lamar," 77–78; Muckleroy, "Indian Policy," 135–38; Roland, *Albert Sidney Johnston,* 90–93; Everett, *Texas Cherokees,* 101–108.

Chapter 9. The Caddos
Return to Texas, 1839–54

1. Minutes of Treaty Council at Tehuacana Creek, May 14, 1844, *TIP* 2:45–46.

2. Col. James B. Many to Joel Poinsett, April 19, 1839, CAL; Kenneth P. Neighbours, "José María, Anadarko Chief," 254–74.

3. Minutes of Final Day of Council at Tehuacana Creek, May 15, 1843, *TIP* 2:55; Robert S. Neighbors to W. Medill, June 22, 1847, *HED* 8, 894.

4. A. S. Liscomb to B. E. Bee, August 8, 1840, *DCRT* 1:464.

5. Benton to Poinsett, January 9, 1839; Garland to Poinsett, January 25, 1839; and Many to Poinsett, April 19, 1839, all in CAL.

6. William Armstrong to T. Hartley Crawford, November 27, 1839; H. G. Rind to Armstrong, February 5, 1840; and Agreement of Caddo Chiefs, January 23, 1840, all in CAL.

7. Armstrong to Crawford, August 28, 1840, CAL.

8. Armstrong to Crawford, March 5, 1841; and Armstrong to Crawford, May 21, 1841, both in CAL.

9. Armstrong to Crawford, May 21, 1841, CAL.

10. Armstrong to Crawford, September 20, 1841; M. G. Lewis to Crawford, February 8, 1842; and Red Bear to the Chief of the Muskogees, July 10, 1842, all in CAL.

11. Red Bear to the Chief of the Muskogees, July 10, 1842, CAL.

12. Muckleroy, "Indian Policy," 145–46; Red Bear to the Chief of the Muskogees, July 10, 1842, CAL; Letter to the Chiefs of the Caddo from Jim Marthler Mieed, Hopochthli Yoholo, Tuscoomah Hargo, and Jim Boy, July 20, 1842, *TIP* 1:137–38.

13. Quoted in Muckleroy, "Indian Policy," 184–85; Appointment of Henry E. Scott, Indian Commissioner, by Sam Houston, July 5, 1842, *TIP* 1:136–37.

14. Grant Foreman, *Advancing the Frontier, 1830–1860*, 167–68.

15. Ethen Stroud, Leonard Williams, and Joseph Hurst to Sam Houston, September 4, 1842, *TIP* 1:139.

16. Minutes of Indian Council at Tehuacana Creek, March 28, 1843, *TIP* 1:149-52, 156–57.

17. Ibid., 149–52.

18. Ibid., 153–56, 160.

19. Eldredge to Houston, June 2, 1843, *TIP* 1:256.

20. Muckleroy, "Indian Policy," 187–88; Proclamation by Sam Houston, September 29, 1843, *TIP* 1:241–46.

21. Statement of Luis Sanchez as Taken by Walter Winn, May 1844, 64–65; and L. H. Williams to Thomas G. Western, July 16, 1845, 291–92, both in *TIP* 2; Anderson, "Delaware and Shawnee Indians," 246–49; Roemer, *Texas*, 200–201.

22. Statement of Sanchez, May, 1844, *TIP*, 2:64–66. For a discussion of the Wichitas during this period, see Elam, "History of the Wichita Confederacy," 256–67.

23. Statement of Sanchez, May, 1844, *TIP* 2:65.

24. Thomas G. Western to Houston, April 15, 1844, 13; J. C. Neill, L. H. Williams, and Thomas Smith to Houston, May 23, 1844, 60–62; Meeting of Waco and Tawakoni Chiefs by Commissioners, May 11, 1844, 30–31; Minutes of a Council at Tehuacana Creek, May 12, 1844, 31–34, 42–55; and Minutes of Final Day of Council at Tehuacana Creek, May 15, 1843, 55, all in *TIP* 2.

25. Western to Houston, July 27, 1844, 84–85; Western to Stephen T. Slater, September 5, 1844, 94–95; and John Conner and James Shaw to Houston, October 2, 1844, 101–102, all in *TIP* 2.

26. L. H. Williams, Jesse Chisolm, and D. G. Watson to Houston, October 9, 1844, *TIP* 2:119–21. The Comanches were hesitant to treat with the Texans because of the "Council House Fight" of March 19, 1840, in which a group of Penatekas were attacked by Texan troops in San Antonio during a peace council. Thirty-five Comanches died, including three women and two children. Twenty-seven women and children and two old men were captured. A first-hand account is presented in Muckleroy, "Indian Policy," 142–44. See also Rupert N. Richardson, *The Comanche Barrier to South Plains Settlement*, 118–23.

27. Minutes of Council at the Falls of the Brazos, October 7, 1844, 2:104–105; and A Treaty Signed in Council at Tehuacana Creek, October 9, 1844, 2:114–19, both in *TIP*; Muckleroy, "Indian Policy," 2:196. The boundary line between the whites and natives was

left unsettled due to the protests of the Penateka headman, Buffalo Hump. Richardson, *Comanche Barrier*, 124.

28. Western to Benjamin Sloat, November 7, 1844, 2:130–31; Western to George Barnard, November 7, 1844, 2:131–32; Western to M. C. Hamilton, November 21, 1844, 2:144–45; and Western to Mrs. Simpson, February 4, 1845, 2:191–92, all in *TIP*.

29. Western to Torrey, January 3, 1845, *TIP*, 2:159.

30. Western to Sloat and Williams, January 4, 1845, 2:160–61; Western to Torrey, January 6, 1845, 2:161; and Western to Williams, April 29, 1845, 2:224–26, all in *TIP*.

31. Juan Fernandez to Jones, January 13, 1845, 2:426; and Western to Sloat and Williams, January 18, 1845, 2:170–72, both in *TIP*.

32. Talk of Red Bear and Vicente, February 6, 1845, 2:193–94; and Western to Sloat and Williams, February 12, 1845, 2:199–200, both in *TIP*.

33. Talk of José María at Tehuacana Creek, January 10, 1845, 2:162–64; and Talk of Bintah at Tehuacana Creek, January 10, 1845, 2:164–65, both in *TIP*.

34. Williams to Western, June 23, 1845, 2:270–72; and Williams to Western, July 16, 1845, 2:290–92, both in *TIP*.

35. Western to Williams, July 24, 1845, *TIP*, 2:296.

36. Minutes of a Council Held at Tehuacana Creek and Appointment of Daniel D. Culp as Secretary, September 27, 1845, *TIP*, 2:236–45.

37. Grant Foreman, ed., "The Journal of Elijah Hicks," *CO* 13 (March 1935): 81, 93.

38. Pierce Butler and M. G. Lewis to W. Medill, August 8, 1846, *HED* 76, 3–7. For an overview of the treaty, see G. Foreman's "The Texas Comanche Treaty of 1846," 314–32, and his edition of "Elijah Hicks," 78–79; Treaty with the Comanche and Other Tribes, May 15, 1846, *TIP* 3:43–52.

39. Butler and Lewis to Medill, August 8, 1846, *HED* 76, 8–9; Treaty between the United States and José María and the Anadarko Indians, July 25, 1846, *TIP* 3:68; Neighbours, "José María," 264; G. W. Hill to Robert S. Neighbors, October 1, 1853, TAL.

40. Three studies include substantial information on the unique situation in Texas. The two best are George D. Harmon's "The United States Indian Policy in Texas, 1845–1860," 377–403; and Robert A. Trennert, Jr., *Alternative to Extinction: Federal Indian Policy and the Beginnings of the Reservation System, 1846–1851*. See also Lena Clara Koch, "The Federal Indian Policy in Texas, 1845–1860."

41. Quoted in Harmon, "Indian Policy," 381.

42. Neighbors to Medill, June 22, 1847, *HED* 8, 894.

43. Ibid., 894–96.

44. Ibid., 895.

45. Neighbors to Medill, September 14, 1847, 899–901; and Neighbors to Medill, October 12, 1847, 905, both in *HED* 8.

46. Neighbors to Medill, September 14, 1847, *HED* 8, 899–901.

47. Neighbors to Medill, October 12, 1847, *HED* 8, 903–904; Neighbors to Medill, March 2, 1848, *HED* 1, 583–85.

48. Neighbors to Medill, October 12, 1847, *HED* 8, 904–906.

49. Neighbors to Medill, September 14, 1847, *HED* 8, 899, 901.

50. Neighbors to Medill, June 15, 1848, 592; Neighbors to Medill, August 14, 1848, both *HED* 1, 594.

51. Neighbors to Medill, March 2, 1848, *HED* 1, 581–85.

52. Ibid., 581–83.

53. Neighbors to Medill, April 28, 1848, 587; and Henry O. Hedgcoxe to Neighbors, February 18, 1848, 575-76, both in *HED* 1; Trennert, *Alternative to Extinction*, 74.

54. C. E. Barnard to Neighbors, Undated, *HED* 1, 588–89.

55. Ibid., 589; Neighbors to Medill, April 28, 1848, TAL.

56. H. G. Catlett to Medill, May 12, 1849, *SED* 1, 969–70.

57. Neighbors to Medill, June 15, 1848, *HED* 1, 591.

58. Neighbors to Medill, August 10, 1848, *HED* 1, 593–95; Agreement between R. S. Neighbors and Colonel P. H. Bell and principal chiefs of the Caddo, José María, Toweash, and Haddabah, September 14, 1848, TAL. No charges were brought against any Rangers, but the Caddos were finally paid the five hundred dollars on February 27, 1849 (Neighbors to Medill, June 18, 1849, TAL).

59. Neighbors to Medill, October 23, 1848, *HED* 1, 597; Neighbors to Medill, February 15, 1849, TAL; Jesse Stem to Luke Lea, Undated, *SED* 1, 522; Ritchie, "Colonel Samuel Cooper," 331.

60. Stem to Lea, Undated, *SED* 1, 521–24; Ritchie, "Colonel Samuel Cooper," 328–29; Mary Idanish Interview; and J. B. Thoburn Deposition, September 22, 1928, both in CRHC; Sadie Weller Interview, DDOIHC. In addition to the Caddo villages, there were three villages of the Wichita bands nearby: the Kichai village was directly across the Brazos from the Kadohadachos', and six miles above these two were the Waco and Tawakoni villages. The total population of the three bands was 293 people, of whom 90 were warriors.

61. Neighbors to Maj. Gen. William J. Worth, March 7, 1849, *SED* 1, 963–65.

62. Trennert, *Alternative to Extinction*, 77–78, 81–82.

63. John Conner to Gen. George M. Brooke, August 30, 1849; and L. W. Williams to Robert S. Neighbors, October 9, 1849, both in TAL.

64. Trennert, *Alternative to Extinction*, 84–87; Harmon, "Indian Policy," 384.

65. Ritchie, "Colonel Samuel Cooper," 328; Stem to Lea, Undated, *SED* 1, 521; Koch, "Federal Indian Policy in Texas," 262.

66. Ritchie, "Colonel Samuel Cooper," 330; Stem to Lea, Undated, *SED* 1, 522; Stem to Lea, February 20, 1852, TAL.

67. Ritchie, "Colonel Samuel Cooper," 331; Stem to Lea, Undated, *SED* 1, 522.

68. Earl Buck Braly, "Fort Belknap," 84; Stem to Lea, November 1, 1851, *SED* 1, 525.

69. Stem to Lea, October 8, 1852, *HED* 1, 435; G. W. Hill to Neighbors, August 10, 1853, TAL.

70. G. W. Hill to Neighbors, August 10, 1853, TAL.

71. Hill to Neighbors, October 1, 1853, TAL.

72. Ibid.

73. Harmon, "Indian Policy," 392–93.

Conclusion

1. Report of an expedition to the sources of the Brazos and Big Wichita Rivers, during the summer of 1854, by Capt. R. B. Marcy, Seventh Infantry, *SED* 60, 2; Hill to Neighbors, April 5, 1855, TAL.

2. Census Roll of Indians, March 31, 1855; and Census Roll of Indians, August 1, 1859, in TAL; Elias Rector to A. B. Greenwood, July 2, 1859, *SED* 1023, 673.

3. Shapely P. Ross to Neighbors, September 11, 1857, 557–58; Samuel Church to Ross, September 9, 1857, 558–59; Neighbors to J. W. Denver, September 16, 1857, 550–51, all in *SED* 1; Murl L. Webb, "Religious and Educational Efforts Among Texas Indians in the 1850's," *SWHQ* 69 (July 1965); Zachariah Ellis Coombes, *Diary of a Frontiersman, 1858–1859.*

4. For Caddo involvement in the campaigns against the Comanches, see John Salmon Ford, *Rip Ford's Texas*; Harold B. Simpson, *Cry Comanche: The Second United States*

Cavalry in Texas, 1855–1861; and William Y. Chalfant, *Without Quarter: The Wichita Expedition and the Fight on Crooked Creek*. For the move to the Indian Territory see *SED* 1023.

5. Berlin B. Chapman, "Establishment of the Wichita Reservation," 1044–55; Ariel Gibson, "Confederates on the Plains: The Pike Mission to the Wichita Agency," 7–16; and Muriel H. Wright, "A History of Fort Cobb," 61.

6. Henry Shanklin to Col. James Wortham, September 1, 1867, *HED* 1, 322; Agreement with the Wichita and Other Indians, *HED* 65, 1–2.

7. Jonathan Richards to Enoch Hoag, August 1, 1874, *HED* 1, 545; Chapman, "Dissolution of the Wichita Reservation," 192–209, 300, 314.

8. Newkumet and Meredith, *Hasinai*, 78, 90–91.

Bibliography

Unpublished Sources

Bexar Archives. Eugene C. Barker Library. University of Texas, Austin.

Blake Supplement to the Bexar Archives. Eugene C. Barker Library. University of Texas, Austin.

Duke, Doris. Oral Indian History Collection. Western History Collections. University of Oklahoma, Norman.

Elam, Earl Henry. "The History of the Wichita Indian Confederacy to 1868." Ph.D. diss., Texas Tech University, 1971.

Gregory, Hiram Ford. "Eighteenth Century Caddoan Archeology: A Study in Methods and Interpretation." Ph.D. diss., Southern Methodist University, 1973.

Houston, Andrew Jackson. Papers. Archives. Texas State Library, Austin.

Hume, C. Ross. Collection. Western History Collections. University of Oklahoma, Norman.

Provincias Internas. Eugene C. Barker Library. University of Texas, Austin.

Records of the Bureau of Indian Affairs. Letterbook of the Natchitoches–Sulphur Fork Factory, 1809-1821. National Archives Microfilm Publication, T1029, Roll 1.

———. Letters Received by the Office of Indian Affairs. National Archives Microfilm Publication, M234, Roll 31 (Caddo Agency, 1824–1842).

———. Letters Received by the Office of Indian Affairs from the Texas Agency. Photostat Copy. Eugene C. Barker Library. University of Texas, Austin.

Rusk, Thomas Jefferson. Papers. Eugene C. Barker Library. University of Texas, Austin.

Schilz, Thomas Frank. "People of the Cross Timbers: A History of the Tonkawa Indians." Ph.D. diss., Texas Christian University, 1983.

Starr, James Harper. Papers (includes Papers of Kelsey H. Douglass). Eugene C. Barker Library. University of Texas, Austin.

Published Sources

Almonte, Juan D. "Statistical Report on Texas." Edited by Carlos E. Castañeda. *Southwestern Historical Quarterly* 28 (Jan. 1925): 177–222.

Allen, Henry Easton. "The Parrilla Expedition to the Red River in 1759." *Southwestern Historical Quarterly* 43 (July 1939): 53–71.

American State Papers, Indian Affairs. 2 vols. Washington: Gales and Seaton, 1832–34.

Anderson, H. Allen. "The Delaware and Shawnee Indians and the Republic of Texas, 1820–1845." *Southwestern Historical Quarterly* 94 (Oct. 1990): 231–60.

Aten, Lawrence E. *Indians of the Upper Texas Coast.* Austin: University of Texas Press, 1983.

Baird, W. David. *The Quapaw Indians: A History of the Downstream People.* Norman: University of Oklahoma Press, 1980.

Bannon, John Francis. *The Spanish Borderlands Frontier, 1513–1821.* Albuquerque: University of New Mexico Press, 1974.

Bender, Averam B. *The March of Empire: Frontier Defense in the Southwest, 1848–1860.* Lawrence: University of Kansas Press, 1952.

Berlandier, Jean Louis. *The Indians of Texas in 1830.* Edited by John C. Ewers. Washington: Smithsonian Institution Press, 1969.

Bienville, M. de. "Journal of the Overland Journey from the Taensas to the Village of the Yataches." In *Iberville's Gulf Journals.* Edited by Richebourg Gaillard McWilliams. Tuscaloosa: University of Alabama Press, 1981.

Bolton, Herbert Eugene, ed. *Athanase de Mézières and the Louisiana-Texas Frontier, 1768–1780.* 2 vols. Cleveland: Arthur H. Clark Company, 1914.

———. "Defensive Spanish Expansion and the Significance of the Spanish Borderlands." In *The Trans-Mississippi West.* Edited by James F. Willard and Colin B. Goodykoontz. Boulder: University of Colorado Press, 1930.

———. *The Hasinais: Southern Caddoans As Seen by the Earliest Europeans.* Edited by Russell M. Magnaghi. Norman: University of Oklahoma Press, 1987.

———. "The Jumano Indians in Texas, 1650–1771." *Texas State Historical Association Quarterly* 15 (July 1911): 66–84.

———. "The Mission as a Frontier Institution in the Spanish-American Colonies." *American Historical Review* 23 (Oct. 1917): 42–61.

———. "The Native Tribes About the East Texas Missions." *Texas State Historical Association Quarterly* 11 (Apr. 1908): 249–76.

———. "The Spanish Occupation of Texas, 1519-1690." *Southwestern*

Historical Quarterly 16 (July 1912): 1–26.

———. *Texas in the Middle Eighteenth Century: Studies in Spanish Colonial History and Administration*. Berkeley: University of California Publications, 1915.

Bosque, Fernando del. "Diary." In *Spanish Exploration in the Southwest, 1542–1706*. Edited by Herbert Eugene Bolton. New York: Charles Scribner's Sons, 1916.

Braly, Earl Buck. "Fort Belknap." *West Texas Historical Association Year Book* 30 (1954): 83–114.

Bridges, Katherine, and Winston DeVille, eds. and trans. "Natchitoches and the Trail to the Rio Grande: Two Early Eighteenth Century Accounts by the Sieur Derbanne." *Louisiana History* 8 (Spring 1967): 239–59.

Brown, James A., and Robert E. Bell. *The First Annual Report of Caddoan Archaeology, Spiro Focus Research*. Norman: University of Oklahoma Research Institute, 1964.

Buckley, Eleanor C. "The Aguayo Expedition into Texas and Louisiana, 1719–1722." *Texas State Historical Association Quarterly* 15 (July 1911): 1–65.

Campbell, Randolph B. *An Empire for Slavery: The Peculiar Institution in Texas, 1821–1865*. Baton Rouge: Louisiana State University Press, 1989.

Canedo, Lino Gómez, ed. *Primeras Exploraciones y Poblamiento de Texas, 1686–1694*. Monterrey: Publicaciones del Instituto Tecnologico y de Estudios Superiores de Monterrey, 1968.

Carter, Clarence E., ed. *The Territorial Papers of the United States*. Vol. 9, *The Territory of Orleans, 1803–1812*. Vol. 15, *The Territory of Louisiana-Missouri, 1815–1821*. Vol. 19, *The Territory of Arkansas, 1819–1825*. Vol. 20, *The Territory of Arkansas, 1825–1829*. Vol. 21, *The Territory of Arkansas, 1829–1836*. 28 vols. Washington: Government Printing Office, published continuous since 1933.

Caruso, John Anthony. *The Mississippi Valley Frontier: The Age of French Exploration and Settlement*. New York: Bobbs-Merrill Company, Inc., 1966.

Castañeda, Carlos E. "Myths and Customs of the Tejas Indians." *Publication of the Texas Folk-lore Society* 9 (1931): 167–74.

———. *Our Catholic Heritage in Texas, 1519–1936*. 7 vols. Austin: Von Boeckmann-Jones Company, 1936–1958.

Cavelier, Jean. "Account of La Salle's Voyage to the Mouth of the Mississippi, His Landing in Texas and March to the Mississippi." In vol. 1 of *The Journeys of René-Robert Cavelier, Sieur de La Salle*. Edited by Isaac J. Cox. 2 vols. New York: A. S. Barnes and Co., 1905.

Céliz, Fray Francisco. *Diary of the Alarcón Expedition into Texas, 1718–1719.* Translated by Fritz Leo Hoffman. Los Angeles: Quivira Society Publications, 1935.

Chafe, Wallace L. "Siouan, Iroquoian, and Caddoan." Edited by Thomas A. Sebeck. In vol. 1 of *Native Languages of the Americas.* New York: Plenum Press, 1976. 527–72.

Chalfant, William Y. *Without Quarter: The Wichita Expedition and the Fight on Crooked Creek.* Norman: University of Oklahoma Press, 1991.

Chapman, Berlin B. "Dissolution of the Wichita Reservation." *Chronicles of Oklahoma* 22 (Summer 1944): 192–209; (Autumn 1944): 300–14.

———. "Establishment of the Wichita Reservation." *Chronicles of Oklahoma* 11 (Dec. 1933): 1044–55.

Chipman, Donald E. *Spanish Texas, 1519–1821.* Austin: University of Texas Press, 1992.

Christian, A. K. "Mirabeau Buonaparte Lamar." *Southwestern Historical Quarterly* 24 (July 1920): 39–80.

———. "Louis Juchereau de Saint-Denis and the Reestablishment of the Tejas Missions." *Texas State Historical Association Quarterly* 6 (July 1902): 1–26.

Clark, Robert Carlton. *The Beginnings of Texas, 1684–1718.* Austin: University of Texas Bulletin no. 98, 1907.

Connor, Seymour V. "The Mendoza-López Expedition and Location of San Clemente." *West Texas Historical Association Year Book* 45 (1969): 3–29.

Coombes, Zachariah E. *Diary of a Frontiersman, 1858–1859.* Edited by Barbara Ledbetter. Newcastle, Texas, 1961.

Cox, Isaac J. *The Early Exploration of Louisiana.* University Studies, Series 2, vol. 2, no. 1. Cincinnati: University of Cincinnati Press, 1906.

———. "The Explorations of the Louisiana Frontier, 1803–1806." *American Historical Association Annual Report* (1904): 151–74, 274–84.

———. "The Louisiana-Texas Frontier." *Quarterly of the Texas State Historical Association* 10 (July 1906): 1–75; 17 (July 1913): 1–42;17 (July 1913): 140–87.

Crane, Verner W. *The Southern Frontier, 1670–1732.* Ann Arbor: University of Michigan Press, 1929.

Crosby, Alfred W. "Virgin Soil Epidemics as a Factor in the Aboriginal Depopulation in America." *William and Mary Quarterly* 3d Ser., 33 (1976): 289–99.

De León, Alonso. "Itinerary of the Expedition of 1689." Edited by Herbert Eugene Bolton. *Spanish Exploration in the Southwest, 1542–1706.* New York: Charles Scribner's Sons, 1916.

———. "Itinerary of the Expedition of 1690." Edited by Herbert Eugene

Bolton. *Spanish Exploration in the Southwest, 1542–1706.* New York: Charles Scribner's Sons, 1916.

Din, Gilbert C., and Abraham P. Nasatir. *The Imperial Osages: Spanish-Indian Diplomacy in the Mississippi Valley.* Norman: University of Oklahoma Press, 1983.

Dobyns, Henry F. *Their Number Become Thinned: Native American Population Dynamics in Eastern North America.* Knoxville: University of Tennessee Press, 1983.

Dorsey, George A. *Tradition of the Caddo.* Washington: Carnegie Institution, 1905.

Douay, Father Anastasius. "Narrative of La Salle's Attempt to Ascend the Mississippi in 1687." In vol. 1 of *The Journeys of René Robert Cavelier, Sieur de La Salle.* Edited by Isaac J. Cox. 2 vols. New York: A. S. Barnes and Co., 1905.

Dunn, William Edward. "The Apache Mission on the San Saba River: Its Founding and Failure." *Southwestern Historical Quarterly* 17 (Apr. 1914): 379–414.

———. "Apache Relations in Texas, 1718–1750." *Texas State Historical Association Quarterly* 14 (Jan. 1911): 198–274.

———. *Spanish and French Rivalry in the Gulf Region of the United States, 1678–1702: The Beginnings of Texas and Pensacola.* Austin: University of Texas Bulletin no. 1705, 1917.

Elvas, The Gentleman of. "The Narrative of the Expedition of Hernando de Soto." *Spanish Explorers in the Southern United States, 1528–1543.* New York: Charles Scribner's Sons, 1907.

Erath, Major George Bernard. "Memoirs." Edited by Lucy Erath. *Southwestern Historical Quarterly* 26 (Jan. 1923): 207–33.

Espinosa, Father Isidro Felíx. *Chrónica apostólica, y seráphica de todos los colegios de propaganda fide de esta Nueva-Espana, de Missioneros Franciscanos observantas: Erigidos con authoridad pontifica, y regia, para la reformaciones de los fieles, y conversion de los gentiles.* Mexico City: Hogal, 1746.

———. "Diary of the Espinosa-Olivares-Aguirre Expedition of 1709." Translated by Gabriel Tous. *Preliminary Studies of the Texas Catholic Historical Society* 1, no. 3 (1930): 1–18.

———. "The Ramón Expedition: Espinosa's Diary of 1716." Edited by Gabriel Tous. In *Preliminary Studies of the Texas Catholic Historical Society* 1, no. 4 (1930): 1–24.

Everett, Dianna. *The Texas Cherokees: A People between Two Fires, 1819–1840.* Norman: University of Oklahoma Press, 1990.

Ewers, John C. "The Influence of Epidemics on the Indian Populations and Cultures of Texas." *Plains Anthropologist* 18 (1973): 104–18.

———. "Symbols of Chiefly Authority in Spanish Louisiana." In *The*

Spanish in the Mississippi Valley, 1762–1804. Edited by John Francis McDermott. Urbana: University of Illinois Press, 1974.

Flores, Dan L. *Jefferson and Southwestern Exploration: The Freeman and Custis Accounts of the Red River of 1806.* Norman: University of Oklahoma Press, 1984.

———. "The Red River Branch of the Alabama-Coushatta Indians: An Ethnohistory." *Southern Studies* 16 (Spring 1977): 55–72.

Folmer, Henry. *Franco-Spanish Rivalry in North America, 1524–1763.* Glendale, Calif.: Arthur H. Clark, Co., 1953.

Ford, John Salmon. *Rip Ford's Texas.* Edited by Stephen B. Oates. Austin: University of Texas Press, 1963.

Foreman, Grant. *Advancing the Frontier, 1830–1860.* Norman: University of Oklahoma Press, 1933.

———. "The Texas Comanche Treaty of 1846." *Southwestern Historical Quarterly* 51 (1948): 314–32.

Freeman, Thomas, and Peter Custis. *An Account of the Red River in Louisiana, Drawn Up from the Return of Messrs. Freeman and Custis to the War Office of the United States, who explored Same in the Year 1806.* Washington: 1806.

Garrett, Kathryn Julia, ed. "Doctor John Sibley and the Louisiana-Texas Frontier, 1803–1814." *Southwestern Historical Quarterly* 45–49 (1942–46).

Garrison, George Pierce, ed. *The Diplomatic Correspondence of the Republic of Texas.* 3 vols. Washington: Government Printing Office, 1908–11.

Gibson, Ariel. "Confederates on the Plains: The Pike Mission to the Wichita Agency." *Great Plains Journal* 4 (Fall 1964): 7–16.

———. *The Kickapooo Indians: Lords of the Middle Border.* Norman: University of Oklahoma Press, 1963.

Gilmore, Kathleen K. *French-Indian Interaction at an Early Eighteenth Century Post: The Roseborough Lake Site, Bowie County, Texas.* Contributions in Archaeology, no. 3. Denton: Institute of Applied Sciences, North Texas State University, 1986.

Giraud, Marcel. *A History of French Louisiana, 1, The Reign of Louis XIV, 1698–1715.* Translated by Joséph C. Lambert. Baton Rouge: Louisiana State University Press, 1974.

———. *Histoire de la Louisiane Francaise, 2, Annees de Transition, 1715–1717.* Paris: Presses Universitaire de France, 1958.

Glover, William B. "A History of the Caddo Indians." *The Louisiana Historical Quarterly* 18 (Oct. 1935): 872–946.

Gregory, Jack, and Rennard Strickland. *Sam Houston with the Cherokees, 1829–1833.* Austin: University of Texas Press, 1967.

Griffith, William Joyce. *The Hasinai Indians of East Texas As Seen by*

Europeans, 1687–1772. Middle American Research Institute, Philological and Documentary Studies, vol. 2, no. 3. New Orleans: Tulane University Press, 1954.

Gulick, Charles A., Katherine Elliott, and Harriet Smither, eds. *The Papers of Mirabeau Buonaparte Lamar*. 6 vols. Austin: Von Boeckmann-Jones, 1921–27.

Hackett, Charles Wilson, ed. *Historical Documents Relating to New Mexico, Nueva Vizcaya, and Approaches Thereto, to 1773*. 3 vols. Washington: Carnegie Institution, 1923–27.

———. *Pichardo's Treatise on the Limits of Louisiana and Texas*. 4 vols. Austin: University of Texas Press, 1931–46.

Haggard, J. Villasana. "The House of Barr and Davenport." *Southwestern Historical Quarterly* 49 (July 1945): 66–88.

———. "The Neutral Ground Agreement Between Louisiana and Texas, 1806–1821." *The Louisiana Historical Quarterly* 28 (Oct. 1945): 1001–1128.

Hanke, Lewis. *The Spanish Struggle for Justice in the Conquest of America*. Philadelphia: University of Pennsylvania Press, 1949.

Harmon, George D. "The United States Indian Policy in Texas, 1845–1860." *The Mississippi Valley Historical Review* 17 (Dec. 1930): 377–403.

Harmon, Jeanne V. "Matthew Leeper, Confederate Agent at the Wichita Agency, Indian Territory." *Chronicles of Oklahoma* 47 (Fall 1967): 242–57.

Harpe, Bénard de la. "Account of the Journey of Bénard de la Harpe: Discovery Made by Him of Several Nations Situated in the West." Translated by Ralph A. Smith. *Southwestern Historical Quarterly* 62 (July 1958–Oct. 1959): 75–86, 246–59, 371–85, 525–41.

———. *The Historical Journal of the Establishment of the French in Louisiana*. Translated by Joan Cain and Virginia Koenig. Edited by Glenn R. Conrad. Lafayette: University of Southwestern Louisiana, 1971.

Harris, Helen Willits. "Almonte's Inspection of Texas in 1834." *Southwestern Historical Quarterly* 41 (Jan. 1938): 135–211.

Hatcher, Mattie Austin, ed. "Descriptions of the Tejas or Asinai Indians, 1691–1722." *Southwestern Historical Quarterly* 30 (Jan. 1927): 206–18; (Apr. 1927): 283–304; 31 (July 1927): 50–62; Oct. 1927): 150–80.

———. "The Expedition of Don Domingo Teran de los Rios into Texas." *Preliminary Studies of the Texas Catholic Historical Society* 2 (Jan. 1932): 1–67.

———. "Myths of the Tejas Indians." *Publication of the Texas Folk-lore Society* 4 (1927): 107–18.

Higginbotham, Jay. *Old Mobile: Fort Louis de la Louisianne, 1702–1711*. Mobile: Museum of the City of Mobile, 1977.

Hudson, Charles T., Chester DePratter, and Marvin T. Smith. "Hernando de Soto's Expedition through the Southern United States." In *First Encounters: Spanish Explorations in the Caribbean and the United States, 1492–1570*. Edited by Jerald T. Milanich and Susan Milbrath. Gainesville: University of Florida Press, 1989. 77–98.

Hughes, Jack T. "Prehistory of the Caddoan-Speaking Tribes." In vol. 3 of *Caddoan Indians*. 4 vols. New York: Garland Publishing Co., 1974. 9–411.

Jackson, Jack, Robert S. Weddle, and Winston DeVille. *Mapping Texas and the Gulf Coast: The Contributions of Saint-Denis, Oliván, and Le Maire*. College Station: Texas A&M University Press, 1990.

Jenkins, John H., ed. *The Papers of the Texas Revolution, 1835–1836*. 8 vols. Austin: Presidial Papers, 1973.

John, Elizabeth A. H. *Storms Brewed in Other Men's Worlds: The Confrontation of Indians, Spanish, and French in the Southwest, 1540–1795*. Lincoln: University of Nebraska Press, 1981.

Johnson, Leroy, and Edward B. Jelks. "The Tawakoni-Yscani Village, 1760: A Study in Archeological Site Identification." *Texas Journal of Science* 10 (Dec. 1958): 405–22.

Joutel, Henri. "Historical Journal." In vol. 2 of *The Journeys of René-Robert Cavelier, Sieur de La Salle*. Edited by Isaac Joslin Cox. 2 vols. New York: A. S. Barnes and Co., 1905.

Kelley, J. Charles. "Juan Sabeata and Diffusion in Aboriginal Terms." *American Anthropologist* 57 (Oct. 1955): 981–95.

Kinnaird, Lawrence, ed. *Spain in the Mississippi Valley, 1765–1794*. 3 vols. Washington: Government Printing Office, 1946.

Kniffen, Fred B., Hiram F. Gregory, and George A. Stokes. *The Historic Indian Tribes of Louisiana, From 1542 to the Present*. Baton Rouge: Louisiana State University Press, 1987.

Koch, Lena Clara. "The Federal Indian Policy in Texas, 1845–1860." *Southwestern Historical Quarterly* 28 (Jan. 1925): 223–34; (April 1925): 259–86; 29 (July 1925): 19–35; (Oct. 1925): 98–127.

LaFora, Nicolás de. *The Frontiers of New Spain: Nicolás de LaFora's Description, 1766–1768*. Edited by Lawrence Kinnaird. Berkeley: The Quivira Society, 1958.

Lange, Charles H. "A Report on Data Pertaining to the Caddo Treaty of July 1, 1835: The Historical and Anthropological Background and Aftermath." In vol. 2 of *Caddoan Indians*. 4 vols. New York: Garland Publishing, Co., 1974. 59–320.

Lesser, Alexander, and Gene Weltfish. *Composition of the Caddoan Linguistic Stock*. Washington: Smithsonian Institution, 1932.

Leutnegger, Benedict, ed. *The Texas Missions of the College of Zacatecas, 1749–1759*. Documentary Series no. 5. San Antonio: Old Spanish Missions Historical Research Library at San José Mission, 1979.

McCann, Elizabeth. "Pénicault and His Chronicle of Early Louisiana." *Mid-America* 23 (Oct. 1941): 288–304.

McCloskey, John. *The Formative Years of the Missionary College of Santa Cruz of Querétaro, 1683–1733*. Washington: Academy of American Franciscan History, 1955.

McGinty, G. W. "Valuating the Caddo Land Cession." *Louisiana Studies* 2 (Summer 1963): 59–73.

Magnaghi, Russell M. "Changing Material Culture and the Hasinai of East Texas." *Southern Studies* 20 (Winter 1981): 412–26.

———, ed. "The Red River Valley, North of Natchitoches, 1817–1818: The Letters of John Fowler." *Louisiana Studies* 15 (Fall 1976): 287–93.

———. "Sulphur Fork Factory, 1817–1822." *Arkansas Historical Quarterly* 37 (Summer 1978): 167–75.

Margry, Pierre, ed. *Découvertes et établissements des Français dans l'ouest et dans le Sud de l' Amérique Septentrionale, 1614–1754*. 6 vols. Paris: D. Jouaust, 1879–88.

Marshall, Thomas Maitland. *A History of the Western Boundary of the Louisiana Purchase, 1819–1841*. Berkeley: University of California Press, 1914.

Massanet, Fray Damian. "Letter to Don Carlos de Sigüenza." Edited by Herbert Eugene Bolton. *Spanish Exploration in the Southwest, 1542–1706*. New York: Charles Scribner's Sons, 1916.

Mendoza, Juan Dominguez. "Itinerary." Edited by Herbert Eugene Bolton. *Spanish Exploration in the Southwest, 1542–1706*. New York: Charles Scribner's Sons, 1916.

Minet. "Journal of Our Voyage to the Gulf of Mexico." In *La Salle, the Mississippi, and the Gulf*. Edited by Robert S. Weddle. College Station: Texas A&M University Press, 1987.

Mooney, James. *The Aboriginal Population of America North of Mexico*. Smithsonian Miscellaneous Collections, vol. 80, no.7. Washington: Smithsonian Institution, 1928.

———. *The Ghost Dance Religion and the Sioux Outbreak of 1890*. Fourteenth Annual Report of the Bureau of Ethnology, 1892–1893. Part 2. Washington: Government Printing Office, 1896.

Morfi, Fray Juan Agustín de. *Excerpts from the Memorias for the History of the Province of Texas*. Edited and translated by Frederick C. Chabot. San Antonio: Naylor Printing Co., 1932.

———. *History of Texas, 1673–1779*. Translated by Carlos E. Castañeda. 2 vols. Albuquerque: Quivira Society Publications, 1935.

Morse, Jedediah. *A Report to the Secretary of War of the United States on Indian Affairs*. New Haven: Howe and Spalding, 1822.

Muckleroy, Anna. "The Indian Policy of the Republic of Texas." *South-*

western Historical Quarterly 25 (Apr. 1922): 229–60; 26 (July 1922): 1–29; (Oct. 1922): 128–48; (Jan. 1923): 184–206.

Murphy, Retta. "The Journey of Pedro de Rivera, 1724–1728." Southwestern Historical Quarterly 41 (October 1937): 125–41.

Nance, Joseph Milton. After San Jacinto: The Texas-Mexican Frontier, 1836–1841. Austin: University of Texas Press, 1963.

Nasatir, Abraham P. Borderland in Retreat: From Spanish Louisiana to the Far Southwest. Albuquerque: University of New Mexico Press, 1976.

Nathan, Paul, and Lesley Byrd Simpson, eds. The San Sabá Papers. San Francisco: John Howell Books, 1959.

Neighbours, Kenneth F. "José María, Anadarko Chief." Chronicles of Oklahoma 44 (Autumn 1966): 254–74.

Neuman, Robert W. "Historical Locations of Certain Caddoan Tribes." In vol. 2 of Caddoan Indians. 4 vols. New York: Garland Publishing, Co., 1974. 9–158.

———. An Introduction to Louisiana Archaeology. Baton Rouge: Louisiana State University Press, 1984.

Newcomb, W. W. The Indians of Texas. Austin: University of Texas Press, 1961.

———, and T. N. Campbell. "Southern Plains Ethnohistory: A Reexamination of the Escanjaques, Ahijados, and Cuitoas." In Anthropological Perspectives of Plains Natives and Their Past. Edited by Don G. Wycoff and Jack L. Hofman. Duncan, Oklahoma: Cross Timbers Press, 1982.

Newell, H. P., and A. D. Krieger. "The George C. Davis Site, Cherokee County, Texas." Society for American Archaeology, Memoirs 5 (1949): 1–271.

Newkumet, Vynola Beaver, and Howard L. Meredith. Hasinai: A Traditional History of the Caddo Confederacy. College Station: Texas A&M University Press, 1988.

Oakes, James. The Ruling Race: A History of American Slaveholders. New York: Vintage Books, 1982.

O'Donnell, Walter J. "Documents: La Salle's Occupation of Texas." Mid-America 18 (Apr. 1936): 96–124.

O'Neill, Charles, ed. Charlevoix's Louisiana: Selections from the History and the Journal of Pierre F. X. Charlevoix. Baton Rouge: Louisiana State University Press, 1977.

Padilla, Juan Antonio. "Texas in 1820: Report of the Barbarous Indians of the Province of Texas, by Juan Antonio Padilla, Made December 27, 1819." Translated by Mattie Austin Hatcher. Southwestern Historical Quarterly 23 (July 1919): 47–68.

Park, Joseph F. "Spanish Indian Policy in Northern Mexico, 1765–1810." In New Spain's Far Northern Frontier: Essays on Spain in the American

West, 1540–1821. Edited by David J. Weber. Albuquerque: University of New Mexico Press, 1979.

Parks, Douglas R., ed. *Caddoan Texts*. Chicago: University of Chicago Press, 1977.

Parson, Edmund Morris. "The Fredonian Rebellion." *Texana* 5 (Spring 1967): 10–52.

Peña, Juan Antonio de la. "Diary of the Aguayo Expedition." Translated by Peter P. Forrestal. *Preliminary Studies of the Texas Catholic Historical Society* 2 (Jan. 1935): 3–68.

Pénicault, André. *Fleur de Lys and Calumet: Being the Pénicault Narrative of French Adventure in Louisiana*. Edited and translated by Richebourg Gaillard McWilliams. Baton Rouge: Louisiana State University Press, 1953.

Perttula, Timothy K. *The Caddo Nation: Archaeological and Ethnohistoric Perspectives*. Austin: University of Texas Press, 1992.

————. "European Contact and Its Effects on Aboriginal Caddoan Populations between A.D. 1500 and A.D. 1680." In vol. 3 of *Columbian Consequences: The Spanish Borderlands in Pan American Perspective*. Edited by D. H. Thomas. Washington: Smithsonian Institution Press, 1991.

Powell, Philip W. *Soldiers, Indians, and Silver: The Northward Advance of New Spain, 1550–1600*. Berkeley: University of California Press, 1952.

Prucha, Francis Paul. *American Indian Policy in the Formative Years: The Indian Trade and Intercourse Acts, 1790–1834*. Cambridge: Harvard University Press, 1962.

————. "Andrew Jackson's Indian Policy: A Reassessment." *Journal of American History* 56 (Dec. 1969): 527–39.

Ramenofsky, Ann F. *Vectors of Death: The Archaeology of European Contact*. Albuquerque: University of New Mexico Press, 1987.

Ramón, Don Domingo. "Diary of His Expedition into Texas in 1716." Translated by Paul J. Foik. *Preliminary Studies of the Texas Catholic Historical Society* 1, no. 4 (1930): 1–24.

Richardson, Rupert N. *The Comanche Barrier to South Plains Settlement*. Glendale, Calif.: Arthur H. Clark Co., 1933.

Ritchie, E. B., ed. "Copy of Report of Colonel Samuel Cooper, Assistant Adjutant General of the United States, of Inspection Trip from Fort Graham to the Indian Villages on the Upper Brazos made in June, 1851." *Southwestern Historical Quarterly* 42 (Apr. 1939): 327–33.

Rivera, Pedro de. *Diario y Derrotero de lo Caminado, Visto, y Observado en la Visita que Hizo a los Presidios de Nueva Espana Septentrional de*

Brigadier Pedro Rivera. Edited by Vito Alessio Robles. Mexico: Taller Autografico, 1946.

Roemer, Ferdinand. *Texas, wtih Particular Reference to German Immigration and the Physical Appearance of the Country*. Translated by Oswald Mueller. San Antonio: Standard Printing Company, 1935.

Rogin, Michael Paul. *Fathers and Children: Andrew Jackson and the Subjugation of the American Indian*. New York: Alfred A. Knopf, 1975.

Roland, Charles P. *Albert Sidney Johnston: Soldier of Three Republics*. Austin: University of Texas Press, 1964.

Rowland, Dunbar, ed. *Official Letter Books of W. C. C. Claiborne*. 6 vols. Jackson: Printed for the State Department of Archives and History, 1917.

————, and Albert Godfrey Sanders, eds. and trans. *Mississippi Provincial Archives: French Dominion*. 3 vols. Jackson:Mississippi Department of Archives and History, 1929–32.

————, Albert Godfrey Sanders, and Patricia Galloway, eds. and trans. *Mississippi Provincial Archives: French Dominion*. Vols. 4–5. Baton Rouge: Louisiana State University Press, 1984.

Ruffin, Thomas F. "Invasion of Caddo Parish by General Thomas Jefferson Rusk's Republic of Texas Army, 1838." *North Louisiana Historical Association Journal 2* (Spring 1971): 71–83.

Sabo, George III. "Reordering Their World: A Caddoan Ethnohistory." In *Visions and Revisions: Ethnohistoric Perspectives on Southern Cultures*. Edited by George Sabo III and W. M. Schneider. Athens: University of Georgia Press, 1987.

Salcedo, Manuel María de. "A Governor's Report on Texas in 1809." Edited by Nettie Lee Benson. *Southwestern Historical Quarterly 71* (Apr. 1968): 603–16.

Sánchez, José María. "A Trip to Texas in 1828." Translated by Carlos E. Castañeda. *Southwestern Historical Quarterly 29*(Apr. 1926): 249–88.

Satz, Ronald N. *American Indian Policy in the Jacksonian Era*. Lincoln: University of Nebraska Press, 1975.

Schilz, Thomas F. *The Lipan Apaches in Texas*. El Paso: Texas Western Press, 1986.

Shelby, Charmion Clair. "Projected French Attacks upon the Northeastern Frontier of New Spain, 1719–1721." *Hispanic American Historical Review 8* (Nov. 1933): 457–72.

————. "St. Denis's Declaration Concerning Texas in 1717." *Southwestern Historical Quarterly 26* (July 1923): 165–83.

————. "St. Denis's Second Expedition to the Rio Grande, 1716–1719." *Southwestern Historical Quarterly 27* (Jan. 1924): 190–216.

Sibley, John. "Historical Sketches of the Several Indian Tribes in

Louisiana, south of the Arkansas, and between the Mississippi and the Rio Grande." *American State Papers, Class II, Indian Affairs.* Washington: Gales and Seaton, 1832.

————. *A Report From Natchitoches in 1807.* Edited by Annie Heloise Abel. New York: Museum of the American Indian Foundation, 1922.

Sibley, Marilyn McAdams. "Across Texas in 1767: The Travels of Captain Pages." *Southwestern Historical Quarterly* 70 (Apr. 1967): 593–622.

Simpson, Harold B. *Cry Comanche: The Second United States Cavalry in Texas, 1855–1861.* Hillsboro, Texas: Hill Junior College Press, 1979.

Solís, Fray Gaspár José de. "Diary of a Visit of Inspection of the Texas Missions made by Fray Gaspár José de Solís in the Year 1767–1768." Translated by Margaret Kenny Kress. *Southwestern Historical Quarterly* 35 (July 1931): 28–76.

Story, Dee Ann, ed. *Archeological Investigations at the George C. Davis Site, Cherokee County, Texas, Summers 1979 and 1980.* Texas Archeological Research Laboratory Occasional Papers no. 1. Austin: University of Texas at Austin, 1981.

Strickland, Rex. "Moscoso's Journey through Texas." *Southwestern Historical Quarterly* 46 (Oct. 1942): 109–37.

Swanton, John Reed. *Final Report of the United States De Soto Commission.* Washington: Government Printing Office, 1939.

————. *Indians of the Southeastern United States.* Bureau of American Ethnology Bulletin 137. Washington: Government Printing Office, 1946.

————. *Indian Tribes of the Lower Mississippi Valley and Adjacent Coast of the Gulf of Mexico.* Bureau of American Ethnology Bulletin 43. Washington: Government Printing Office, 1911.

————. *Indian Tribes of North America.* Bureau of American Ethnology Bulletin 145. Washington: Government Printing Office, 1945.

————. *Source Material on the History and Ethnology of the Caddo Indians.* Bureau of American Ethnology Bulletin 132. Washington: Government Printing Office, 1942.

Talon, Pierre, and Jean-Baptiste Talon. "Voyage to the Mississippi through the Gulf of Mexico." In *La Salle, the Mississippi, and the Gulf.* Edited by Robert S. Weddle. College Station: Texas A&M University Press, 1987.

Tanner, Helen Hornbeck. "The Territory of the Caddo Tribe of Oklahoma." In vol. 4 of *Caddoan Indians.* New York: Garland Publishing Co., 1974. 9–144.

Taylor, Allan R. "The Classification of the Caddoan Languages." *Pro-*

ceedings of the American Philisophical Society 107 (Feb. 1963): 51–59.

————. "Comparative Caddoan." *International Journal of American Linguistics* 29 (Jan. 1963): 113–51.

Taylor, Virginia H., ed. *The Letters of Antonio Martínez, Last Spanish Governor of Texas, 1817–1822*. Austin: Texas State Library, 1957.

Thornton, Russell. *American Indian Holocaust and Survival: A Population History Since 1492*. Norman: University of Oklahoma Press, 1987.

Tonty, Henri de la. "Memoir by the Sieur de la Tonty." In vol. 1 of *Historical Collections of Louisiana*. Edited by B. F. French. 5 vols. New York: Wiley and Putnam, 1846–53.

Trennert, Robert A., Jr. *Alternative to Extinction: Federal Indian Policy and the Beginnings of the Reservation System, 1846–1851*. Philadelphia: Temple University Press, 1975.

U.S. Congress. House. *Executive Documents*. 25th Cong., 2d Sess., 1838, H. Doc. 351.

————. *Executive Documents*. 25th Cong., 3d Sess., 1838, H. Doc. 71.

————. *Executive Documents*. 29th Cong., 2d Sess., 1846, H. Doc. 76.

————. *Executive Documents*. 30th Cong., 1st Sess., 1847, H. Doc. 8.

————. *Executive Documents*. 30th Cong., 2d Sess., 1848, H. Doc. 1.

————. *Executive Documents*. 32d Cong., 2d Sess., 1852, H. Doc. 1.

————. *Executive Documents*. 40th Cong., 2d Sess., 1867, H. Doc. 1.

————. *Executive Documents*. 42d Cong., 3d Sess., 1872, H. Doc. 65.

————. *Executive Documents*. 43d Cong., 1st Sess., 1873, H. Doc. 1.

————. *Executive Documents*. 27th Cong., 2d Sess., 1841, H. Doc. 1035.

U.S. Congress. Senate. *Executive Documents*. 31st Cong., 1st Sess., 1849, S. Doc. 1.

————. *Executive Documents*. 32d Cong., 1st Sess., 1851, S. Doc. 1.

————. *Executive Documents*. 32d Cong., 2d Sess., 1852, S. Doc. 14.

————. *Executive Documents*. 34th Cong., 1st Sess., 1855, S. Doc. 60.

————. *Executive Documents*. 35th Cong., 1st Sess., 1857, S. Doc. 1.

————. *Executive Documents*. 36th Cong., 1st Sess., 1859, S. Doc. 1023.

————. *Reports*. 30th Cong., 1st Sess., 1847, S. Rept. 171.

Usner, Daniel H., Jr. *Indians, Settlers, and Slaves in a Frontier Exchange Economy: The Lower Mississippi Valley Before 1783*. Chapel Hill: University of North Carolina Press, 1992.

Vigness, David M. "Don Hugo Oconor and New Spain's Northeastern Frontier, 1764–1766." *Journal of the West* 6 (Spring 1966): 27–40.

Wallace, Ernest, and E. Adamson Hoebel. *The Comanches: Lords of the South Plains*. Norman: University of Oklahoma Press, 1952.

Webb, Clarence H. "House Types among the Caddo Indians." *Texas Archeological and Paleontological Society* Bulletin 12 (1940): 49–75.

Weber, David J. *The Spanish Frontier in North America*. New Haven: Yale University Press, 1992.

Weddle, Robert S. *The French Thorn: Rival Explorers in the Spanish Sea, 1682–1762*. College Station: Texas A&M University Press, 1991.

———. *The San Sabá Mission: Spanish Pivot in Texas*. Austin: University of Texas Press, 1964.

———. *Wilderness Manhunt: The Spanish Search for La Salle*. Austin: University of Texas Press, 1973.

Wedel, Mildred Mott. *La Harpe's 1719 Post on Red River and Nearby Caddo Settlements*. Austin: University of Texas Press, 1978.

Whittington, G. P. "Doctor John Sibley of Natchitoches, 1757–1832." *The Louisiana Historical Quarterly* 20 (Oct. 1927): 467–512.

Williams, J. W. "New Conclusions on the Route of Mendoza, 1683–1684." *West Texas Historical Association Year Book* 38 (1962): 111–34.

Williams, Stephen. "The Aboriginal Location of the Kadohadacho and Related Tribes." Edited by Ward Goodenough. *Explorations in Cultural Anthropology*. New York: McGraw-Hill, 1964.

Wilmsen, E. N. "A Suggested Development Sequence for House Forms in the Caddoan Area." *Bulletin of the Texas Archaeological Society* 30 (1959): 35–49.

Winfrey, Dorman, ed. *The Indian Papers of Texas and the Southwest, 1825–1916*. 5 vols. Austin: Texas State Library, 1959–1961.

Winkler, Ernest William. "The Cherokee Indians in Texas." *Southwestern Historical Quarterly* 7 (Oct. 1903): 95-165.

Wood, Peter H. "La Salle: Discovery of a Lost Explorer." *American Historical Review* 89 (Apr. 1984): 294–323.

Worcester, Donald E. "Spaniards, Frenchmen, and Indians." Edited by Philip Weeks. *The American Indian Experience*. Arlington Heights, Ill.: Forum Press, Inc., 1988.

———. "The Spread of Spanish Horses in the Southwest." *New Mexico Historical Review* 19 (July 1944): 225–32.

Wright, Muriel H. "A History of Fort Cobb." *Chronicles of Oklahoma* 34 (Spring 1956): 53–71.

Wycoff, Donald G. "The Caddoan Cultural Area: An Archaeological Perspective." In vol. 1 of *Caddoan Indians*. New York: Garland Publishing, Co., 1974. 25–280.

———, and Timothy G. Baugh. "Early Historic Hasinai Elites: A Model for the Material Culture of Governing Elites." *Midcontinental Journal of Archaeology* 5 (1980): 225–88.

Zavala, A. de. "Religious Beliefs of the Tejas or Hasinai Indians." *Publication of the Texas Folk-lore Society* 1 (1916): 39–43.

Index

Bird's Fort, 148, 149
Blanco, 86, 98, 99
Blondel, Phillipe, 41, 46
Bonnell, G. W., 139
Bonnell, J., 122, 129
Bosque, Fernando del, 18
boundary disputes, 88; Kadohadachos and, 193; Louisiana-Texas, 84, 85, 92, 97, 102, 106; U.S.-Spanish, 89
Brazos Reserve, 166, 167
British: and Caddos, 37; and Osages, 77
Brooks, Jehiel, 115–18, 120, 122, 123, 132; swindling by, 132, 134
Brossaut brothers, 41
Brucaiguais, 76
Bucareli (town), 73
Bucareli y Ursua, Antonio María, 70, 73
buffalo, 12–14, 156
Buffalo Hump, 200
burials, 8, 10, 30, 34, 176
Burnet, David G., 119, 127
Butler, Pierce M., 148, 154

Cabello, Domingo, 73, 79, 80
Cabezon, 83
caddi: defined, 10; and French, 25; importance of, 85; Kadohadacho, 33; Nabedache, 23; respect for, 27, 33; role of, 27, 55; Spanish appointment of, 99; succession to, 178
Caddoan language, 171
Caddo confederacies, 9
Caddo County, Okla., 167, 168
Caddo Lake, 83
Caddos: and abandonment of lands, 131; allegiance of, 99, 100; ancestors of, 6; and Anglo-American settlers, 103; and Apaches, 59; and benefits from Europeans, 51; and British, 37; and Cherokees, 115, 119; and Choctaws, 131; and Comanches, 167; constitution of, 168; culture of, 104; as emissaries, 148; and European goods, 4, 54;

farming by, 163; first contact of, with Europeans, 3; and French, 26, 37, 38, 49, 52; gifts for, 41; importance of, 57, 88; in Indian Territory, 147, 166, 167; in Kansas, 167; Kadohadachos as, 189; and Kiowas, 167; and land issues, 158; location of, 5; as mediators, 60, 68, 69, 143, 150, 151, 153; origin myth of, 5; as peacemakers, 60; and peace with Texans, 162; raids by, 116; reservation for, 165, 166; reunification of, 167, 168; school for, 166; settlements of, 153, 154; and Spanish, 26, 59, 64, 66, 67; strategy of, 4; structure of, 55; and Texan hostility, 125; and Texans, 147, 149, 153, 163; and Texas Revolution, 129; and tribal customs, 52, 86, 88, 149, 176; tribal interrelations of, 9, 51, 85; tribal name of, 171; and United States, 64, 129, 163; and U.S.-Spanish conflict, 99, 103; and Wacos, 155
Caddo Treaty, 123; and Texas Revolution, 125
Cadillac, Sieur de, 39, 40, 42
Cahinnios, 25
Calahorra, José, 56–58, 60, 61
canahas, 5, 10
Canalizo, Valentin, 136
Canos, 60, 61
Cantonas, 24
Carondelet, Barón de, 82
Carter County, Okla., 147, 161
Casañas de Jesús María, Fr. Francisco, 30–32
Castillo, Diego del, 17
Castro, José Manuel de, 91
cavalry, U.S., 167
Cavelier, Jean, 23
Cavelier, René-Robert, 21
Chacaiauchia, 57
chayas, 10
Chef Blanc, 38, 39
Cheocas, 44, 47
Cherokees: abandon Texas lands, 142;

106; in Indian Territory, 161; introduction of, 163; and Kadohadachos,
139; as mediators, 70; and Nadacos,
131, 144; and peace negotiations,
148; population of, 86; settlement
of, 149; and Spanish, 61, 98; and
Texans, 134, 141, 153; and Texas
Revolution,, 127
Hardee, William J., 162
Harris, C. A., 134, 135
Harrison, Thomas J., 121
Hasinai confederacy, 8, 9, 54
Hasinais, 8, 65; agriculture of, 56; allegiance of, 92; and Apaches, 72, 78;
and arms trade, 57; caddices of, 85;
conversion of, 177; described, 18,
23, 27; disease among, 74, 78; and
French, 24, 35, 39, 40, 49, 51, 78;
hostility of, toward Spanish, 33–35;
intermediary role of, 42; and Ka-
dohadachos, 86, 97, 108; lifestyle of,
30; meaning of, 171; as mediators,
61, 68, 69, 71; and Osages, 77; and
other tribes, 114; population of, 54,
65, 74, 105, 106, 126, 183, 184; and
Spanish, 18, 28–30, 34, 35, 37, 51,
60, 81, 93, 98, 99, 178; U.S. relations with, 92
Henderson, J. Pinckney, 156, 158
Herrera, Simon, 95, 96
Herring, Elbert, 118
Hidalgo, Fr. Francisco, 39, 40
Hidalgo revolt, 99
hierarchical society, 9
Highsmith, Samuel, 158
Hill, George W., 164
Hood County, 163
horses, 15, 16, 24; theft of, 98
horticulture: introduction of, 7
Houhan, 64, 67
House Committee on Indian Affairs,
123
houses, 12, 104, 174
Houston, Sam: Indian policy of, 133,
136, 137, 138, 147; at peace coun-
cil, 151
Hunt, Memucan, 133

hunters and gatherers, 14
hunting, 12

Iberville, Sieur d', 38
Iesh, 144; death of, 167; as intertribal
leader, 155, 159, 163, 166; and land
issues, 158, 163, 164; as mediator,
151, 152, 159; and Neighbors, 156;
and peace negotiations, 148–50;
and U.S. treaty, 154
Indian policy, U.S., 116, 117
"Indian question," 161
Indian Removal Act, 116
Indian Territory: Caddos in, 141;
Cherokees in, 142
Irion, Robert A., 127
Iscanis, 56, 60, 70
Iturbide, Agustín de, 111
Izard, William, 114

Jackson, Andrew, 102; Indian policy
of, 132
Jamison, John, 106–108, 110
jewelry, 104
Johnston, M. T., 159
Jones, Anson: Indian policy of, 151
Jones, Robert M., 147, 148
José María. See Iesh
Joutel, Henri, 24, 25
Jumanos, 15, 32

Kadohadachos, 4, 8, 25, 52, 54, 77;
abandon Texas lands, 141; agriculture of, 56; allegiance of, 85, 90, 94,
96, 102; as allies against British,
102; and Americans, 94, 111; and
annuity payments, 146; arming of,
82; attacked, 140; attacks by, 135,
139, 140; on Brazos Reserve, 166;
caddices of, 85; and Chickasaws, 41,
52; and Choctaws, 146; dependence
of, 130–32; disease among, 75; and
French, 37, 41, 42; importance of,
76, 85, 86, 88, 91, 125, 171; in Indian Territory, 145, 146, 161; influence of, 68; intermediary role of, 42;
as intertribal leaders, 110; and in-

settlement patterns, 7, 11

settlements, Anglo-American, 107, 109; raids on, 113; and slavery, 11

settlements, European, 40

Sewall, Charles A., 139–41, 144

Sewall, James, 144, 145

shamans, 10

Shawnees, 137, 194; and Caddos, 110; and Mexicans, 137; and peace negotiations, 148

Shreve, Henry, 117

Sibley, Henry H., 162, 163

Sibley, John, 88, 189; and Dehahuit, 97, 99, 100; and intertribal council, 97; and Kadohadachos, 85, 89; as Indian agent, 90–92, 96, 98, 106, 190; importance of, 98

Silva, Fr. Miguel de Santa María y, 69, 70

Simpson, Nancy, 151

Slater, Samuel, 151

slaves, 15, 37, 41, 42

Sloat, Benjamin, 152

smallpox, 86, 131

Smith, James, 134

smuggling, French, 67

sociopolitical system, 8

Solís, Fr. Gaspar de, 53, 56

Soto, Marcel, 99, 100

Spanish: and Apaches, 15; and Caddos, 26, 31, 32, 59, 64, 66–67, 71, 73; entry of, 15; formal ties with, 68; gifts from, 32, 44, 68, 82; and Hasinais, 41, 81, 89, 178; and Kadohadachos, 89, 106; and Norteños, 78; as protectors, 16, 64; and United States, 84, 91, 92, 95

Spiro Mound Site Park, 172

Spy Buck, 130

Standing Committee on Indian Affairs, 134

Stem, Jesse, 162, 163

Stroud, Ethan, 148

Taensas, 25

Talapoon, Lucas, 94

Talon, Pierre, 24, 25, 28

tammas, 5, 10

Taovayas, 56, 70, 86; and Comanches, 99; and Osages, 77; and Spanish, 61; as Wichitas, 194

Tarrant, Edward H., 140

Tarshar, 117, 120, 121, 128, 129, 131, 134, 137, 139, 144; and annuity payments, 132, 135, 136, 146

Tawakonis, 56, 60, 87, 150; and Americans, 102; and Indian alliance, 137; and Kadohadachos, 97; and Osages, 77; and peace, 70, 148, 150; raids by, 130

Taylor, Zachary, 161

Tehuacana Creek: councils at, 148–54

"Tejas," 17, 175

Terán de los Ríos, Domingo, 31–33

Terrell, G. W., 148

Terreros, Alonso Giraldo de, 185

Texans: attacks by, 159, 167; Indian attacks on, 161; and Indians, 155, 158; and land issues, 158

Texas, Republic of, 134; and annuity payments, 135; and Indians, 134, 136–38; and Mexicans, 138

Texas, state of: and federal Indian policy, 162; Indian policy of, 164, 165; and public lands, 154

Texas Emigration and Land Company, 158

Texas Rangers, 135: ambushed, 133; Caddo aid to, 167; and Indians, 140, 158; Indians killed by, 158, 159, 160; and Kadohadachos, 141; and land dispute, 158; slaughter by, 158

Texas Revolution, 125–28

Texita, 73, 78, 79

Thorn, Frost, 112

Tinah, 164, 167

Tinhioüen, 63, 64, 66, 68, 69, 75–78, 85; death of, 187; and Norteños, 70

Tonkawas, 14, 57, 60, 61, 81, 174

Tonti, Henri de, 9, 16, 23, 25, 26, 28, 29

Torrey's Trading House, 148; attack planned on, 150; Caddos and, 151, 152; councils at, 156; and land dis-

Williamson, Thomas, 138
Winthuisen, Tomás Felipe, 52, 55, 56
women, 12: role of, 11, 13
Wright, Jeff, 137

xinesi, 9, 10, 29, 42; discontinuance of, 55; respect for, 24

Yatasis, 8, 25, 37, 38, 40, 52, 54, 55, 58, 64; and Americans, 101; disease among, 74; and Kadohadachos, 85, 86; population of, 54, 75, 86
Ybarbo, Gil, 73, 74, 81
Yojaunes, 14, 42, 61
Young County, 163, 166